TRIUMPH AND DEFEAT

The Vicksburg Campaign

Volume 2

Books by Terrence J. Winschel

Triumph and Defeat:
The Vicksburg Campaign (1998)

Vicksburg:
Fall of the Confederate Gibraltar (1999)

The Civil War Diary of a Common Soldier:
William Wiley of the 77th Illinois Infantry (2001)

Vicksburg is the Key:
The Struggle for the Mississippi River (2003)

TRIUMPH
AND DEFEAT

The Vicksburg Campaign

Volume 2

[signature: Terrence J. Winschel]

Terrence J. Winschel

SB

Savas Beatie

New York and California

Cataloging-in-Publication Data is available from the Library of Congress.

ISBN 1-932714-21-9

05 04 03 02 01   5 4 3 2 1
First edition, first printing

Published by
Savas Beatie LLC
521 Fifth Avenue, Suite 3400
New York, NY 10175
Phone: 610-853-9131

Editorial Offices:

Savas Beatie LLC
P.O. Box 4527
El Dorado Hills, CA 95762
Phone: 916-941-6896
(E-mail) editorial@savasbeatie.com

Savas Beatie titles are available at special discounts for bulk purchases in the United States by corporations, institutions, and other organizations. For more details, please contact Special Sales, P.O. Box 4527, El Dorado Hills, CA 95762, or you may e-mail us at sales@savasbeatie.com, or visit our website at www.savasbeatie.com for additional information.

For Therese, my love;

Jennifer, our angel;

Bert, our pride; and Evan, our joy.

God has blessed me through you.

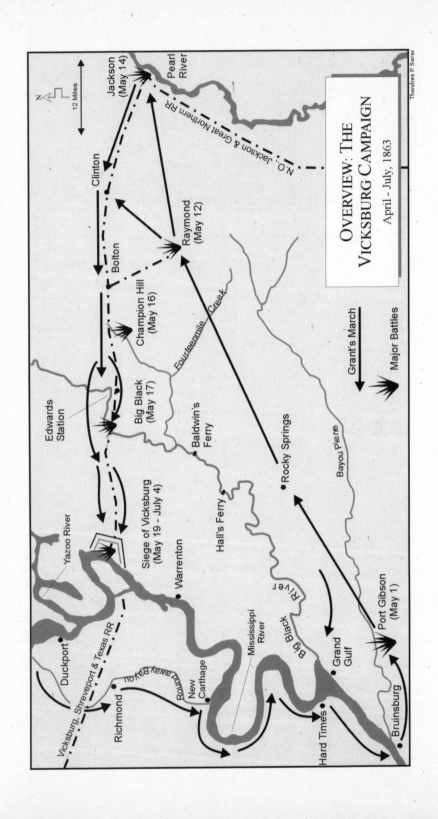

OVERVIEW: THE VICKSBURG CAMPAIGN
April - July, 1863

Theodore P. Savas

Grant's March

Major Battles

Jackson (May 14)

Pearl River

N.O., Jackson & Great Northern RR

Clinton

Raymond (May 12)

Bolton

Champion Hill (May 16)

Fourteenmile Creek

Edwards Station

Big Black (May 17)

Baldwin's Ferry

Rocky Springs

Bayou Pierre

Siege of Vicksburg (May 19 - July 4)

Hall's Ferry

Warrenton

Yazoo River

Big Black River

Grand Gulf

Port Gibson (May 1)

Duckport

Vicksburg, Shreveport & Texas RR

Roundaway Bayou

Richmond

New Carthage

Mississippi River

Hard Times

Bruinsburg

N

12 Miles

Contents

Contents (continued)

Maps and illustrations have been distributed throughout the text
for the convenience of the reader.

Preface

The 1998 release of *Triumph & Defeat: The Vicksburg Campaign*, my first hard-bound volume, marked in many ways my coming of age as a historian. Although employed by the National Park Service since June 1977, my first eleven years with the agency were spent as an interpreter, during which period I held different job titles: park aide, park technician, and park ranger. My duties varied from title to title and from park to park (I worked in four different parks during this time frame: Gettysburg, Fredericksburg, Valley Forge, and Vicksburg), but mostly they consisted of manning the park's information desk, distributing brochures, and doing interpretive programs. It was not until 1988 that I moved into the ranks of the professional historians within the agency. Two men were largely responsible for my promotion: Bill Nichols, who then served as superintendent at Vicksburg National Military Park, and Edwin C. Bearss, who was at that time chief historian of the National Park Service. I shall ever be grateful to these men for their support, mentoring, and friendship that have molded my career and will always guide my stewardship of the national treasures entrusted to my care by the American people.

Life as a public historian is vastly different than the stereotype most people have of historians. Rather than spend my time with musty old books and documents doing research and writing, my days are devoted to public relations work, managing the cultural resources of the park (which are vast and complex), land acquisition initiatives, restoration projects, producing exhibits, doing interpretive programs, and an array of other fascinating and fun activities. (A visitor to my office upon seeing a hard hat and Swedish brush ax behind my desk asked, "What are those things doing in here?" to which I replied, "Oh, that's standard equipment for a field historian.") But mostly, my time is consumed by the mind-numbing bureaucracy associated with the processes required in all Federal undertakings, processes such as GPRA, PMIS, NEPA, NHPA, and an endless stream of other acronyms that academic historians have never heard of, let alone the visitors who enjoy our national military parks and national battlefields. Yet, these time consuming and obscenely expensive processes have somehow become "mission critical," and largely replace common sense and pragmatism in the management of our resources. For those of us in the field, these processes are the bane of our existence. (My friend and former boss at Fredericksburg, Bob Krick, told me upon his retirement that he "no longer grinds corn for the Philistines." After almost thirty years of Federal service, how well I have come to appreciate that sentiment.) Although I look forward to the day when I too can stop grinding corn, there is much I still desire to achieve while working for the Philistines and will suffer through the bureaucratic nonsense for a few more years at least.

In order to promote my career and break into the historian ranks of the NPS, I have over the years had to sacrifice the very people for whom I was working so hard to provide—namely my family. In addition to my work at the park, I attended night school for eight years and completed two graduate degrees, then taught night school for fifteen years to help put my wife through college and to provide for our children's education. During this time I missed so many family moments—which I shall always regret, but take consolation in knowing that my absence did produce some benefits for them that otherwise would not have been realized. This book, as with my previous works, is as much a credit to my family and their sacrifices as it is to my own efforts. Thus, it is fittingly and lovingly dedicated to them.

I also traveled extensively over the years speaking at Civil War Round Tables around the country—further sacrificing family time. (My wife, who is envious of my travels, frequently comments, "You must see a lot of fascinating places," to which I reply, "Mostly airports and hotels.") This is my favorite aspect of the job, dealing with people who share a similar interest in the Civil War and a passion for battlefield preservation. The friendships I have developed with many of you who read these pages are cherished. Please know that my gratitude and admiration are always yours, as are my heartfelt thanks for the wonderful work and accomplishments we have achieved together. (In fairness to my wife, I must confess that I have also seen some fascinating places in my travels.)

It is the dream of most historians to write a book, or at least get published in a journal or magazine. (Public historians are no different in this desire than our counterparts in academia.) Fortunately for me, there is more interest in the Civil War than any other aspect of world history, and thus better chances of getting published in one of the many fine magazines and journals devoted to the conflict that engulfed our nation from 1861-1865. My first magazine article appeared in 1980 and a steady stream of articles has followed ever since. Scores of articles (and many years) later, my dear friend and former coworker, Will Greene, encouraged me to finally write a book. (I always had a mental block when it came to writing books. Writing articles of 10-30 pages in length is one thing, but writing a book is . . . well, that is a much greater and far more difficult challenge.) Will, I can never thank you enough for encouraging me to reach my potential.

Surprisingly, *Triumph & Defeat* came about relatively easy for, rather than being a book-length narrative, it is a collection of academic-style essays that I produced on various aspects of the Vicksburg campaign. (Many of these essays were originally written as speeches to present on the Round Table circuit. Thus, the effort was more like writing a bunch of articles, yet resulted in the publication of a book.) It begins with an overview of the operations that focused on the Hill City, which laid the foundation on which the other essays then built. The essays that followed dealt with Grant's march through Louisiana—the opening stage of the campaign, Grierson's Raid, the battle of Port Gibson, the battle of Champion Hill, and the May 19, 1863, assault against the Vicksburg defenses that highlighted the action of the Thirteenth United States Infantry. The essays continued with treatments of Union approach operations, the experience of Vicksburg's citizens under siege, the efforts of the Trans-Mississippi Confederates to rescue the city and its garrison, and the final days of the siege leading up to the surrender of Vicksburg on July 4, 1863.

In the years since the release of *Triumph & Defeat*, I have remained active on the Round Table circuit. This necessitates continued research and the development of new material for presentations. (Besides, I constantly challenge myself to delve into aspects of the campaign with which I have little knowledge in order to better comprehend—and in turn present to varied audiences, the' complexities of the Vicksburg operations.) The number and subject matter of these additional presentations warrant the development of a second collection of essays and gave birth to the idea for this book.

Triumph & Defeat: The Vicksburg Campaign, vol. 2, covers aspects of the operations for Vicksburg not addressed in the first collection of essays. As with the previous set of essays, this collection is presented in chronological order so that readers can better follow the campaign as it unfolded. It also includes essays on Confederate General Joseph E. Johnston and the relief operations conducted under his command. It further provides an essay on the significance of Vicksburg to the war efforts of the North and South, and concludes by bringing the story of Vicksburg to the present with an essay on the establishment of Vicksburg National Military Park—one of America's premier historic sites.

* * *

Permit me to take this opportunity to convey my heartfelt thanks to the many people who have contributed to my understanding of the Vicksburg campaign: National Park Service Historians Al Scheller, Edwin C. Bearss, Stacy Allen, and Tim Smith; Drs. Michael Ballard and John F. Marsalek at Mississippi State University; Dr. William Shea of the University of Arkansas at Monticello; fellow authors Brig. Gen. (ret) Parker Hills and Warren Grabau; Jim Woodrick of the Mississippi Department of Archives and History; and Gordon Cotton, Blanche Terry, and Jeff Giambrone of the Old Court House Museum in Vicksburg. Thank you all for your friendship and for sharing with me your love of history.

Special thanks are extended to my dear friend and mentor Ed Bearss for his guidance and support over the years. My position and whatever stature I may have in this agency are due largely to him. Thanks Ed for all that you have done and continue to do for me and for providing the Foreword to this volume (as he did for the first collection of essays).

Special thanks are extended to Theodore P. "Ted" Savas, another dear friend who, in addition to this book, published the first installment of *Triumph & Defeat* back in 1998. Ted has always been willing to promote my writing career, for which I am truly grateful. (Ted, please tell Alexandra Maria that the Elfin King sends his best wishes.) May God bless and keep both of you always in His loving care.

It is my fervent hope that you will enjoy this collection of essays and that someday you will have the opportunity to visit the many sites associated with the Vicksburg campaign.

Foreword

I have been privileged to know Terrence J. "Terry" Winschel as a colleague and friend for more than a quarter of a century. In those years I have seen him master the diverse skills expected of a dedicated public historian. These include meeting the public, answering diverse questions, representing the National Park Service (NPS) and giving off-site presentations, interpreting and protecting the park's resources, etc.

Beginning in 1976 as a Licensed Battlefield Guide at Gettysburg National Military Park, Winschel during the next two years served at several other NPS flagship parks, before signing on as a permanent member of the NPS family at Vicksburg in 1978. By 1980 he had honed his research and writing skills and his first Civil War monograph was published. It was well received and Terry was encouraged to continue. In the ensuing years he became a frequently published public historian with an impressive bibliography. As to be expected, in view of his interest, the focus of these articles was on the Civil War and the Vicksburg campaign and personalities.

His initial ventures appeared in magazines. He soon made the transition to scholarly journals and then in July 1989 he authored a monograph in the inaugural issue of *The Gettysburg Magazine* of which I am senior editor. He became a popular member of the magazine's distinguished authors' corps, his byline being found in the next nine issues of *Gettysburg*. He returned to the pages of the Youngers' publication in issue No. 12 off the press in 1995. Winschel's contributions were popular with readers, and all featured Mississippians and their significant role in the Gettysburg campaign.

Because of my position as the Service's Chief Historian and the Youngers' editor, I became familiar with the superior quality of Winschel's scholarship, his passion for the Civil War, his graceful style, and keen insights. All these positive attributes were underscored when I read and authored the "Foreword" for *Triumph & Defeat: The Vicksburg Campaign*, published in 1998 by Savas Publishing Company. My penultimate sentence in the Foreword read, "If *Triumph & Defeat* had been on the shelves of the Park library in September 1955, when I first entered on duty at Vicksburg, it would have provided the missing one volume introduction to the campaign and siege that I craved." That sentiment is as true today as it was eight years ago.

Winschel enriched his bibliography and expanded his horizons in 2003 when he coauthored with William Shea *Vicksburg is the Key: The Struggle for the Mississippi River* in the applauded Great Campaigns of the Civil War series published by the University of Nebraska Press.

Needless to say, in view of my long standing interest in Gen. U. S. Grant's masterful Vicksburg campaign and my association with Winschel, I again looked forward to reading and if deemed warranted preparing the "Foreword" for his eagerly awaited Volume II of *Triumph & Defeat* to be published by Savas Beatie.

As in his first volume, Winschel's latest features ten essays, several of which he earlier researched and developed for presentation to Civil War Round Tables which constitute formidable venues for knowledgeable speakers with a flare for the dramatic, a key element in Terry's popularity.

Again Winschel follows the successful but challenging format of his initial volume which proved popular with both readers and reviewers. It is not a detailed campaign study of which there are several. It features ten stand alone essays, as well honed and focused as those found in his earlier endeavor. The first three essays pick-up in the hours following the May 1, 1863, battle of Port Gibson and focus on the first 15 days of Grant's campaign east of the Mississippi. Too often ignored these two weeks show Grant at his best possessing attributes, among them flexibility, that mark all great captains. Not only do his troops defeat the Confederates twice at Raymond and Jackson, but Grant on three occasions at Hankinson's Ferry, at Dillon's plantation, and at Jackson out thinks and outmaneuvers Confederate leaders by changing the direction of his march to go for the jugular. Here Winschel pulls no punches and does Grant proud.

In the fourth essay highlighting Grant's "Fighting Corps commander," he comes down on the side of the political ambitious John A. McClernand, but sides with Grant when push comes to shove and McClernand becomes too big for his britches.

Close cooperation of the army and navy ensured Union success. To give Adm. David D. Porter and the "brownwater" navy their due, Winschel tells it through an essay titled "Companion to the Fishes: The Saga of the Gunboat *Cincinnati*."

The story of the city under first the guns and mortars of the "bluewater" navy in May-July 1862, then under siege as seen through the eyes and words of the family and friends of the Episcopal rector the Rev. William W. Lord highlight the next essay. No one better blends and integrates the words of the people who were there into an historical narrative that catches the temper of the times and the people's emotions during these trying and dreadful days.

Essays 7 and 8 shift to Gen. Joseph E. Johnston and what were for him unhappy times in Mississippi. The first "I Am Too Late: Joseph E. Johnston and the Army of Relief" is a companion essay to the ninth essay in Volume I "To Rescue Gibraltar: Efforts of the Trans-Mississippi Confederates to Relieve Fortress Vicksburg." They center stage efforts by the trans- and cis-Mississippi Confederates to relieve the gallant Vicksburg defenders. The second takes us back to Jackson. With the July 4 surrender of Vicksburg, Gen. William T. Sherman goes after Johnston, lays siege to Jackson (July 10-16) only to see Johnston and his army evacuate the city and retreat eastward.

Winschel in essay 9 accepts the challenge to the significance of Vicksburg raised by respected Civil War historian Albert Castel in the November 2003 issue of *North & South* article titled "Vicksburg: Myth and Realities." His choice of title is thought-provoking, "Crucial to the Outcome: Vicksburg and the Trans-Mississippi Supply Line." Winschel, as readers will discover, in the words of the late Governor Al Smith, "looks at the record[s]," probes the past, marshals his evidence, and comes up with compelling arguments to refute Castel's position.

The final essay is "Stephen D. Lee and the Making of an American Shrine." Evident in his monograph is Winschel's deep feeling and respect for Vicksburg National Military Park, the city, Warren County, the State of Mississippi, and the soldiers and sailors and civilians of the 1860s. Coupled with that is a similar feeling for Brig. Gen. Stephen D. Lee and all those who worked so long and hard to have this shrine to valor and sacrifice established as the last of the five 1890s War Department Civil War Parks. Once the park was authorized, no one labored harder than General Lee and Resident Commissioner William T. Rigby, late captain in the 24th Iowa and future chairman of the Vicksburg National Military Park Commission, to put their stamp on the park to give it an identity in regards to monumentation that sets it aside from the other War Department Parks.

Terry Winschel, in his love for the Vicksburg Park and what it stands for, in many ways—but particularly as an enthusiast for preservation—reminds me of Captain Rigby, who was intimately associated with the park from 1899 to his death in 1929 three decades later. Terry has now logged 28 years at the park, more than any uniformed employee except Captain Rigby. I, for one, trust that his tenure will exceed Rigby's, whom he so greatly admires.

Edwin C. Bearss
Historian Emeritus, National Park Service

CHAPTER ONE

Beyond the Rubicon:
The Union Army Secures
its Beachhead on Mississippi Soil

V oices that cried so piteously for water pierced the darkness from every direction and served to hail the Angel of Death who throughout the night of May 1, 1863, stalked the battlefield west of Port Gibson. Before the gray streaks of dawn brightened the eastern sky, most of those voices had been forever stilled and the mangled and torn bodies from whence they came were motionless—their souls mercifully released from the pain and suffering dictated them by a cruel fate. Lingering clouds of white-blue smoke that had shrouded the fields and forest the previous day when two armies clashed in furious combat still drifted under the canopy of trees and gave a ghostly appearance to those who searched for killed or wounded comrades. Pervading the horrific scene of carnage and destruction was the stench of death from which there was no escape. The sights and sounds and smells experienced that fateful day would forever haunt those who survived the opening clash of arms in the campaign for Vicksburg.

At the cost of less than 900 men, the Union Army of the Tennessee under the command of Maj. Gen. Ulysses S. Grant had won a resounding victory at Port Gibson on May 1. The significance of his triumph cannot be overstated as it secured Grant's beachhead on Mississippi soil and provided his army with a base from which to launch its inland drive against Vicksburg. Of greater impact than the reported 787 casualties inflicted on the Confederate army, the action threw his opponent, Lt. Gen. John C. Pemberton, off balance. Reeling in shock, the commander of the Department of Mississippi and East Louisiana embraced a defensive posture and relinquished the offensive to a dangerous adversary. Michael Ballard, biographer of the general in gray, asserts that "when Grant crossed the Mississippi, he pushed Pemberton across his personal Rubicon." Confused, uncertain, and with his confidence shattered, Pemberton would stumble through the unfolding crisis with predictable indecision.[1]

Such character, however, was not woven into the fabric of the Union commander who moved quickly to further his initial success. Grant had seized the initiative in his bold march through Louisiana and had gained the upper hand with his amphibious landing at Bruinsburg and victory on the battlefield at Port Gibson. Seeking to exploit the situation, Grant decided to march on Vicksburg with his entire force and ordered the gruff commander of his XV Corps and most trusted subordinate, Maj. Gen. William T. Sherman, to join him with all possible dispatch.

With the rising sun on Saturday, May 2, blue-clad soldiers of the XIII Corps commanded by Maj. Gen. John A. McClernand formed ranks and advanced cautiously on the town, expecting the battle to be resumed with renewed fury. As they crossed Willow Creek and pushed up the steep slopes from where stiff resistance had been offered the previous afternoon, the soldiers encountered only discarded arms and equipment which littered the road and evidenced that their enemy had fled. Realizing there was no danger, the men moved fluidly from line of battle into column formation and marched into Port Gibson.

As the long column began descending from the heights overlooking Bayou Pierre, the deserted streets of Port Gibson came into view. A magnificent panorama spread before the men for the town wore a lavender crown furnished by the chinaberry trees that lined its streets. Stately homes greeted their gaze and rising toward Heaven through the colorful umbrella were the spires of Port Gibson's diverse houses of worship. Pvt. Israel Ritter of the Twenty-fourth Iowa Infantry marveled at such elegance and recorded his impression of the town in the pages of his diary: "A most beautiful place, high and fine buildings, four large churches, Meth., Presby., and Catholic, etc. Nearly all the citizens are gone. Much property taken but still the town is well protected." He declared emphatically that Port Gibson was the "best place I ever saw."[2]

The Federal soldiers quickly filed through the tree-shaded streets only to discover that the retreating Confederates had burned the suspension bridge across Little Bayou Pierre on the north edge of town. In order to open the direct route to Vicksburg, pioneers and fatigue parties under the direction of Lt. Col. James H. Wilson and Capt. Stewart R. Tresilian were set to work bridging the deep and sluggish stream. One soldier noted that "teams soon brought the dry trunks of trees, logs, rails and boards, anything that would float and piled them into the water." Cotton gins and nearby buildings were also torn down to provide material for the bridge that was thrown across the bayou by early afternoon. But the improvised bridge failed under the strain as a cannon pulled by four mules eased out onto the span only to tip and sink. "It was rather an expensive trial," admitted Thomas B. Marshall of the Eighty-third Ohio who witnessed the incident and selfishly theorized, "but better than a column of infantry."[3]

Grant was anxious to push across Little and Big Bayou Pierre and keep the momentum going lest the Confederates move into position to deter his efforts and block his drive on Vicksburg. Rather than wait for the engineers to complete their task, elements of Maj. Gen. James B. McPherson's XVII Corps were directed to ascend the bayou and, if need be, force a crossing at Askamalla Ford three miles above town. The brigades of Brig. Gens. John E. Smith and Elias Dennis were ordered to shoulder their knapsacks and swing into column. Guided by a local black the rugged soldiers marched out of town and off to the southeast. An hour later they reached the bank of Little Bayou Pierre and were relieved to find that the ford was unguarded. The two brigades quickly splashed across the stream and, pushing on, were soon in position on Confederate Colonel Benjamin Grubb Humphrey's plantation where they secured possession of the Port Gibson-Vicksburg road. Here they discovered a commissary depot that contained 8,000 pounds of bacon which, much to their delight, was distributed among the men to augment their limited supplies. (The Confederates would later lament loss of this bacon as by the end of June the Vicksburg garrison was issued mule meat.)[4]

Grant also ordered Maj. Gen. John A. Logan to move with one brigade of his division and investigate the possible use of the road and railroad bridges across Bayou Pierre west of Port Gibson that led to

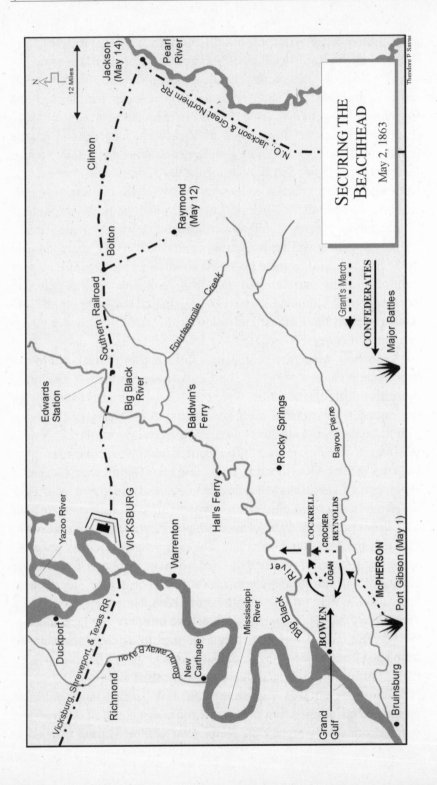

SECURING THE BEACHHEAD

May 2, 1863

Maj. Gen.
John A. Logan

National Archives

Grand Gulf. As the Federals expected, the highway bridge that had served as the avenue of escape for Brig. Gen. John S. Bowen's force from the battlefield the previous afternoon had been torched by the retreating Confederates. To further deter the bluecoats, a brigade of infantry led by the aggressive Col. Francis Cockrell, four guns of Capt. Henry Guibor's Missouri Battery, and the two remaining guns of the Botetourt (Virginia) Artillery guarded the crossing. Logan had no desire to force a crossing in the face of determined opposition and so simply held the Confederates in position for several hours then retired to Port Gibson.

Back in town, Wilson and Tresilian completed a more-sturdy span that was a continuous raft which measured 166 feet long and 12 feet wide. As the approaches were over quicksand, the engineers had fatigue parties corduroy the road and cover the planks with dirt. By 4:00 p.m. the bridge was open and the XVII Corps division of Brig. Gen. Marcellus Crocker crossed over the bayou. Turning east, Crocker's men pushed past Humphreys' plantation, where the brigades of Smith and Dennis joined the column, and on toward Grindstone Ford in hope of securing intact the suspension bridge across Big Bayou Pierre.

It was near 7:30 p.m. and the last light of day was rapidly fading when the vanguard reached Grindstone Ford. To their disappointment flames were licking at the far end of the bridge and threatened to engulf the structure. Captain Tresilian, who was traveling with the vanguard, organized men into a firefighting brigade and hurried onto the span to extinguish the flames. Their valiant effort managed to put out the blaze and save the bridge, but repairs were needed before troops could cross.

Throughout the night as soldiers of Crocker and Logan's divisions caught some much needed sleep, the corps' pioneer company and soldiers from the Fourth Minnesota labored to make repairs. Charred sections were planked over to form a new roadway and long pieces of timber were lashed to the suspension rods by wire to strengthen the bridge. As the new floor was ten inches above the old surface, ramps also had to be raised to facilitate the passage of wagons and artillery. Tresilian pushed the men hard and by 5:30 the following morning the bridge was declared open.

Watching the Federal activity from a safe distance were the weary soldiers of Col. Arthur E. Reynolds' demi-brigade who had moved into position on the high ground overlooking the bayou after a grueling march from Big Black River Bridge, east of Vicksburg. Consisting of the Fifteenth and Twenty-sixth Mississippi Infantry and the four guns of Company C, Fourteenth Mississippi Artillery Battalion, Reynolds' men were no match for the powerful Federal force that gathered on the opposite side of the stream. The Mississippians realized that they were all that stood between the enemy and Hankinson's Ferry on the Big Black

River, thus blocking the direct road to Vicksburg. Despite the disparity of numbers they mustered their courage and settled in for a long night during which they prayed that succor would arrive in the morning.

Accompanying the Mississippians to Big Bayou

Brig. Gen.
John S. Bowen

National Archives

Pierre were Maj. Gen. William W. Loring and Brig. Gen. Lloyd Tilghman who rode on to Grand Gulf to confer with Bowen. The fiery Bowen was visibly shocked when informed of the paucity of troops then en route to his aid. He had hoped to establish a formidable line of defense behind Bayou Pierre, a position he felt he could hold indefinitely. But with the enemy now north of Little Bayou Pierre and threatening Grindstone Ford, it was apparent to the Confederate generals that Grand Gulf had to be abandoned lest the command be trapped in a cul-de-sac from which there could be no escape. The success of their movement would depend on getting across Big Black River at Hankinson's before the Federals brushed Reynolds' Mississippians aside and seized the flatboat bridge at the strategic ferry.

Throughout the night of May 2 Southern soldiers worked feverishly to dismount and spike the heavy guns that had inflicted heavy damage to R. Adm. David Dixon Porter's ironclads on April 29 and removed the commissary stores and quartermaster supplies. As a parting gesture, the bastion's three magazines were exploded, the sound of which reverberated among the hills and along the Mississippi River for miles, announcing to the world that Grand Gulf was open. (The explosions were heard at Bruinsburg where Porter's fleet was tied up for the night. In the light of dawn on May 3, his squadron stood upriver and Union sailors took possession of the fortress that their guns could not silence.)

Though disheartened by the necessity of abandoning the fortress they had worked so hard to construct and valiantly defend, the men of Bowen's command were still full of fight and took up the line of march by the light of the moon. Daylight, however, found them still many miles from the safety of Big Black River and the ominous rumble of artillery could be heard in the direction of Grindstone Ford. In an effort to stave off disaster, Tilghman was directed to take the brigade of Alabamans and hasten to the assistance of Reynolds' small command. Despite this reinforcement, there were still too few Confederates to offer stiff resistance to the Federal juggernaut which at that moment was crossing the bayou below.[5]

With the first light of day, Logan's Union division pushed across the bridge and started up the steep grade that led to the important road junction of Willow Springs (also referred to as Willows) two miles away. From Willows, a road ran west through Ingleside to Grand Gulf where contact could be made with Porter's fleet and thus enable Grant to more

Brig. Gen.
John E. Smith

National Archives

easily supply his army. Roads also ran northeast to Rocky Springs and north to the important ferry crossing at Hankinson's. The troops of Crocker's division followed in support in expectation that battle would soon be joined.

Such expectations were well grounded. As the Federals neared the crest, the long column was fired upon by the cannoneers from Mississippi, whose guns were concealed from view. The lead brigade under John E. Smith scurried into line of battle and was hurled forward with the Forty-fifth Illinois on the left, Thirty-first Illinois in the center, and the Twenty-third Indiana on the right. As they formed line of battle three of the Hoosiers were wounded when a shell exploded in their midst. Once formed the line swept forward with a vengeance but only met token resistance and soon gained the crossroads.

Yielding the crossroads compelled the Confederates to fight on two fronts in order to safeguard the army as it crossed Big Black River at Hankinson's Ferry. Arthur Reynolds' Mississippians attempted to form line astride the Ingleside-Grand Gulf Road while the Alabamans under Brig. Gen. Stephen D. Lee covered the direct road to Hankinson's. But terrain prevented these two brigades from forming a connection. With their flanks in the air, both brigades were soon hard pressed and forced back farther.

Having occupied Willows, the Federals pressed their advantage. Logan's division was sent west in pursuit of Reynolds along the

Ingleside-Grand Gulf Road, while Crocker's division advanced north toward Hankinson's Ferry. Logan's men pushed relentlessly which prevented the Confederates from establishing a roadblock and kept them on the run. Before they reached Ingleside, the soldiers clad in uniforms of butternut and gray turned north, crossed Kennison Creek, and continued on toward Big Black River with the enemy nipping at their heels. The heat of the day sapped their strength as the Southerners scurried along and the thick clouds of dust that rose from the road made it difficult to breath. Their ranks soon lost semblance of order and the men straggled as the grueling pace continued. Those who fell by the wayside were picked up by the score as Logan's troops closed on their prey. Sgt. Henry S. Keene of the Sixth Wisconsin Battery noted of the stragglers collected, "They were a tough, hearty set of men," and added, "better than most we have seen."[6]

Reynolds' men were exhausted as they reached Hardscrabble Crossroads, where the roads from Willows and Ingleside met, and turned north toward Hankinson's Ferry which was still a long 3.5 miles away. With the Federals closing in overwhelming numbers from two directions, the situation facing the Confederates was critical as the army hurried to get across Big Black River. To bolster the defense of Hankinson's Ferry, Loring deployed Cockrell's Missouri Brigade near the crossroads, facing south, from which direction the enemy's approach was most alarming. His fighting blood up, Cockrell formed line of battle on a ridge overlooking Kennison Creek where he was in position to support the brigade of Alabamans whose line was overlapped on both flanks and falling back slowly.

Cockrell secured his position with little time to spare for Lee's men soon drew abreast of the Missourians and turned to face the enemy. The combined brigades unloosed a savage volley that stopped the Federals cold as it ripped through their ranks. Stunned by the murderous fire, Crocker's division scurried for cover and returned fire as officers sought to restore order among the troops. Within minutes the lines were reformed and as the soldiers in blue slowly advanced they felt for the flanks of the Confederate line.

The determined stand made along Kennison Creek enabled the Confederate army to make good its escape across the Big Black. With the main force now north of the river, Lee's Alabamans disengaged and fell back to the ferry leaving the rugged Missourians to cover their

Col.
Francis Cockrell

National Archives

withdrawal. But pressed in front and threatened on both flanks, Cockrell's men were forced back to Hardscrabble Crossroads where they attempted to reform their line. Scouts, however, informed the colonel that a powerful Federal force (Logan's division) was pushing rapidly along the road from Ingleside and posed a grave threat to his right flank. As further resistance would only threaten his brigade, Cockrell ordered his men to retire which was done in good order under the protective fire of Capt. John Landis' Missouri battery and its two 12-pdr. howitzers. One Missouri infantryman later captured the scene when he wrote with pride: "The rapid and skillful management of this battery, and the style in which the boys handled their pieces, were certainly splendid. Covered with black stains of powder, and almost enveloped in smoke, they worked in a manner and with a will, that indicated plainly they were in their element, and their hearts in the work they were doing."[7]

As the report of the guns thundered along the river, Sgt. George Harrison of the battery shouted to John Hanger, a friend in the Second Missouri Infantry, "Johnny, did you see us lam into them that time? Wasn't it handsomely done?"

The rapid and well-directed fire of Landis' guns held the enemy at bay and secured the time needed for Cockrell's men to safely cross the river, after which the battery then limbered up and retired. The artillerymen breathed a sigh of relief as the wheels of their guns rumbled over the bridge and onto the north shore. With great energy and skill, the escape of Loring's command had been consummated.[8]

The men of Company G, Second Missouri Infantry, and twenty pioneers from Alabama were instructed to take up the bridge which would effectively cut off pursuit and leave the enemy stranded south of the river. One soldier from Missouri recalled, "The boat was cut to pieces and we were just in the act of prizing and floating it out, when the crack of a gun was heard a few hundred yards from us, up the road, on the other side." The enemy was much closer than the sound indicated and almost immediately the whiz of bullets was fast and uncomfortably close. A pioneer from Alabama declared, "They have got us this time," and asked of one of the Missourians, "How in the name of Heaven are we to get out." Non-pulsed, Ephraim Anderson replied, "For myself, I expect to run out; and the rest of the boys, I suppose will get out the same way." As fast as their legs would go Anderson and his comrades fled from the bridge, but the unfortunate men had 300 yards to go across low flat bottomland to reach shelter in the trees. "Zip, zip went the bullets in the dust," recalled one Missourian, "and if ever I stepped briskly to the lively music of minie balls, it was then and there."[9]

In driving the Confederates from their work of destruction, soldiers of the Twentieth Ohio raced forward under the cover of artillery fire and scrambled over the bridge securing it intact. Manning Force, the regiment's hard-fighting colonel, boasted in his report of the speed of his Buckeyes noting that they even "secured many working implements, which the enemy was forced to abandon in his hasty flight." It was a stunning achievement that was equally significant for the Army of the Tennessee, for it now had a means by which to cross the Big Black and advance directly on Vicksburg. Historian Edwin C. Bearss likened it to the coup scored by the First Army in its dash across the Rhine at Remagen 82 years later. Although the officers were elated by this achievement, the men in the ranks focused on activities of less strategic importance as expressed by Sgt. Osborn Oldroyd of the Twentieth Ohio who wrote following capture of the bridge "we closed up business for the night and sought our blankets."[10]

On this Sunday Grant rode in the wake of Logan's division as it pursued Reynolds' Mississippians from Willow Springs toward the Big Black. At Ingleside, the Union commander, escorted by twenty troopers of the Fourth Independent Company, Ohio Cavalry, continued west to Grand Gulf, which he found occupied by the Union navy. "The first thing I did was to get a bath, borrow some fresh underclothing from one of the naval officers, and get a good meal on the flag-ship," recalled Grant, who had been without his personal baggage since April 27.[11]

The general also took the time to write his wife, Julia, whom he last wrote from Perkins' plantation in Louisiana on April 28. "My victory at this place, over Bowen, is a most important one," Grant boasted of the day's accomplishments. "Management I think has saved us an immense loss of life and gained all the results of a hard fight." Indeed, it certainly had, for the Federal beachhead on Mississippi soil was now secure and would enable Grant to unite his army in preparation for the inland movement against Vicksburg. Of equal importance, the movement across the bayous Pierre to the Big Black compelled the evacuation of Grand Gulf, which provided the Union army with a good all-weather landing from which point roads radiated deep into the interior of the Magnolia State. This would expedite the movement of supplies from Milliken's Bend and enhance the security of his tenuous supply line through Louisiana. In light of these results, the normally stoic Grant confided to his wife, "I feel proud of the Army at my command. They have marched day and night, without tents and with irregular rations without a murmur of complaints."[12]

In addition to his wife, Grant also wrote several dispatches and a report for Washington in which he informed General-in-Chief Henry W. Halleck, "I shall not bring my troops into this place but immediately follow the enemy, and if all promises as favorably hereafter as it does now, not stop until Vicksburg is in our possession."[13]

Refreshed by a good meal and clean clothes, Grant swung back into the saddle and rode through the night to Hankinson's Ferry where the troops of McPherson's XVII Corps were bivouacked. As Pemberton in a cloud of confusion and indecision desperately sought to concentrate his widely-scattered forces, Grant methodically consolidated his position along the Big Black and awaited Sherman's arrival. With grim determination the Federal commander prepared his men for the hard fighting that surely lay ahead in which he would drive his army as a stake into the heart of his enemy.

CHAPTER TWO

Blitzkrieg, U. S. Grant Style

T he most pressing question for Grant following the victory of his forces at Willow Springs and Hankinson's Ferry on May 3, 1863, was the direction in which to lead his army. The road north led directly to Vicksburg, but his keen appreciation of geography argued against this route. After crossing Big Black River his army would be in a narrow triangle of land bordered by the Mississippi River on the west and the Big Black River to the east and south that would restrict his ability to maneuver. Besides, he expected John Pemberton to concentrate his forces south of Vicksburg, which is exactly what the Confederate commander struggled to do that first week of May as the rugged and densely wooded area afforded him many excellent defensive positions.

Rather than march north on Vicksburg, Grant, a master of the indirect approach, ordered his troops in a northeasterly direction and used the Big Black River to screen the movements of his army and serve as a shield on his left. (Ironically, Pemberton also used the river as a shield against Grant as he struggled to concentrate his scattered forces for the defense of Vicksburg.) It was Grant's intention to get astride the Southern Railroad of Mississippi, which connected Vicksburg with Jackson, and sever that vital line of communications and supply. He would thus cut the Confederate garrison off from supplies and reinforcements. The long march would carry his men deep into the heart of Mississippi and be boldly made with the precision of a modern warrior—a boldness that has

Lt. Gen.
John C. Pemberton

National Archives

earned Grant the coveted distinction of being one of the great battle captains of history.[1]

As only two of his three corps were on Mississippi soil, however, the Federal commander could not launch the next phase of his operations until the army was united. While he anxiously awaited the arrival of Sherman's men, Grant had McPherson consolidate his hold on Hankinson's with the XVII Corps while the XIII Corps under McClernand settled down in the vicinity of Willow Springs. He also directed his subordinates to send out patrols to reconnoiter the approaches to Vicksburg from the south and southeast to keep Pemberton off balance and the enemy guessing where the next blow would fall.

In response to Grant's orders, the XV Corps with Sherman at the helm was at that moment pushing south through Louisiana to Hard Times from camps at Milliken's Bend, Young's Point, and Duckport Landing. "It is unnecessary for me to remind you of the overwhelming importance of celerity in your movements," Grant emphasized to Sherman on May 3. Delay could be costly as it would provide the enemy time to recover from the initial blow of the campaign. His trusted lieutenant recognized this and drove his men hard. Still, several days passed before Sherman was in position to cross the Mississippi River.[2]

With Grand Gulf now in Union hands, there was no need for Sherman's men to march all the way to Disharoon's plantation and cross the river to Bruinsburg. Thus, when the XV Corps reached Hard Times on May 6, it was ferried across the river to Grand Gulf (May 6-7) from where the hard–marching veterans of Sherman's command hastened to join their comrades in the vicinity of Willow Springs.

Once Sherman's men were across the river, Grant's eager soldiers shouldered their rifle-muskets and resumed the invasion of the Magnolia State. In another diversion intended to keep his opponent off balance, Grant ordered McPherson to make a strong demonstration at Hankinson's Ferry to keep Pemberton's attention focused south of Vicksburg while he started for the railroad east of the Hill City with his other corps. With his opponent confused and uncertain, Grant unleashed the inland phase of the campaign that would lead his army to the gates of the fortress city. Over the seventeen-day period from May 1 to May 17, in what is often described as the "blitzkrieg" of the Vicksburg campaign, Grant's army would march more than 200 miles, fight five battles, and drive the Confederates into the Vicksburg defenses.

Rather than a "lightning war" in which speed is essential, it is apparent that the pace of the advance and the daily distance traveled by the various units of Grant's army were determined in large part by the availability of water. In the late spring and early summer of 1863 this precious resource was rather scarce in Mississippi and was a major concern for the men and animals of the Union army. Ironically, too much water had hampered Grant's operations throughout the winter and early spring. Now, a scarcity of water almost controlled his movements.

(It is important to note that the level of the Mississippi River along its lower stretch is determined more so by rainfall and snowmelt in the Ohio River valley and upper reaches of the Mississippi than by precipitation locally. Thus, although the Mississippi River itself was still high and floodwaters in Louisiana were receding, water levels in the interior of the Magnolia State were low and there was no rain in this portion of the state from April 27 until May 14.)

The Union army advanced on a broad front with McClernand's corps on the left, closest to the Big Black River, Sherman's in the center, and McPherson's on the right. The alignment of his army during this phase of the operations reveals much about Grant's perception of his subordinates and the role that they played during the campaign. It also helps dispel the popular image of both McClernand and McPherson.

McClernand is usually depicted as bombastic, egotistic, inept, and reckless. Yet it is interesting to note that during the Vicksburg campaign the XIII Corps under McClernand led the march through Louisiana (arguably the most important assignment of the campaign) and was first to cross the Mississippi River. In addition, as the Union army pushed inland, McClernand's corps formed the army's left flank and thus, at all times, was at the point of danger being closest to the enemy. Contrary to Grant's later claim that he doubted McClernand's fitness for command, the politician-turned-soldier was his senior and most experienced corps commander in the spring of 1863 and had demonstrated his willingness to fight at Belmont, Fort Donelson, Shiloh, and Arkansas Post. During the campaign Grant was confident that the energetic and aggressive McClernand would fight well and entrusted him with a high level of responsibility.

James McPherson, on the other hand, a man whom popular historians heap with credit during the campaign for Vicksburg, was the junior corps commander in Grant's army. The Ohio native graduated at the top of his class at West Point in 1853 and spent the pre-war years teaching at the academy or working on harbor improvements and coastal fortifications. Following the outbreak of hostilities, he was elevated through the ranks from a lieutenant of engineers to major general over just a fourteen-month period. His meteoric rise was based largely on his winning personality, by which he became a favorite with Grant on whose staff he had served as chief engineer in the

Maj. Gen.
James B. McPherson

National Archives

campaign for Forts Henry and Donelson and at Shiloh. Due to McPherson's inexperience as a field commander, Grant sought to shield him throughout this campaign by placing the XVII Corps in a supporting role. Fate, however, would bring McPherson to the fore in this stage of the Vicksburg campaign and his performance would be less than stellar.

Grant placed his most trusted subordinate, William T. Sherman, and his XV Corps in the center as the army pushed inland. In this vital "swing" position Sherman's corps could move right or left should the need arise to support either wing of the army. After Grant's army reached a line between Old Auburn and Raymond, the Union commander planned to wheel to the north and strike the Southern Railroad between Edwards and Bolton.

With buoyant spirits and confidence in their leaders, the men of the Union army swung into column and left their encampments at Willow Springs and Hankinson's Ferry early on the morning of May 7. "This is quite a hilly region," noted Surgeon Benjamin F. Stevenson of the Twenty-second Kentucky in the XIII Corps division led by Brig. Gen. Peter Osterhaus, "and I have been surprised to find growing here, side by side, the beech, the elm, the maple, the sugar tree, the oak, the sycamore, and the pine." In the letter written to his wife Lida, the good doctor added, "The soil is rather thin and poor, but the country is one of much beauty, and, if I were to recast my fortune in the South, I would much prefer a location here in the hills to one on the [Mississippi] river." William Bentley, also of the XIII Corps, who marched with the Seventy-seventh Illinois Infantry, was equally impressed by the countryside. With romantic flare he recorded in the pages of his journal, "As we passed along, the dark green foliage of the Magnolia waved in the breeze, as if to welcome our advent, and bid us God-speed in our laborious campaign."[3]

The Union route of march carried the dusty soldiers through the hamlet of Rocky Springs to Big Sand Creek where three divisions of McClernand's corps, which formed the vanguard of the army, bivouacked that evening and remained for several days. The soldiers took advantage of the rest on May 8 to bathe in the cool water, clean their equipment, and wash their clothes for the first time in weeks. The "Big Wash," as it was called by Thomas Bringhurst of the Forty-sixth Indiana, was propitious as these divisions in martial array passed in review before Generals McClernand and Grant later that day. "Our Generals reviewed the troops today," read the diary entry of Henry Clay Warmoth of

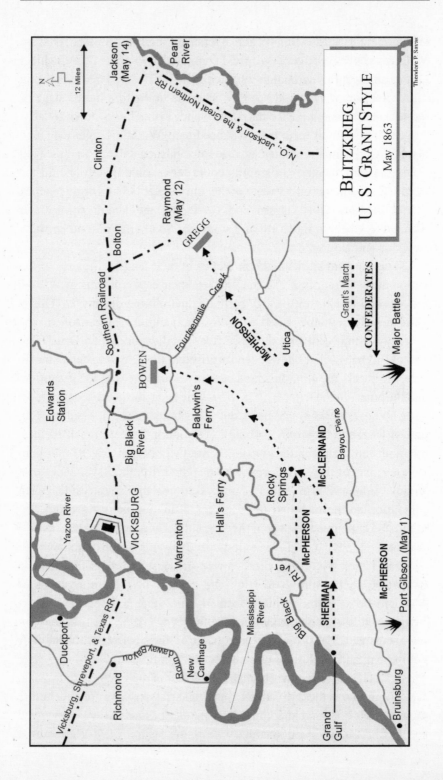

McClernand's staff, who wrote with pride, "The woods reverberated with their shouts of applause."[4]

   In addition to cleaning equipment and reviewing the troops, there were other serious concerns to be addressed as the army prepared to move deeper into Mississippi. The lengthy supply line that wound its way through Louisiana from Milliken's Bend to Hard Times was tenuous at best and, as flood waters in the Bayou State receded, became more exposed. Grant realized that if the line was cut, it could embarrass or even terminate his operations in Mississippi. The Union commander looked to shorten the line by constructing a new road from Young's Point (above Vicksburg) to Bower's Landing (below the Warrenton casemate) from where the supplies could be moved by boat to Grand Gulf. The new road would not only shorten his land route from 63 to 12 miles but, with the protection afforded by the fleet, would provide greater safety to the vital supplies his army needed to conduct the inland campaign against Vicksburg.

   Until the new road was open, supplies of food and ammunition had to be conserved. In response to concerns expressed by Sherman, Grant acknowledged that it was not possible to provide the desired quantities of food and that his men would have to stretch two days rations to last ten days. "What I do expect, however, is to get up what rations of hard bread, coffee, and salt we can," he said. Grant then offered a solution to his worried subordinate that he "make the country furnish the balance."[5]

   A soldier in A. J. Smith's division grumbled that the men of his regiment had been issued the "excessive amount" of one and a half crackers that had to last as many days. But hungry soldiers are always resourceful and in their quest for food Thomas Marshall and John Beard of the Eighty-third Ohio managed to find a sheep. "Taking it to camp, we sliced it up, fried it, and ate it all for supper and breakfast, the two of us," recalled Marshall, who added "One thing is certain, either the sheep was a small one or we were very hungry."[6]

   In order to augment the army's limited food supplies, fatigue parties were sent out daily to gather in the produce of the land—which was found in abundance. Capt. John A. Bering of the Forty-eighth Ohio characterized the foragers as "a jolly, mischievous set, eager and ready for any adventure." One soldier who benefited from the skill and precision with which the foragers kept the army fed marveled at their work: "No sooner were they beyond the lines than they began their work.

They slaughtered the pigs in the pens; the cattle and horses were driven from the fields, smokehouses and cellars were ransacked for flour, meal and bacon; the chickens and turkeys were captured in the yard; the mules were hitched to the family carriage, and the provisions stowed away in it; when it was driven to the next plantation, where the same ceremony was repeated." In this manner the foragers stripped the country clean and each night returned with their bounty. With a soldier's delight, Captain Bering noted of the daily routine, "Toward evening the foragers returned to camp, driving the cattle before them, followed by a long line of vehicles of every description, loaded with all kinds of provisions, which was equally distributed among the different regiments."[7]

By May 10, McClernand's and Sherman's corps were concentrated along the road from Willow Springs to Big Sand Creek, while McPherson's had turned and swung east toward Utica. On that day, with their haversacks and cartridge-boxes full, the Union soldiers resumed the advance over dusty roads under a blazing sun. The XIII Corps, which continued in the lead, pushed through Cayuga and bivouacked along the banks of Fivemile Creek (the next major watercourse). He also established a fortified camp at the intersection of the Telegraph and Raymond Roads, well in advance of his main force, and sent combat patrols farther out both roads to scout for the enemy. Sherman's troops, which followed in McClernand's wake, marched through Rocky Springs to Big Sand Creek. And over on the Federal right flank, the handsome and jovial McPherson directed his corps to Utica which was reached around noon that Sunday. The men of the XVII Corps continued through the town and bivouacked that night four miles east of Utica on the Weeks' plantation—their only source of water being Tallahala Creek, a mile to the southeast.

The following day Grant moved his corps to perfect the alignment of his army preparatory for its lunge toward the railroad. Consequently the soldiers of the XIII Corps, who were to act as the hinge for the army as it wheeled north to strike the Confederate lifeline, remained in their camps and took great amusement in throwing gibes at and heckling the men of Sherman's command as they took the lead and headed toward their destination for the day—Old Auburn. William B. Halsey, one of Sherman's men who served in the Seventy-second Ohio, complained of the region through which they marched: "Water scarce; weather hot;

roads dusty; land poor; rations short; houses, poor shabby things. Don't like the country."[8]

The weather was hot—even for Mississippi, and the scarcity of water along the route was cause for growing alarm within the army's high command. The next watercourse of any size was Fourteenmile Creek that flowed east-west across the Federal line of advance. The stream was also the last natural barrier between the Union army and its immediate objective—the Southern Railroad of Mississippi. As such, the sluggish stream that originated near Raymond (on the Federal right) and emptied into Big Black River (on the Federal left), provided the Confederates with a potentially strong defensive position and an opportunity to strike the enemy a telling blow. Appreciative of geography and recognizing the potential for danger, McClernand and Sherman at least were satisfied that they would have to fight for the water and its crossing points.

Indeed, Pemberton divined Grant's objective and ordered a brigade from Jackson to Raymond with instructions to strike the enemy in the right flank or rear as they moved toward the railroad and drive them against the Big Black River. (At that moment the Confederate commander was shifting the main body of his army from south of Vicksburg into position along Big Black River, east of the city, to serve as the anvil against which to smash Grant.) If the Union army could be defeated and kept from reaching the shelter of Porter's gunboats in the Mississippi River, it could be destroyed and thus eliminate the most significant threat to Vicksburg.

The Confederate brigade charged with this hazardous assignment was composed of Texans and Tennesseans commanded by Brig. Gen. John Gregg. Although he was born, raised, and educated in Alabama, Gregg moved to Texas in 1852 where he rose to prominence in the practice of law and was elected district judge in 1856. As the nation drifted closer to war, he espoused the principles of states' rights and was elected a member of the Texas secession convention. Following dissolution of the Union, Gregg became a member of the Provisional Confederate Congress where he generally favored legislation that strengthened the central government in Richmond.

The halls of Congress, however, could not content a man of his temperament—a man who thirsted for bloodier fields of battle. Without resigning his seat, he recruited the Seventh Texas Infantry and was elected colonel. His first taste of battle came at Fort Donelson on

Brig. Gen.
John Gregg

National Archives

February 15, 1862, when his regiment participated in the desperate breakout attempt that was recalled at the moment of success. Surrendered with the balance of the garrison, Gregg was imprisoned at Camp Chase in Ohio and later at Fort Warren in Boston harbor. Following his exchange in August of that same year, he was promoted to brigadier general and given command of a Tennessee brigade that fought along the banks of Chickasaw Bayou, north of Vicksburg, in December.[9]

Transferred to Port Hudson, Louisiana, early in 1863 to strengthen the Confederacy's southern bastion on the Mississippi River, Gregg's Brigade was directed to return to the Magnolia State for the defense of Vicksburg—and time was of the essence. His movements, however, were impeded by the havoc wrought by Grierson's Union raiders upon the tracks of the New Orleans, Jackson & Great Northern Railroad that caused the men to march around the gap in the line between Summit and Brookhaven. From Brookhaven the men were able to ride the cars all the way into Jackson where they detrained on May 8 and were able to rest for a couple of days.

But the events of which they were now a part continued to rapidly unfold, and Gregg's Brigade was given its marching orders on Monday, May 11. The men shouldered their weapons and took up the line of march southwest to Raymond, where the white-column courthouse identified the village as one of the seats of government for Hinds County. As they marched, the soldiers from Texas and Tennessee fell victim to the oppressive heat and suffocating clouds of dust that rose from the road and covered them with a thick coating of fine powder. By the time it tramped into Raymond around 4 p.m., Gregg's 3,000-man brigade had dwindled significantly, and the men continued to straggle into town individually or in small clusters for the remainder of the day.

Gregg, however, was not deterred by the situation and set about gathering intelligence on the enemy's movements and local geography, and formulating his plan of action. From Capt. J. M. Hall, whose company of state troops was patrolling out the Utica Road, Gregg learned that the enemy was encamped on the Roach plantation about ten miles from Raymond. Unfortunately the "graybeards and striplings" of the state troops were not able to penetrate the Federal cavalry screen to ascertain the size and composition of the enemy force. Based on Pemberton's evaluation of the intelligence coming into army headquarters, Gregg was notified that the column heading his way was a feint and to expect nothing more than a brigade-strength unit behind a screen of cavalry. The Confederate brigadier acted accordingly and prepared his regiments to spring a trap on the Federals in the morning—unaware of the peril that would soon engulf his command.

May 12 was to be a defining day in the Vicksburg campaign as the armies again clashed at several points along the banks of Fourteenmile Creek. Sensing the approach of battle, Pemberton penned a circular to his troops in which he announced, "The hour of trial has come." He reminded the soldiers of the issues at stake. "The enemy fights for the privilege of plunder and oppression!" he wrote. "You fight for your country, homes, wives, children, and the birth-right of freemen!" In an expression of his Christian faith—a faith shared by thousands in the rank and file of the Army of Vicksburg, he assured the men of his command that "God, who rules in the affairs of men and nations, loves justice and hates wickedness. He will not allow a cause so just, to be trampled in the dust." "In the day of conflict," the Pennsylvanian in gray continued, "let each man appealing to Him for strength, strike home for victory, and our triumph is at once a sured [sic]. A grateful country will hail us as deliverers, and cherish the memory of those who may fall as martyrs in her defense." In closing, he charged his men to "Be vigilant, brave and active; let there be no cowards or laggards, nor stragglers from the ranks—and the God of battle will certainly crown our efforts with success."[10]

As Pemberton sought to inspire his men with lofty words, his opponent was busy maneuvering his three corps into the desired alignment for the strike against the railroad. On Tuesday, May 12, Grant's army advanced along four roads over a 10-mile front. If all went according to plan, by day's end the army would be positioned to hit the railroad the following morning between Bolton and Edwards.

On the left, a division of the XIII Corps led by Brig. Gen. A. J. Smith left its encampment near Cayuga and marched north crossing Fivemile Creek en route to Montgomery's Bridge over Fourteenmile Creek. Smith's division managed to catch the Confederate bridge guards unaware. As the Federals neared the span, the startled Southerners fled, and Smith's men seized the structure which they quickly crossed. After establishing a strong line of pickets, his main force bivouacked south of the creek.

McClernand's other three divisions, commanded by Brig. Gens. Alvin Hovey, Eugene Carr, and Peter Osterhaus in order or march, left their bivouac on the banks of Fivemile Creek at 5:30 a.m. and advanced through Old Auburn where the long column swung north onto the Telegraph Road that led to Edwards Station on the Southern Railroad. Despite the oppressive conditions, the column pushed steadily onward until it was fired upon as the men approached Whitaker's Ford across Fourteenmile Creek. Opposing the advance were three companies of the First Missouri Cavalry (dismounted) supported by a section of artillery. The lead Federal brigade was deployed and advanced through a field and into the woods lining the stream. Only after a spirited fight were the stubborn Confederates forced to retire and fell back to within two miles of Edwards, where they were reinforced. The Northerners did not vigorously pursue, but rather secured their position and improved the approaches to the ford before bedding down for the night south of the creek.

While McClernand's troops brushed aside enemy resistance to establish their bridgehead across Fourteenmile Creek, the soldiers of Sherman's corps—accompanied by General Grant and his staff, pushed east along the main Port Gibson-Raymond Road. Screening the advance were the hard-riding troopers of the Fourth Iowa Cavalry. As the horsemen approached the bridge across Fourteenmile Creek, an unexpected volley zipped through their ranks which, fortunately, only toppled one man from his saddle. Startled by the sudden encounter, the

Iowans dismounted and scurried for cover from where they returned fire with their carbines.

Hearing the sound of gunfire, Sherman ordered forward his lead brigade, which was commanded by Col. Charles Woods. Also galloping forward were the six guns of Capt. Clemens Landgraeber's Battery F, Second Missouri Light Artillery which dropped trail and began spraying the opposite bank with canister. Deploying into line of battle under the protective fire of Landgraeber's guns, Wood's regiments stormed across the stream and drove the enemy away, but not before the Southerners set fire to the bridge which collapsed into the stream in a cloud of smoke and flame.

Federal engineers and pioneers were set to work replacing the bridge in order for the artillery and wagons to roll as the infantrymen splashed across the creek. Sgt. Maj. Edward Reichhelm of the Third Missouri Infantry was angered to see one of his men leave the ranks, but his anger turned to astonishment as the man knelt by a badly wounded Confederate and tenderly embraced him. Reichhelm later learned that the men were brothers whose situation—far from unique, reflected the divided sympathies of border states such as Missouri.

Pleased by the day's events, after his corps had crossed the stream Sherman placed his troops into bivouac in line of battle. But as Grant and his most trusted subordinate settled into their headquarters in the home of Col. W. F. Dillon, the ominous sound of artillery fire rumbling as distant thunder was heard in the direction of Raymond, six miles to the east. The two generals knew instinctively that McPherson's men had run into stiff resistance and anxiously awaited word as to the outcome of the fight.

The morning of May 12 found McPherson's XVII Corps, out on the Federal right flank, marching along the road from Utica toward Raymond. Shortly before 10 a.m., the Union skirmish line swept over a ridge and moved cautiously through open fields into the valley of Fourteenmile Creek, southwest of Raymond. Suddenly a deadly volley ripped into their ranks from the woods that lined the almost-dry stream. Artillery also roared into action announcing the presence of Brig. Gen. John Gregg's battle-hardened Confederate brigade.

The ever-combative Gregg decided to strike with his 3,000-man brigade, turn the Federal right flank, and capture the force in his front. Faulty intelligence had led him to believe that he faced only a small contingent of Union troops when, in reality, McPherson's 10,000-man corps was on the road before him. Regardless of the odds, Gregg's fighting blood was up and he directed his troops to advance.

Shortly after noon, Gregg's regiments advanced across the creek en echelon from right to left and slammed into the opposing ranks with a vengeance. The blue line wavered and broke in places. Some men even cast their weapons aside and raced to the rear in panic. Among the units caught in the gray surge was the Twentieth Ohio which sought shelter in the creek, the banks of which stood fifteen feet high. Just moments before someone noticed Cpl. Calvin Waddell of Company E, looking at his reflection in a mirror and grooming himself as if it truly mattered at this time. "Cal, you needn't fix up so nice to go into battle," he yelled, "for the rebs won't think any better of you." A few moments later a ball crashed through Waddell's brain and he fell into the muddy water now mixed with the blood of his comrades. Sgt. Osborn Oldroyd sadly recorded, "With the assistance of two others I picked him up, carried him over the bank in our rear, and laid [him] behind a tree, removing from his pocket, watch and trinkets, and the same little mirror that had helped him make his last toilet but a little while before." The Twentieth Ohio would count 10 killed and 58 wounded by day's end.[11]

Seeing panic spread among his troops, Maj. Gen. John A. Logan, whose Federal division was the first to arrive and deploy on the field, rode forward at this critical moment and with "the shriek of an eagle" turned them back to their places. The battle grew in intensity as soldiers in blue and gray sought the shelter of the creek from where they fired away at one another separated, in some areas, only by a small meander loop. Col. Manning Force of the Twentieth Ohio observed "one tree in front of my line was stripped and hacked near the root by balls, though not a mark was found more than 2 feet above the ground."[12]

Although the Confederates enjoyed initial success, as Gregg's regiments attacked en echelon across the creek, Union resistance stiffened. But the thick clouds of smoke and dust that quickly obscured the field prevented either commander from accurately assessing the size of the force in his front. The ferocious nature of the Southern attack and the manner in which it unfolded compelled McPherson, despite his numerically superior strength, to react to the situation rather than control the battle. Thus, in his first test as a combat commander, McPherson yielded the initiative to the more aggressive, determined, and dangerous John Gregg.

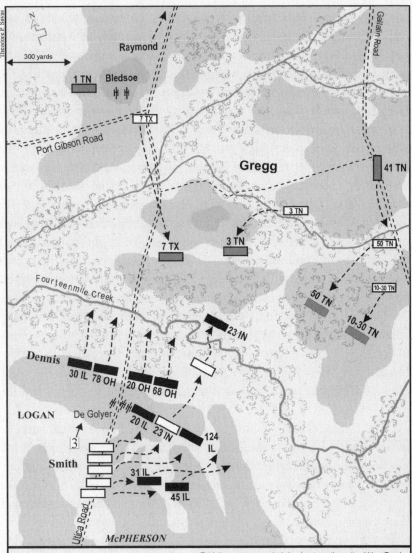

BATTLE OF RAYMOND

Deploy and Engage
10:30 a.m.-12:30 p.m., May 12, 1863

Told the enemy was in brigade strength on the Utica Road, Gregg deploys his regiments to stop them. His artillery fire and skirmishers bring the vanguard of McPherson's corps (Logan's division) to a halt. Logan deploys Dennis and Smith and moves into the bottomland around Fourteenmile Creek. The wooded terrain, creased by ravines filled with brush, makes maneuvering and reconnaissance difficult for both sides.

Additional Union regiments, however, continued to arrive and deploy into line of battle on the high ground south of Fourteenmile Creek, from where they were thrown into the fray. Union guns rolled into position and increased in number until 22 pieces were pounding the enemy. By early afternoon, Gregg's attack ground to a halt. The brigadier from Texas realized a much larger Federal force was on the field.

This fact also became apparent to McPherson by mid-afternoon when wind associated with a weather front began pushing through the area and lifted the shroud of smoke obscuring the field. Somewhat embarrassed that his powerful corps had been bested thus far by an inferior force, the Union commander launched a counterattack. In piecemeal fashion, McPherson's men pushed forward at 1:30 p.m. and drove the Confederates back across the creek. The fighting that ensued was of the most confused nature. The dense vegetation lining the stream and lingering smoke of battle made it difficult for the commanders to know where their units were or what they were doing. Referred to as a "soldier's battle," the fight was directed by regimental and company commanders more than by general officers on either side. Union strength of numbers, however, prevailed and the Southern line began to buckle. Under tremendous pressure the Confederate right flank along the Utica road finally broke and Gregg had no alternative but to retire from the field.

The fight at Raymond cost Gregg 73 killed, 252 wounded, and 190 missing, most of whom were from the Third Tennessee and Seventh Texas. As his regiments retreated through the tree-shaded streets of town with the enemy in close pursuit, Gregg's soldiers were unable to partake of a feast prepared for them by the citizens of Raymond in anticipation of their victory. Rather, much to the townspeople's chagrin, soldiers from Ohio with voracious appetites enjoyed the picnic as their "victors" fled out the Jackson road to the east. Exhausted by the day's events, the weary Confederates fell to the ground and bivouacked for the night along Snake Creek. The following day, Gregg's Brigade broke contact with the enemy and tramped into Jackson.

There was no Federal pursuit past Raymond and McPherson's troops bedded down for the night in and around the town. In the engagement on May 12, McPherson lost 446 men of whom 68 were killed, 341 wounded, and 37 missing. Pleased with the outcome of battle, the commander of the XVII Corps had his men bury the dead and remove the wounded from the

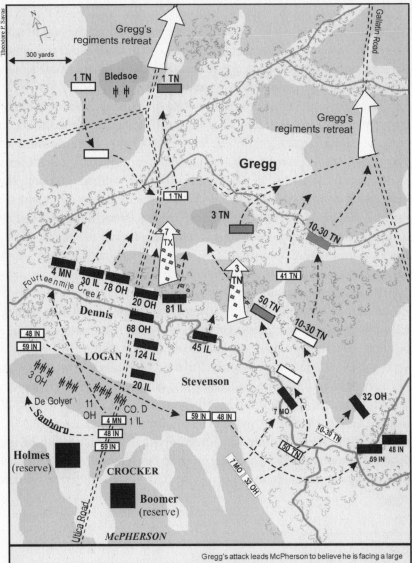

Theodore P. Savas

300 yards

N

Gregg's
regiments retreat

1 TN   Bledsoe   1 TN

Gallatin Road

Gregg's
regiments retreat

Gregg

1 TN

3 TN

10-30 TN

7
TX

41 TN

4 MN 30 IL 78 OH

Fourteenmile Creek

Dennis

20 OH   81 IL

68 OH

45 IL

50 TN

10-30 TN

124 IL

LOGAN

20 IL

Stevenson

3
TN

48 IN
59 IN

3 OH

De Golyer 11
OH

32 OH

Sanborn

CO. D
4 MN 1 IL
48 IN
59 IN

59 IN   48 IN

7 MO

10-30 TN

48 IN
59 IN

Holmes
(reserve)

CROCKER

50 TN

7 MO   32 OH

Boomer
(reserve)

Utica Road

McPHERSON

BATTLE OF RAYMOND

Repulse & Counterattack
1:30 p.m. - 4:00 p.m., May 12, 1863

Gregg's attack leads McPherson to believe he is facing a large
opponent. Logan uncoils his division and once deployed,
moves forward and sweeps back Gregg's fragmented
brigade. Crocker's division arrives behind Logan; one brigade
(Sanborn) joins the action. With a masterful tactical touch,
Gregg pulls back his bloodied regiments and withdraws from
the field. McPherson does not vigorously pursue.

field. That evening he sent a courier to Grant to inform the army commander of his clash with enemy forces and detail the day's action. In his report, however, McPherson (perhaps out of embarrassment) doubled the size of the enemy force engaged that day, crediting the Confederates with 6,000 men supported by two batteries.

Regardless of numbers the Battle of Raymond was a relatively minor engagement by Civil War standards, yet one that had a profound effect on the Vicksburg campaign. With the XVII Corps in possession of Raymond, the Army of the Tennessee had achieved the desired alignment and was now in position to strike the railroad. But with his objective within easy reach, Grant changed the direction of his army's march based on McPherson's report of Gregg's strength. Fearful lest he leave a sizeable enemy force in his rear after he cut the railroad then wheeled west toward Vicksburg, the ever-adaptive Grant decided to turn east and instead move on Jackson, the state capital.

It was a bold decision fraught with many dangers as the Union army would push even deeper into Mississippi. In so doing Grant was putting himself—as Sherman expressed his concerns early in the campaign, "in a position voluntarily which an enemy would be glad to maneuver a year—or a long time" to get him in. But it was a decision consistent with the manner in which Grant waged his unique style of warfare during the Vicksburg campaign—a style that Historian Edwin C. Bearss compared to Gen. George S. Patton and the Third Army's sweep across Europe following the Allies' landing at Normandy in 1944. In writing of the decision to march on Jackson, Bearss noted "such audacity was unheard of in modern military annals," yet was the hallmark of blitzkrieg—Grant style.[13]

CHAPTER THREE

The National Colors Are Restored O'er the Capitol

The focus of Grant's operations now shifted to Jackson, Mississippi's capital city, which was situated on the Pearl River approximately 14 miles northeast of Raymond. The city served as a funnel through which most of the supplies of men and war materiél passed to Vicksburg. It was his intention to destroy Jackson as a rail and communications center and scatter any Confederate reinforcements that might be en route to Vicksburg. (At that very moment several gray-clad brigades coming from the south and east were moving rapidly by rail toward the city.) To neutralize Jackson, therefore, was essential to safeguard the rear of his army as it marched west toward Vicksburg and would make the task of capturing the Confederate Gibraltar that much easier.

The Union commander boldly decided to march on the capital with two of his three corps—those of McPherson and Sherman. The movement required the Army of the Tennessee to wheel 90 degrees to the east—a difficult maneuver under any circumstance. Of greater concern, the movement would leave Confederate General Pemberton with his Vicksburg field army situated at Edwards, perched dangerously in his rear. To protect the troops marching on Jackson, Grant directed General McClernand to position his corps on a line from Bolton to Raymond facing west to serve as a shield against Pemberton's force at Edwards.

McClernand had the far more difficult assignment. Three of his divisions were in proximity to the enemy near Whittaker's Ford, only four miles south of Edwards where Pemberton's forces were concentrating, while his remaining division was in contact with the enemy farther west at Montgomery's Bridge. The former congressman would have to break contact with the enemy and move his divisions quickly to avoid entanglement with Confederate forces, which outnumbered him 2-1. "The movement ordered was a delicate and hazardous one," wrote McClernand, "but was calculated to deceive the enemy as to our design." The operation required diligence, skill, and precise execution and would be carried out flawlessly by the rugged soldiers of the XIII Corps.[1]

Early on Wednesday, May 13, the lead division of McClernand's corps, commanded by Brig. Gen. Alvin P. Hovey, splashed across Fourteenmile Creek at Whittaker's Ford and deployed into line of battle astride the road that led to Edwards. With their banners snapping in the breeze and bayonets glistening in the morning light, Hovey's troops presented quite a spectacle. Yet, it was nothing but an elaborate feint to hold the enemy in check and enabled the divisions of Generals Eugene Carr and Peter Osterhaus to also cross the creek then turn southeast and head to Dillon's plantation and on to Raymond. "The movement was happily executed," reported McClernand, "and had the effect to throw the enemy upon his defense against apprehended attack."[2]

Having accomplished his task, Hovey retired from his advance position by successive regiments and marched rapidly to distance the division from its foe. One soldier recorded, "About Noon, having driven in all the advanced posts of the enemy, we faced to the right and moved rapidly to the east, leaving the rebel army in line of battle awaiting our attack." An officer from Ohio, who took delight in their accomplishment, boasted, "Our route through the woods was very pleasant and the men enjoyed it, also the joke we had played on the rebels, holding their army in line with two or three regiments, while our main force marched on their scarcely protected capitol." By the time the Confederates realized they had been fooled and sent troops in pursuit, Hovey's division was safely across Bakers Creek and McClernand's corps went into bivouac west of Raymond.[3]

Farther west, the XIII Corps division led by Brig. Gen. A. J. Smith that had stormed across Fourteenmile Creek the previous day and captured Montgomery's Bridge intact, was also ordered to move lest it be isolated and left dreadfully exposed. Smith, who became recognized as "one of the most competent division and [later] corps commanders in the service," withdrew his command across the creek without difficulty and burned the bridge behind him to prevent pursuit. The division marched south then east to New Auburn where the men went into camp for the night. Here they were joined next afternoon by the soldiers of Maj. Gen. Frank Blair's XV Corps division who were escorting a 200-wagon train filled with ammunition and hardtack. (This ammunition served to replenish the army's supply which, in the aftermath of the battles at Jackson, May 14, and Champion Hill, May 16, was dangerously low.)[4]

While McClernand skillfully disengaged his command, in accordance with instructions received from army headquarters, McPherson's corps moved north through Raymond to Clinton on May 13, while Sherman pushed northeast from Dillon's plantation through Raymond to Mississippi Springs. These movements were accomplished without incident and by nightfall both corps were positioned to strike at Jackson the following morning.

"We were astir early and ready to move," recorded H. S. Keene of the Sixth Wisconsin Battery, one of McPherson's men, "but it was 7 or 8 o'clock before we started." As the soldiers of the XVII Corps marched out of Raymond, their advance was screened by the troopers of Capt. John S. Foster's Provisional Cavalry Battalion who bumped into Confederate cavalry patrols along the way. "There was some skirmishing in front from time to time," recalled Keene, "so we moved slowly and cautiously." The march was further slowed by the weather which was hot and sultry, and a blazing Mississippi sun beat down unmercifully upon the men who trudged along enveloped by suffocating clouds of dust.[5]

By midafternoon the spires of Clinton's houses of worship came into view. "The Yankees are coming, the Yankees are coming," was the cry heard throughout town as the long blue column approached. "The news spread terror to all hearts," remembered Alice Shirley, a nineteen-year-old native of Vicksburg who attended the Central Female Institute in Clinton. "The people of the village were hurrying hither and yon, the women hysterical, many hiding their jewels and their money."[6]

McPherson's lead division pushed through town and established its camp one mile east of Clinton on the road to Jackson. His other division occupied the village and the men were set to work destroying all of military value. The tracks of the Southern Railroad of Mississippi were torn up and the depot burned, telegraph lines were cut, and military stores were seized. Alice Shirley committed to the pages of her diary all that she witnessed:

> The usually quiet village of Clinton was now all confusion. The soldiers were bent on destruction, stables were torn down, smoke houses invaded and emptied of their bacon and hams, chicken houses were depopulated, vehicles of all kinds were taken or destroyed, barrels of sugar and molasses . . . were emptied, the molasses running in streams in the yard. The sugar was carried off. The bees, not liking to be disturbed, and attracted also by the flowing molasses, hovered around in large numbers and directed much of their attention to the soldiers, adding still more to the confusion, and then, too, the soldiers were chasing hens around the yard trying to catch them, and the frightened fowls squawked and lent their voices to the uproar. The dry goods stores were broken into, the beautiful goods given to negroes or destroyed, crockery broken, making sad havoc with the merchants' stock.[7]

Though unheralded at the time, the occupation of Clinton was significant as the Federals cut the railroad, which was Grant's interim objective, preventing reinforcements and supplies from reaching Vicksburg. But perhaps of greater importance, by severing the telegraph lines they forced the enemy to rely on mounted couriers for communications between Pemberton and Confederate forces in Jackson. According to logistician Warren Grabau, "They would need some twelve hours to send a dispatch and receive a reply. That would be far too long a time to permit adequate coordination of forces in a situation as fluid as this one." (This situation led in part to the fall of Jackson on May 14 and the Confederate disaster at Champion Hill two days later. And, during the siege of Vicksburg the lack of timely and effective communications between Pemberton and Gen. Joseph E. Johnston in Jackson ensured that cooperation between their two armies for the relief of the city and its garrison was not achieved.)[8]

That same morning, Grant awoke at Dillon's plantation and following a meager meal accompanied Sherman's corps on the march to Raymond. (Grant had lost his false teeth on February 11 when his servant inadvertently threw them into the Mississippi River when he emptied the general's washbasin. Grant ate mostly soft foods until his new set of teeth arrived.) The commanding general established his headquarters at Waverly, the home of Maj. John Peyton, located just north of the town square on the road to Clinton, while Sherman's men pushed through town and continued northeastward to Mississippi Springs where the XV Corps bivouacked for the night.

*   *   *

Following the battle at Raymond on May 12, Confederate Brig. Gen. John Gregg, whose troops had bivouacked along Snake Creek just east of the village, was instructed to fall back on Jackson. In so doing, he broke contact with the Federals which led to misperception and confusion during the fight for the capital. On May 13, Southern cavalry picked up McPherson's march on Clinton and further reported that two Union divisions (Sherman's) had reached Raymond. Without direct contact to accurately monitor enemy movements, however, it was falsely assumed these divisions were also en route to Clinton. Thus as Sherman's troops continued in a northeasterly direction toward Mississippi Springs, Gregg had no knowledge of their movements.

Late in the afternoon of May 13, as the Federals closed on Jackson, a train arrived in the capital city carrying Confederate Gen. Joseph E. Johnston. Ordered to Jackson by President Jefferson Davis, Johnston was to salvage the rapidly deteriorating situation in Mississippi. Establishing his headquarters in the Bowman House, the general was apprised of available troop strength and the condition of the fortifications around Jackson. He immediately wired the authorities in Richmond; "I am too late." Instead of fighting for Jackson, Johnston ordered the city evacuated. (In response to the Federal threat, Governor John J. Pettus had already moved the seat of state government to Enterprise, located near the Alabama line, south of Meridian.) He instructed Gregg to fight a delaying action to cover the evacuation then, along with his staff, Johnston also departed the city. The general and his entourage left Jackson as a heavy rain fell and rode to Tougaloo, seven miles north of the capital.[9]

Gregg wasted no time in getting his troops into position to resist the enemy onslaught. Believing that the Federals would be advancing from

Clinton, he directed Col. Peyton Colquitt's small brigade to move beyond the city's fortifications where it assumed a defensive position on the O. P. Wright farm, three miles northwest of city center. The two remaining brigades available to Gregg were moved to within supporting distance and ordered to be ready at a moment's notice to advance to Colquitt's assistance. Once in position, the troops settled down for a long, wet night as the rain fell now in torrents.

*   *   *

"Oh, how it did rain," complained S. C. Beck of the 124th Illinois Infantry as McPherson's men awoke on Thursday, May 14. "Marching in the rain and mud, shoe-mouth deep was fearful." H. S. Keene of the Sixth Wisconsin Battery lamented, "I don't think rain ever fell much faster, even in the south. The water was soon sweeping over everything and the roads were very muddy." "But," boasted the artilleryman from Wisconsin, "this did not check the advance of our troops." "During the forenoon we got perfectly soaked," recalled Richard C. Hunt of the Twentieth Ohio about the march on Jackson. A fellow member of his regiment, Sgt. Osborn Oldroyd, recorded:

> Started again this morning for Jackson. When within five miles of the city we heard heavy firing. It has rained hard to-day and we have had both a wet and muddy time, pushing at the heavy artillery and provision wagons accompanying us when they stuck in the mud. The rain came down in perfect torrents. What a sight! Ambulances creeping along at the side of the track—artillery toiling in the deep ruts, while generals with their aids and orderlies splashed mud and water in every direction in passing. We were all wet to the skin, but plodded on patiently, for the love of country.[10]

Inexorably, though slowly, McPherson's water-soaked column closed on Jackson. Around 9:00 a.m., the four guns of the Brookhaven Light Artillery posted on the O. P. Wright farm fired on the lead elements of his corps, announcing to everyone within earshot that the battle had been joined. "We found the enemy in force, on the crest of a ridge which extends a considerable distance along the west side of the city," wrote Harvey Trimble of the Ninety-third Illinois Infantry. "The division [Crocker's] was immediately formed in line of battle, extended to the right and left across the road, at the foot of the western slope of that ridge, full three-quarters of a mile from the enemy's position." Despite the projectiles whistling over head, the sergeant-major from Princeton, Illinois, took note of the countryside. "That slope, covered with green grass and dotted here and there with small groves and short stretches of young timber," he wrote, "was as beautiful as nature could make it. It was the subject for an artist's pencil."[11]

Instantly there was a flurry of activity as the Union corps commander deployed his men into line of battle and prepared to attack. The rain, however, continued to fall in sheets which compelled McPherson to postpone the attack until the rain stopped. He later explained "that there was great danger of the ammunition being spoiled if the men opened their cartridge-boxes." The handsome young corps commander from Ohio reported, "The time, however, was well employed in putting the troops in position and bringing up [Maj. Gen. John A.] Logan's division as a reserve."[12]

In conjunction with McPherson's march on Jackson, Sherman's veterans were also en route to the capital city from Mississippi Springs. At 3 a.m. the men of the XV Corps were awakened by the clarion call of bugles which echoed through the camps and pierced the pre-dawn darkness as did the rain. "The bugles sang reveille as sweetly as though the sun was shining on the drenched violets by the muddy roadside and in the dripping woods," noted Robert J. Burdette of the Forty-seventh Illinois. By comparison he observed that, "The drums beat sullenly, for like many more delicate musicians they are very sensitive to changes in the weather, and never like to get their heads wet." With words less poetic, Byron Bryner, a fellow soldier in the Forty-seventh, lamented, "The weather was tempestuous and when the march was resumed in the morning the roads were muddy and the rain falling in torrents."[13]

As his rain-soaked soldiers inched their way to within three miles of the capital, the cavalry advance reported the enemy in position at the bridge across Lynch Creek, only two miles southwest of the State House. (Fortunately for the Confederates their scouting forces were functioning properly and detected Sherman's advance in time to react. The Third Kentucky Mounted Infantry, First Georgia Sharpshooter Battalion, and the four guns of Capt. Robert Martin's Georgia Battery were rushed into position arriving in time to contest the Federal advance. This quick action averted disaster at Jackson, otherwise the XV Corps would have entered the capital unopposed, thus cutting off Gregg's forces on the Clinton Road.) Shortly after 10:00 a.m., as Sherman's advance started down a slope toward the creek, the shrill whistle of artillery shells announced the presence of Confederate troops in the open fields north of the stream. Union batteries were run forward, dropped trail, and roared into action in angry response. "The regiment followed to the brow of the hill that looked down on the creek winding in muddy swirls and many meanderings across the level meadows," wrote a soldier from Illinois whose regiment deployed as part of the lead brigade. "Far to our right we could hear our own battery, the Second Iowa, its bronze Napoleons throbbing like a heart of fire. And at our left the Waterhouse Battery, of Chicago [Company E, First Illinois Light Artillery], was baying like a wolf-hound at the gray battalions."[14]

Robert Burdette of the Forty-seventh Illinois described the Federal deployment this way: "A dull staccato thunder of guns in the distant front, a galloping staff-orderly giving an order to Colonel [John] Cromwell, which he shouted to us; a sudden barking of many commands from the line officers; a double-quicking of the column into the line, and almost in the time I have written it we were in line of battle in the woods before Jackson, Mississippi." In short order the overwhelming numbers of Union soldiers coupled with the accurate fire of Federal batteries compelled the Confederates to seek shelter behind the city's defenses, one-half mile to the northeast. Due to the heavy rain, however, the Southerners made no attempt to fire the narrow wooden bridge across the bank-full stream, thus providing Sherman's men with the means to cross Lynch Creek.[15]

Reforming his troops into column formation Sherman ordered his men to push across the creek. The time was a little after 11 a.m. and, thankfully, the rain ceased, eliminating an unpleasant factor from the day's equation. "Crossing the bridges and emerging from the woods, far away to the left, could be seen a line of entrenchments, bristling with guns behind, which pressed the intense, earnest faces of a brave soldiery," wrote Byron Bryner from Peoria, Illinois. "A brisk fire from their guns opened and continued for some time."[16]

The Federal advance ground to a halt as a hailstorm of canister ripped through the air. As the men hugged Mother Earth for self preservation, they peppered the works with a shower of their own to drive the enemy

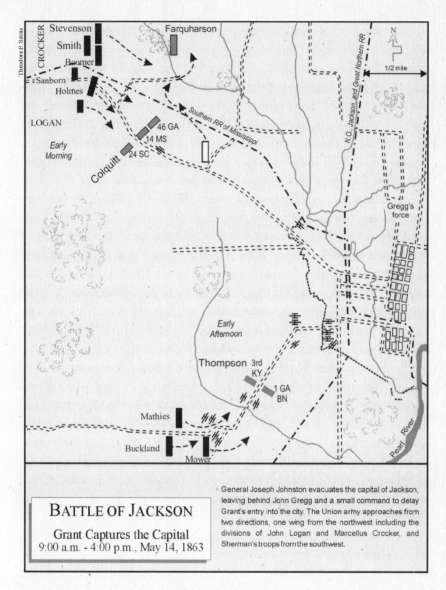

BATTLE OF JACKSON

Grant Captures the Capital
9:00 a.m. - 4:00 p.m., May 14, 1863

General Joseph Johnston evacuates the capital of Jackson, leaving behind John Gregg and a small command to delay Grant's entry into the city. The Union army approaches from two directions, one wing from the northwest including the divisions of John Logan and Marcellus Crocker, and Sherman's troops from the southwest.

from their guns. A regiment of soldiers from Illinois complied with the request of their colonel who directed the men to "Keep up a rapid fire in the general direction of the enemy, and yell all the time." One man recalled that the colonel "was very specific regarding the kind of 'yelling,' which was to be emphatically sulphurous."[17]

Not wishing to expose his men to such deadly fire, Sherman sent one regiment to the right (east) at 2 p.m. in search of a weak spot in the defense line. The men of the Ninety-fifth Ohio moved off through the woods until they reached the tracks of the New Orleans, Jackson & Great Northern Railroad then turned north and nervously approached the enemy fortifications. Tension mounted as they neared the works and, as they scaled the parapet, the Ohioans were greatly relieved to find them deserted. Col. William McMillen, commander of the regiment, reported with pride that he "planted my colors in full view of the city."[18]

An elderly black man waving his hat greeted the soldiers in blue from Ohio saying, "Ise come to tell you-all that the Rebels is left the city, clear done gone. You jes go on and you will take the city." In disbelief, one Ohioan asked, "Why are the Rebs still firing their battery if they had left the place?" Laughing, the black man replied, "Oh! There is only a few cannoneers there to work the guns to keep you back." True enough, the Buckeyes discovered only a handful of state troops and civilian volunteers manning the guns in Sherman's front and took them prisoner clearing the way for their comrades to enter Jackson.[19]

Seeing the men from Ohio go over the parapet, the other units of Sherman's command surged forward. "The bugles called sweetly and imperiously, the colonel's voice rang out stern, peremptory, inspiring, the line sprang to its feet, and with mighty shouting rushed forward like unleashed dogs of war," recorded a soldier from Illinois. An infantryman in the Twelfth Iowa remarked that "the yell that those wet Northern boys gave was enough to scare even the ghosts of the Southern Confederacy." One man who charged the works forever remembered the scene: "Thundering guns, rattling musketry, cheering and more cheering, a triumphant charge, a wild pursuit, a mad dash—we were over the works and into the city."[20]

The ease with which Sherman's men entered Jackson was a different experience than the fighting that erupted on the Clinton Road as the XVII Corps battled its way into the capital city. As McPherson's troops braved the elements waiting for the rain to stop, one of his soldiers noted in frustration by noting, "Their infantry was secreted just over the brow of the hill from our forces, where their sharpshooters were making sad havoc among our men." The battle-tested veterans, however, knew their time would come and they would soon be able to wreak their revenge on the pesky foe.[21]

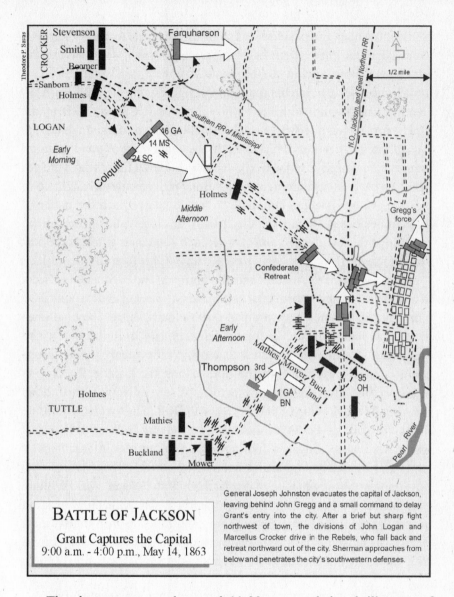

Theodore P. Savas

BATTLE OF JACKSON

Grant Captures the Capital
9:00 a.m. - 4:00 p.m., May 14, 1863

General Joseph Johnston evacuates the capital of Jackson, leaving behind John Gregg and a small command to delay Grant's entry into the city. After a brief but sharp fight northwest of town, the divisions of John Logan and Marcellus Crocker drive in the Rebels, who fall back and retreat northward out of the city. Sherman approaches from below and penetrates the city's southwestern defenses.

The downpour ceased around 11:00 a.m. and the shrill notes of bugles sounded the advance. Raising a mighty cheer, the Federals sprang forward with bayonets fixed and banners unfurled. "With a shout they started up the hill amid a perfect shower of balls that rapidly thinned their ranks, but nothing seemed to check their progress," remembered H. S. Keene of the Sixth Wisconsin Battery. "Not a Co.—hardly a man—was seen to waver, but in a straight line they rushed over the hill with one continuous shout. Every effort was made by the rebels to check them, but to no purpose. They swept everything before them, soon having the butternuts double quicking to the woods."[22]

Clashing in a bitter hand-to-hand struggle with the soldiers from Georgia and South Carolina who comprised Colquitt's Brigade, McPherson's men overwhelmed the Southerners and forced them back toward the fortifications of Jackson. In the excitement of victory Union infantrymen chased after the Confederates, capturing those who were not fleet of foot. Even artilleryman Keene from Wisconsin was caught up in the race. "Capt. [Henry] Dillon also made a charge with the battery," Keen remembered, "following the infantry up closely, he opened on the retreating rebels with shell and canister, and soon their whole force was on the retreat."[23]

The disorganized pursuit compelled brigade and regimental officers to halt their men and reform their commands. It was not until around 2:30 p.m. that the advance was resumed under cloudy skies. The blue lines moved cautiously toward the city's defenses only to find (no doubt to their relief) that they had been abandoned by the enemy whose troops could be seen evacuating to the north along the Canton Road. One member of the advancing brigades wrote, "When ready, we were ordered forward and did not stop until we reached the R.R. depot with the Rebs on the run. I shall never forget that sight on looking back after the rebel works were taken, Logan's div. moving up in our rear in four lines of battle was a grand and imposing sight."[24]

Among the regiments that marched with Logan was William Crummer of the Forty-fifth Illinois Infantry. Although his regiment did not get the chance to burn powder during the battle, the men from Illinois suffered a number of casualties and were ingloriously routed—not by the sting of enemy bullets, rather, as Crummer detailed:

> We were in line of battle and had moved up to the vicinity of a plantation around which were scattered a number of bee hives. Now, had we not been engaged with the enemy, our boys would have liked nothing better than to have despoiled those bees and supped on honey, but for the present we had important work at hand. The bees were quiet enough until the minie-balls went crashing through their hives, when they came out and rushed at us with terrible ferocity. Men can stand up and be shot at, all day, with the deadly musket, but when a swarm of bees pounces upon a

company of men in concert, it's beyond human nature to stand it, and so two or three companies retired from the field. . . . They had no "rebel yell" but their charge on us was a successful one.[25]

The Federal soldiers swept over the earthworks, capturing four pieces of artillery which had been left by the fleeing graycoats and pushed into the heart of Jackson. As he moved past the city's stately residences, Sergeant Oldroyd of the Twentieth Ohio viewed a number of dead or dying enemy soldiers lying in the city streets. "I never saw finer looking men than the killed and wounded rebels of to-day, and with the smooth face of one of them, lying in a garden mortally wounded, I was so taken, that I eased his thirst with a drink from my own canteen. His piteous glance at me at that time I shall never forget." The twenty-one-year-old sergeant philosophized, "It is on the battle field and among the dead and dying we get to know each other better—nay, even our own selves. Administering to a stranger, we think of his mother's love, as dear to him as our own to us. When the fight is over, away all bitterness. Let us leave with the foe some tokens of good will, that, when the cruel war at last is over, may be kindly remembered."[26]

The Confederates were well out the Canton Road to the north when Union troops entered Jackson around 3:00 p.m. Once inside the defense perimeter the race was on between Sherman and McPherson's men to place their colors atop the capitol. Participating in the race was young Fred Grant, son of Ulysses, who, accompanied by newspaperman Sylvanus Cadwallader was after a different honor. The men in the ranks found it a laughable sight as the twelve-year-old boy in a mud splattered uniform and the dapperly attired reporter "started for the Capitol at full speed to secure the large Confederate flag which waves from a staff on the roof." Dismounting in front of the building, the pair raced up the steps only to meet "a ragged, muddy, begrimed cavalryman descending with the coveted prize under his arm." His vision of fame and glory dashed, the *Chicago Times* reporter lamented, "To say that our disappointment was extreme but mildly expresses the state of our feelings."[27]

McPherson's men won the race between the corps. Colonel Jesse Alexander, commanding the Fifty-ninth Indiana, reported with justifiable pride, "At this point Capt. L. [Lucien] B. Martin rode up and asked for the colors of the Fifty-ninth. I ordered them given to him, when he placed our colors on the dome of the capitol, where they remained in charge of my color-guard whom I had ordered to guard them till next morning. They were the first and only colors planted on the capitol of Jackson."[28]

In the short but spirited engagement at Jackson, Union casualties totaled 300 men of whom 42 were killed, 251 wounded, and 7 missing. Confederate casualties were not accurately reported but estimated at 845 killed, wounded, and missing. In addition, 17 pieces of artillery fell into Federal hands. Of greater importance, Confederate forces that were streaming toward Jackson to bolster the defenders of Vicksburg were scattered to the winds and effective communications between those forces and Pemberton's army destroyed, which would dramatically impact the campaign as it continued to unfold.

As the Hoosiers unfurled their coveted banner, the Stars and Stripes which proudly snapped in the breeze not only symbolized Union victory, but identified Jackson as the third capital of a seceded state to have the national colors restored to its place of honor above the State House. "To-night the stars and stripes float proudly over the cupola of the seat of government of Mississippi," Sergeant Oldroyd from Ohio scribbled in the pages of his diary that night, "and if my own regiment has not had a chance to-day to cover itself with glory it has with mud."[29]

Union soldiers quickly filled the streets of Jackson and began a search for enemy soldiers and war materiél. "In the evening I was sent out after rebs hiding in houses," wrote an artilleryman from Wisconsin serving under McPherson. "I found four in one house in bed with their clothes on and guns between them. We took them with us." Some soldiers explored the city or went sightseeing among who was George W. Huff of the Eightieth Ohio, another one of McPherson's men. He observed, "Jackson is a very nice place and has not been damaged much by artillery." H. S. Keene of the Sixth Wisconsin Battery expressed a different view: "Jackson is hardly what might be expected of the capitol of a proud state like Mississippi." Still others, such as Enoch Williams of the Eighth Iowa Infantry, simply sought a degree of comfort. "[Although] we were muddy and tired," he admitted, "we found plenty of cotton and good quarters which afforded us a good nights rest."[30]

Not wishing to waste combat troops on occupation, Grant ordered Jackson neutralized militarily. The torch was applied to machine shops and factories, telegraph lines were cut, and railroad tracks destroyed. All facilities that supported the war effort were burned, including a textile factory in which women rolled out cloth marked "C.S.A." Grant, who was visiting the facility with Sherman, turned to his trusted corps commander and suggested that the women had done enough work. Prior to burning the factory, the generals permitted the women to leave and take with them all the cloth they could carry.

"In Jackson the Arsenal Buildings, the Government Foundry, the Gun Carriage Establishment, including the carriages for two complete six gun batteries, stable, carpenter and paint shops, were destroyed," recorded Byron Bryner of the Forty-seventh Illinois. "The penitentiary was burned, I think, by some convicts who had been set free by the Confederate authorities, also a very valuable cotton factory." He further noted, "Other buildings were destroyed in Jackson by some mischievous soldiers (who could not be detected) which was not justified by the rules of war, including the Catholic Church and the Confederate Hotel, the former resulting from accidental circumstances and the latter from malice."[31]

Indeed, the proprietor of the hotel, which was located near the railroad depot, inquired of Sherman on May 15 as the general was leaving town if he intended to burn the structure. In a gruff voice Sherman replied, "We have no intention to burn it, or any other house, except the machine-shops, and such buildings as could easily be converted to hostile uses." Greatly relieved, the owner professed to be a strong Union man only to have the general rebuke him stating that his sympathies were evident from the sign on front. It read "Confederate Hotel," but under the first word could be seen "United States" imperfectly painted over.

Despite Sherman's assurance, as the general rode out of Jackson the hotel burst into flames. Although no one has identified the culprits, the commander of the XV Corps believed that it was infantrymen from Iowa. Those suspected of the blaze had been captured the previous year at Shiloh and, while passing through Jackson, had been permitted to go to the Confederate Hotel for supper. However, having only greenbacks with which to pay, they were refused supper and insulted by the proprietor. The men now feasted on revenge.[32]

The destruction of Jackson's military capabilities continued unabated throughout May 15 as Sherman's men freely applied the torch.

(McPherson's corps returned to Clinton accompanied by Grant and his staff.) Unfortunately for the citizens of Jackson, the fires were fanned by strong winds associated with the storm that had practically drowned the city the previous day and the flames spread to residential areas. Much of Jackson was left a smoldering ruin, earning the capital city the name "Chimneyville." "It was sad indeed to see great quantities of valuable supplies given over to the flames. They would have been a boon to our army, but there was no way to take them along," commented Charles A. Willison of the Seventy-sixth Ohio Infantry.[33]

Willison was a seventeen-year-old private from Massillon who served in Company I. (In 1864, his twin brother Benjamin joined him in service.) "What grieved me most I think was to see the sugar warehouses with their tiers upon tiers of sugar hogsheads, going up in fire and smoke," the young man wrote regretfully. At 5 feet 4 ½ inches tall, Willison was not robust, but had a large appetite and evidently a sweet tooth. "I loved sugar—it had always been a luxury with me, how great was evidenced by my carrying eight or nine canteens of it, hung to my shoulders, as we marched out of the city." He later confessed, "But my endurance proved not equal to my zeal for sugar. One by one the canteens had to go as the straps cut into my shoulder."[34]

To complete the task of destruction and ensure that Confederate forces could never again fully utilize Jackson as a supply and communication center, Sherman's troops destroyed the railroads that radiated from the capital city. He reported on the effectiveness of his men: "The railroads were destroyed by burning the ties and warping the iron. I estimate the destruction of the roads 4 miles east of Jackson, 3 south, 3 north, and 10 west." A soldier from Ohio added one final detail: "Pearl river bridge having been burnt by the enemy, its abutments were battered down by our artillery. This ruthless destruction was necessary for the protection of our rear, as we turned to the hard task yet before us toward Vicksburg."[35]

With Jackson in flames and Johnston's forces continuing in flight toward Canton, Grant turned west with confidence toward his objective—Vicksburg. On May 16, the Army of the Tennessee clashed with Pemberton's Confederates at Champion Hill (near Edwards Station) in what was the largest, bloodiest, and most significant action of the Vicksburg campaign. Anticipating battle that morning, Grant sent a courier racing to Sherman in Jackson directing him to march immediately to support the other corps. Without delay, Sherman instructed one of his divisions to march at 10 a.m., the other by noon. Prisoners were paroled, and the wounded men who would be left behind were made as comfortable as possible.

As the last of the Federal troops were leaving Jackson, Col. John N. Cromwell of the Forty-seventh Illinois rode back into the city to speak with Surgeon Henry S. Hewett. Cromwell, who had been captured at Iuka in September 1862, and later exchanged, also wanted to offer words of comfort to the wounded men who were being left behind as they would soon be taken prisoner. As he left the hospital and rode along Capitol Street, a squadron of Confederate horsemen came off a side street and demanded his surrender. "Half turning in his saddle, with a laugh upon his lips, he shook his head in answer and setting his spurs deep in his horse's sides sprang ahead," noted the regimental historian. "Instantly carbines were leveled, a flash and volley and the heroic form of Cromwell, pierced by a dozen bullets, lay rolling in the dust." The last casualty in the Battle of Jackson, the colonel's loss was lamented by his men, one of whom wrote in praise, "Popular throughout the whole brigade, brave, generous and handsome, he was one of the noblest of men and best of soldiers."[36]

The tragic loss of Colonel Cromwell was overshadowed by the death that same day of hundreds of men who wore the blue and gray at Champion Hill. In a fierce struggle that raged throughout the day, the Union army was again victorious and drove the Confederates back toward Vicksburg. The following morning, May 17, the Federals overwhelmed Southern forces at Big Black River Bridge and Pemberton's demoralized and weary soldiers staggered to the shelter of the Vicksburg defenses. On May 19 and again three days later, Grant hurled his army against the city's ring of forts only to sustain a heavy loss of human life and be denied entrance into Vicksburg. The failure of these costly assaults convinced Grant that the Confederate defenses could not be taken by storm, at least not yet. To avoid another bloodbath, he decided to "out camp the enemy," as he termed it, by laying siege to the city. "With the navy holding the river, the investment of Vicksburg was complete," wrote the general in his *Memoirs*. "As long as we could hold our position the enemy was limited in supplies of food, men, and munitions of war to what they had on hand. These could not always last."[37]

As his army settled into a war of attrition, Grant's attention would be distracted by two men. One was Joseph E. Johnston, the general in gray whose Army of Relief assembled in the Jackson/Canton area and posed a threat to Federal operations at Vicksburg. The other was the irascible John Alexander McClernand, the commander of his XIII Corps, whose actions precipitated a crisis within the Union army and threatened to undermine the unity of command that was so vital for success.

CHAPTER FOUR

John A. McClernand:
Fighting Politician

Embroiled in controversy throughout much of his military career, Maj. Gen. John A. McClernand remains a shadowy figure around whom controversy still swirls. He was a victim of his own actions as much as those of others, and history has all too easily come to accept and present the popular image of McClernand without questioning its validity or fairness. A troublesome subordinate, he has been characterized by his more famous contemporaries as inept, incompetent, and insubordinate. He continues to be maligned by his critics and writers of popular history and is nowadays all but ignored by even devout students of the Civil War. McClernand biographer Richard Kiper concedes that the fighting politician "has become a footnote in the story of the American Civil War." Indeed, the politician-turned-soldier was a prominent figure in the Western Theater of operations, whose service was worthy of note; yet a clear and accurate portrait of the general remains to be painted by historians.[1]

McClernand's path to relative obscurity began in the spring of 1861 when he first met then Col. Ulysses S. Grant. It culminated at Vicksburg on June 18, 1863, when by Special Orders No. 164 issued by Major General Grant, he was relieved of command of the XIII Corps then stationed in the trenches before the Confederate Gibraltar. Less than two weeks later, McClernand requested that a Court of Inquiry be convened

Maj. Gen.
John McClernand

National Archives

to examine the circumstances surrounding his removal from command. That court was never formed, and McClernand's reputation— hence his legacy— was never salvaged or refined.

The pretext for which McClernand was removed from command was the issuance of General Orders No. 72, a congratulatory order in which he praised the men of the XIII Corps for their accomplishments in the opening stages of the Vicksburg campaign. Army regulations stipulated that any such orders be cleared by the War Department prior to publication. Either by design or error, the order was never submitted by the corps commander for such clearance.[2]

On the surface, it was a petty offense hardly justifying McClernand's removal from command. But, the incident reveals not only the deep animosity which existed between the army commander and his senior subordinate, but also the jealous relationship between professional soldiers and volunteer officers that was prevalent during the Civil War. How did their relationship, which began with such promise in 1861, erode to this extent? It was a complex relationship, deeper and more intimate than popular history leads us to believe, and thus one that warrants further evaluation, particularly in the context of the Vicksburg campaign.

Frustration and death plagued the Union Army of the Tennessee throughout the winter of 1862-1863, as it maneuvered under the command of General Grant to seize the fortress city of Vicksburg. The Confederate citadel on the Mississippi River remained defiant, seemingly impervious to capture by Union land and naval forces. From Yazoo Pass and Holly Springs in north Mississippi, to Lake Providence in Louisiana, along the banks of Chickasaw Bayou north of the city, and the abortive canal across De Soto Point opposite Vicksburg, Grant's efforts had ended in failure. The only result of his operations thus far being an ever lengthening casualty list. The Northern press ridiculed Grant and clamored for his removal. Even members of the Cabinet urged President Abraham Lincoln to find a new commander for his western army. The president, however, answered those critical of Grant by saying, "I can't spare this man, he fights. I'll try him a little longer."[3]

At forty-one years of age, Sam Grant was at a crossroads in his military career. An 1843 graduate of the United States Military Academy at West Point and veteran of the Mexican War, Grant was no stranger to adversity. Having battled his way to national prominence at Belmont, Fort Donelson, and Shiloh, he struggled with rumor and innuendo to establish a reputation of respectability. Cognizant of the criticism which swirled around him in both military and political circles, Grant appeared stoic, but confided the torment he felt to his wife Julia. Determined to persevere, he ignored the critics and remained focused on his objective—Vicksburg. After months of frustration and failure, Grant examined his options.

Three options were discussed at army headquarters. The first option was to launch an amphibious assault across the Mississippi River and storm the Vicksburg stronghold. The second was to pull back to Memphis and try once again the overland route which had failed miserably the previous year. And the third option was to march the army down the west side of the river, search for a favorable crossing point, and transfer the field of operations to the area south and east of Vicksburg. In characteristic fashion and with grim determination, Grant boldly opted for the march south. On March 29, 1863, he directed General McClernand of the XIII Corps to open a road from Milliken's Bend to New Carthage on the Mississippi River below Vicksburg. The movement started on March 31, and thus the Vicksburg campaign began in earnest.[4]

Energetic, aggressive, and ambitious, John Alexander McClernand was also bombastic, egotistical, and extremely irritating to those around him. Standing almost six feet tall, he was sparse of frame, heavily bearded with a rather large nose and scraggly hair, but was of "tough and wiry fiber." He had piercing eyes, a hearty laugh, and an engaging smile, yet at all times was calculating and deceitful. A lawyer by training and a politician by profession, McClernand looked to the field of battle to win victories and headlines in his quest for the White House.[5]

The man selected and entrusted by Grant for what was arguably to be the most important assignment of the campaign had been born near Hardinsburg, Kentucky, on May 30, 1812. The commander of the XIII Corps was the only child of John and Fatima McClernand and his life prior to the Civil War mirrored that of Abraham Lincoln. (They were neighbors later in Springfield, which may perhaps explain why the two men got along so well.) McClernand's family moved to Shawneetown, Illinois, when he was quite young, and his father died not long after in 1816. Although he attended a village school in Shawneetown and benefited from some private tutoring, McClernand was largely self-educated. Throughout his youth, first as a boy then as a young man, he worked at various jobs to support his mother. McClernand went on to study law at a local attorney's office and was admitted to the bar in 1832.

As with most young men on the frontier in the summer of that year, he served as a private in the Black Hawk War. He was later involved in Mississippi River trading and came to appreciate the economic importance of the great river to America. McClernand also edited the *Gallatin Democrat and Illinois Advertiser*, but it was politics that attracted the young man and his many talents. A fiery orator, he proved to be a gifted politician. He served as an Illinois assemblyman for seven years beginning in 1836 and was elected to the United States House of Representatives as a Jacksonian Democrat in 1843—the same year that he married Sarah Dunlap of Jacksonville.

In Congress, he joined the faction led by Stephen A. Douglas whose doctrine of popular sovereignty was embraced by McClernand's constituents in southern Illinois, many of whom like himself were natives of slave holding states. McClernand was reelected four times serving until 1851. Harboring a strong dislike for abolitionists, he watched with mounting anxiety as the nation drifted to the brink of civil war. Entering the political arena once again, he won election to Congress in 1859 and quickly rose to the pinnacle of power in the House of Representatives, only to be narrowly defeated for the speakership by a coalition which opposed his moderate sentiments on slavery and disunion.

Upon the election of Abraham Lincoln and the dissolution of the Federal Union, McClernand threw his considerable influence behind the administration's war policy. Although McClernand was a Democrat, the president considered him as an ally who would help maintain Midwestern support for the Union. McClernand was rewarded with an appointment as a brigadier general of volunteers in August, to rank from May 17, 1861. Reluctant to yield the power he wielded as a member of Congress, the self-serving general did not resign his seat in the House of Representatives until October 28.[6]

He first served in the District of Southeast Missouri commanding the 1st Brigade stationed around Cairo, Illinois. As part of Grant's force, McClernand moved down the Mississippi and led his brigade in the battle of Belmont on November 7, 1861. McClernand distinguished himself in this bizarre little action, where untested Union troops drove equally green Confederate soldiers from their encampment. "In this charge," wrote Col. John A. Logan, a fellow political officer, "I saw General McClernand, with hat in hand, leading as gallant a charge as ever was made by any troops unskilled in the arts of war." Victory, however, was short-lived as the Confederates, reinforced from across the river by the garrison at Columbus, Kentucky, counterattacked. Soon the Federals were retreating toward their transports, narrowly averting disaster.[7]

In a manner that became characteristic of McClernand, he placed the best possible light on events in his report and claimed great credit for his command, and thus for himself. He boasted of his brigade's action in his report: "We beat them, fighting all the way into their camp immediately under the guns at Columbus; burned their encampment, took 200 prisoners, a large amount of property, spiked two or three guns, and brought away two." In this, his first test in combat, the politician-turned-soldier earned the praise of General Grant. "General McClernand was in the midst of danger throughout the engagement, and displayed both coolness and judgment," wrote the Federal army commander. "His horse was three times shot under him." Grant went on to state that McClernand "acted with great coolness and courage throughout, and proved that he is a soldier as well as statesman."[8]

On February 1, 1862, in a reorganization of Grant's force, he assumed command of the 1st Division, District of Cairo, in the Department of the Missouri. The feisty officer next fought at Fort Donelson where, on February 13 he launched a premature attack in an attempt to silence a Confederate battery that was playing on his command. The attack was easily repulsed, and he was criticized by Grant for recklessness, who reported that McClernand attacked "without orders or authority." Two days later, on the 15th, the Confederates attempted to break through Grant's encircling lines and withdraw toward Charlotte, on the road to Nashville. The attack was directed against McClernand's sector of the line, on the Federal right, and the battle soon raged in fury. Although his troops fought with grim determination, they were not supported and he complained bitterly in his report that "up to this and a still later hour a gun had not been fired either from the gunboats or from any portion of our line, except that formed by the forces under my command." Poor staff work at all levels throughout the inexperienced army further placed his men in a precarious situation and resulted in the troops of McClernand's division running out of ammunition—although tons of it were lying around in cases. His troops were outflanked and forced to fall back—the road to Nashville was temporarily open to the Confederates.[9]

Grant, who had been absent from the field throughout the morning, arrived on the scene and, in his words, witnessed "great confusion in the ranks." Although relieved to see the commanding general, McClernand expressed his displeasure with Grant, muttering, "The army needs a head." (This is the first indication of the rift that developed between the two generals.) Grant ignored this rebuke and simply replied, "It seems so." Along with McClernand he brought order to the troops, saw to it that ammunition was distributed, and directed the men to seal the breach. The Federal commander later wrote of McClernand's advance, "notwithstanding the hours of exposure to a heavy fire in the forepart of the day, was gallantly made, and the enemy further repulsed." The following day, Fort Donelson surrendered resulting in the capture of 13,000 Confederate soldiers.[10]

In the wake of victory there was much glory to go around. McClernand, however, irritated Grant and his fellow division commanders by claiming the fruits of victory for his division in his lengthy report filed on February 28, 1862. Grant forwarded the report to his immediate superior, Maj. Gen. Henry W. Halleck, commander of the Department of the Missouri, with the observation that the account was "a little highly colored." McClernand's experience as a politician, coupled with a rather large ego and thirst for higher office, helps explain—though does not justify—this tendency for self-aggrandizement, a tendency that would grow more irritating to his fellow officers as the war progressed and prove to be the cause of his undoing. Regardless, his actions at Donelson helped seal for him the confidence of his men and gain the respect of his superiors. In his report, Grant informed the War Department, "I must do the justice to say" that General McClernand was with his command in the midst of danger and was always ready to execute all orders, no matter what the exposure to himself. A future critic, Charles A. Dana, noted that McClernand "behaved with the most conspicuous gallantry."[11]

The Union victory at Fort Donelson was hailed across the nation and the political general basked in the public acclaim he received in the papers. In this bloody affair, McClernand had again demonstrated that he was an aggressive and courageous officer. In recognition of his service he was elevated to the rank of major general of volunteers on March 21, 1862. It was a promotion that Grant admitted was well deserved.

Following up on this victory, the Federal force moved downriver and less than two months later was again engaged at Pittsburg Landing. In the first day of fighting in the battle of Shiloh on April 6, 1862, McClernand's division moved quickly to the support of Maj. Gen. William T. Sherman's hard-pressed troops and established a formidable line of defense. Throughout the day he and his men fought with both valor and skill, but were forced to fall back from one position to another as the Federal army was driven toward the Tennessee River. Grant noted that the "hardest fighting was in front of these two divisions." Despite the confusion and casualties of the day, McClernand's exertions worked to ensure that his division retained a semblance of order and combat capability when the sun set. His performance in the bloody fray had been solid and again earned for him the praise of Grant, who stated in his report that McClernand maintained his place with credit to himself and the cause.[12]

Reinforced during the night by Maj. Gen. Don Carlos Buell and his Army of the Ohio, the combined Federal force counterattacked the next morning. In close cooperation with Sherman, McClernand's division advanced over much of the same ground yielded the previous day. Overcoming obstinate resistance, the Illinois politician exhorted his men forward and by late afternoon reoccupied the lost ground as Confederate troops fled south toward Corinth, Mississippi.

Union victory at Shiloh polished his reputation as a fighting general. Yet despite the acclaim he received, it was a spring and summer of frustration for McClernand, who rankled under the harness imposed by subordination to Grant and others, who, he felt, treated him unfairly while showing favoritism to West Pointers. A series of incidents occurred in which McClernand believed Grant was meddling in his authority and questioning his actions. There was considerable disagreement between the two generals, even signs of hostility that strained their relationship. McClernand yearned for an independent command and wrote letters to both Lincoln and his political ally Gov. Richard Yates of Illinois for assistance.

At the request of Governor Yates, he was sent home in mid-August to raise troops in Illinois, Indiana, and Iowa, a role in which he was highly successful. McClernand seized upon his popularity and traveled to Washington in search of greater opportunity for political gain following the battle of Antietam. Accompanying the president to the battlefield near Sharpsburg, Maryland, he played a subversive role in the army seeking to supplant Maj. Gen. George B. McClellan in the East and criticized Grant's operations in the West for his failure to pursue the enemy after Shiloh. Such criticism only worked to widen the rift between McClernand and Grant.[13]

Although he failed to gain command in the East, McClernand did receive authorization from the president and Secretary of War Edwin M. Stanton to raise and command a force for operations on the Mississippi River aimed at Vicksburg. While the force he raised assembled at Memphis, the general, who by this time was a widower, courted Minerva Dunlap, his sister-in-law, and was married on December 26, 1862. The honeymooners traveled south only to learn that McClernand's command had been commandeered by Sherman and led to defeat on the banks of Chickasaw Bayou.[14]

Rushing to the vicinity of Vicksburg, McClernand assumed command on January 4, 1863, and christened his force the Army of the Mississippi. Anxious for combat, the general embraced Sherman's recommendation to seize Arkansas Post—a suggestion that concurred with his own estimation of the strategic situation. Located 50 miles up the Arkansas River from its confluence with the Mississippi, Arkansas Post was a point from which the Confederates had sent gunboats into the Mississippi. Moving with remarkable speed, McClernand's force reached its objective on January 9 and two days later forced the surrender of Fort Hindman and almost 5,000 enemy soldiers. Although the victory secured headlines for McClernand, his victory was downplayed by Grant who said it was not the proper theater of operations and termed it "a wild goose chase"—that is, until he found out that his friend Billy Sherman had recommended the campaign. In all fairness to McClernand, it must be recognized that his actions eliminated a major threat to Union operations on the Mississippi River aimed at Vicksburg and a potential source of trouble for Grant's operations in Louisiana and Mississippi in the campaign soon to be initiated.[15]

Fearful lest McClernand launch an operation of greater consequence, Grant hastened from his headquarters in Memphis to the front. On January 30, 1863, Grant issued General Orders No. 13 in which he announced, "I hereby assume immediate command of the expedition against Vicksburg, and department headquarters will hereafter be with the expedition." By such action, McClernand's command was limited to that of the XIII Corps, a reduction in authority that did not sit well with the fiery political general. McClernand, however, replied that he would "acquiesce in the order for the purpose of avoiding a conflict of authority in the presence of the enemy" and asked that his protest be forwarded to General Halleck and through him to the secretary of war and President Lincoln. Along with McClernand's protest, Grant sent a cover letter in which he expressed a lack of confidence in McClernand's "ability as a soldier to conduct an expedition," and by that he meant an independent expedition. (Unfortunately for McClernand, Washington remained deathly quiet on the matter and he had to content himself with corps command.)[16]

In spite of his expressed lack of confidence in McClernand and an obvious personality clash that severely strained the relationship between the two men, Grant selected the commander of the XIII Corps to lead the army's vanguard through Louisiana in the spring of 1863. The selection of McClernand to lead the march through Louisiana is a source of controversy still today. As a political appointee in the military, he was at times inept in the handling of troops. The former congressman had repeatedly demonstrated his disdain for administrative details and contempt for military protocol. He did not work well with superiors or subordinates and his hatred for West Pointers did not endear him to his fellow corps commanders—William T. Sherman and Maj. Gen. James B. McPherson. McClernand, however, had proven to all his willingness to fight at Fort Donelson and Shiloh and had developed into an able combat officer. Although Grant knew of the widespread distrust of the corps commander which existed within the combined force operating against Vicksburg, and later wrote that he "doubted McClernand's fitness," in the spring of 1863 he was confident that the former congressman could and, if necessary, would fight.[17]

On March 29, 1863, Grant directed McClernand to open a road from Milliken's Bend to New Carthage on the Mississippi River below Vicksburg. The troops of the XIII Corps were in high spirits as they pushed south from Milliken's Bend, followed by McPherson's XVII Corps. Over the next month, McClernand's veterans marched through 60 miles of Louisiana swamp and bottom lands corduroying roads and building bridges practically each step of the way. He later wrote, "The 2,000 feet of bridging which was hastily improvised out of materials created on the spot . . . must long be remembered as a marvel." He justly boasted of his men with pride that their labors produced "the highest examples of military energy and perseverance."[18]

By the end of April, the XIII Corps was concentrated at Hard Times Landing and boarded the transports of the invasion armada in preparation for a landing at Grand Gulf. The Union fleet, however, was unable to silence all the guns at Grand Gulf. Not wishing to send the transports and barges, loaded to the gunwales with troops, to attempt a landing in the face of enemy fire, the troops were disembarked, marched five miles farther down the levee, and rendezvoused with the fleet at Disharoon's plantation, below Grand Gulf. On April 30, Grant hurled his army across the mighty river and onto Mississippi soil at Bruinsburg. Soldiers and sailors gave a mighty cheer when a band aboard the flagship *Benton* struck up "The Red, White, and Blue" as McClernand's men jumped ashore. By noon, much of the XIII Corps—17,000-strong—was ashore and the inland campaign begun.

Over the next 17 days, in what is often referred to as the blitzkrieg of the Vicksburg campaign, the Union army would march more than 200 miles, fight and win five engagements, and drive the Confederates into the defenses of Vicksburg. The XIII Corps played a stellar role in these operations during which the Confederacy was struck a fatal blow.

Having landed at Bruinsburg, the XIII Corps pushed inland through the night until Confederate resistance was encountered west of Port Gibson. In a furious battle which raged throughout the day on May 1, 1863, McClernand's troops fought with grim determination to secure the Federal beachhead on Mississippi soil while Confederate soldiers fought with equal determination to drive the invaders into the river. His force, later augmented with one division of the XVII Corps, overwhelmed the Southern troops and drove them from the field. In the opening action of the campaign, McClernand reported the loss of 125 killed, 678 wounded, and 23 missing, whereas the XVII Corps lost a total of 49 men. The XIII Corps had carried the day and McClernand would boast with justification that this was "the most valuable victory won since the capture of Fort Donelson."[19]

Rather than move north, directly on Vicksburg, Grant pushed his army deep into Mississippi. His objective was to strike the railroad between Vicksburg and Jackson, sever that vital line of communications and supply, and isolate the fortress city on the river. During this phase of the campaign, McClernand's corps was on the left—closest to the enemy at the point of danger. Throughout this critical period, he handled his troops with consummate skill and was prepared to meet the enemy at all times confident of the results.

By May 12, elements of the XIII Corps had crossed Fourteenmile Creek and moved to within four miles of Edwards where Confederate Lt. Gen. John C. Pemberton was massing his army. In response to the sharp engagement at Raymond that day, a battle fought entirely by the soldiers of McPherson's corps, Grant decided to move on Jackson. McClernand's crops would be used as a shield to cover the movement. The crusty officer skillfully disengaged his command from the enemy near Edwards (always a potentially hazardous operation) and crossed Bakers Creek to the east, taking up a blocking position on a line running from Bolton to Raymond. Thus protected in rear, the other corps of Grant's army marched on Jackson and seized the capital city of Mississippi on May 14. Not wishing to detach combat troops for occupation, Grant neutralized Jackson with the torch then turned his army west toward Vicksburg—the XIII Corps was again in the lead.

En route from Jackson to Vicksburg, Grant's army encountered Pemberton's force near Edwards on May 16. McClernand's divisions led the three Federal columns that converged on the small town. Cautioned not to bring on a general engagement until the army was well in hand, the commander of the XIII Corps acted accordingly when they encountered the enemy, first along the Raymond-Edwards Road, then along the Middle Road farther to the north. The third Federal column, with which Grant traveled, advanced on the Union right along the Jackson

Road. Undetected at first by the Confederates, this column was in position to flank the Southerners. Grant seized the opportunity and ordered his columns to advance all along the front.

In the largest, bloodiest, most significant action of the Vicksburg campaign, Grant's men overcame stiff Confederate resistance at Champion Hill, inflicting devastating casualties on the enemy, and drove Pemberton's army from the field. The XIII Corps was engaged all along the front and in the bitter fight suffered the loss of 218 killed, 987 wounded, and 145 missing. McPherson's corps reported 300 fewer casualties than did McClernand, while elements of the XV Corps engaged that day suffered no reported loss. Yet, Grant gave credit for the victory—as have most historians—to McPherson, whose actions that day revealed that his meteoric rise through the ranks from first lieutenant to major general had not prepared him for the level of command responsibilities he now faced.[20]

Pursuing the routed enemy on the following morning, the XIII Corps again formed line of battle and overwhelmed Pemberton's rear guard at the Big Black River. In this brief affair fought by his corps alone of the Union army, McClernand's troops captured almost 1,800 prisoners, 18 cannon, 6 limbers, 4 caissons, 1,400 stands of arms, and 4 battleflags while suffering a combined loss in killed, wounded, and missing of less than 300 men. Bridging the stream on May 18, he then pushed his men to the outskirts of Vicksburg.[21]

The campaign thus far had been a stunning success for the Union army thanks largely to the hard-marching, hard-fighting soldiers of the XIII Corps and their commander. Anxious for a quick victory, Grant ordered an attack against the city's defenses on May 19. His three corps, however, were unable to concentrate in time and only Sherman's troops were in proper position to make the attack. Although his men fought with commendable valor and succeeded in planting several stands of colors on the exterior slope of Stockade Redan, Sherman's troops were repulsed. In this assault, Sherman's corps lost more than 700 men. McPherson reported 130 casualties, while McClernand, whose troops were only lightly engaged, suffered the loss of 100 men.[22]

Realizing that he had been too hasty, Grant decided to make a more thorough reconnaissance and gathered his forces in hand for a second strike. Three days later, on May 22, he hurled his army over a broad three-mile-front against the Vicksburg fortifications. Sherman and

McPherson were stopped cold by the deadly fire which poured from Confederate rifle-muskets. But, McClernand's troops withstood the galling fire and, advancing with sheer determination, reached the ditches that fronted the Confederate fortifications. Although his troops penetrated Railroad Redoubt and threatened to enter at Second Texas Lunette, he had few reserves with which to exploit the situations. (McClernand was a puncher who always threw in everything he had. His failure to hold a ready reserve was perhaps his most significant tactical weakness.) He knew they could not consolidate their gains without reinforcements or a diversion in their favor. "We are hotly engaged with the enemy," McClernand quickly penned Grant. "We have part possession of two forts, and the Stars and Stripes are floating over them. A vigorous push ought to be made all along the line."[23]

Grant was skeptical and not inclined to accept the note at face value. Although he doubted its veracity, the information had been provided by his subordinate on the scene of action. Grant ordered the attacks renewed all along the front. Beneath a blistering sun, Federal soldiers surged forward with a mighty cheer only to be checked and driven back with heavy loss. McClernand was also forced to relinquish the ground gained and the bodies of his dead and wounded littered the field in abundance. Death had reaped a bountiful harvest. In the assault on May 22, the XIII Corps suffered the heaviest casualties in Grant's army. The returns on this bloody day tallied McClernand's loss as 1,275 men killed, wounded, or missing. Yet, he could boast that his was the only corps to gain a lodgment in the enemy works.[24]

Failing to carry Vicksburg by storm, the Union army settled into the routine of siege life. As the army completed its dispositions around the beleaguered city and perfected its alignment, Lt. Col. James Harrison Wilson delivered an order from Grant to the commander of the XIII Corps. Wilson, another West Pointer—Class of 1860, was astonished when McClernand exclaimed, "I'll be God damned if I'll do it—I am tired of being dictated to—I won't stand it any longer, and you can go back and tell General Grant." The corps commander then issued a stream of oaths against Grant and West Pointers in particular to which Wilson took umbrage. The young officer remarked angrily, "in addition to your highly insubordinate language, it seems to me that you are cursing me as much as you are cursing General Grant." He then added, "If this is so, although you are a major general, while I am only a lieutenant colonel, I will pull you off that horse and beat the boots off of you." McClernand attempted to placate Wilson saying, "I am not cursing you. I could not do that. Your father was my friend and I am yours. I was simply expressing my intense vehemence on the subject matter, sir, and I beg your pardon." (From that time on, whenever anyone around army headquarters raised their voice it was referred to as "simply expressing intense vehemence on the subject matter.") The incident was indicative of the rising storm clouds that were gathering over the unsuspecting corps commander.[25]

On May 30, 1863, McClernand issued General Orders, No. 72 in which he congratulated his troops on their achievements and, in typical fashion, claimed credit for the victories thus far achieved in the campaign. The order is provided here in its entirely for the benefit of readers:

General Orders, HDQRS. Thirteenth Army Corps

No. 72 Battle-field, in rear of Vicksburg, May 30, 1863.

COMRADES: As your commander, I am proud to congratulate you upon your constancy, valor, and successes. History affords no more brilliant example of soldierly qualities. Your victories have followed in such rapid succession that their echoes have not yet reached the country. They will challenge its grateful and enthusiastic applause. Yourselves striking out a new path, your comrades of the Army of the Tennessee followed, and a way was thus opened for them to redeem previous disappointments. Your march through Louisiana, from Milliken's Bend to New Carthage and Perkins' plantation, on the Mississippi, is one of the most remarkable on record. Bayous and miry roads, threatened with momentary inundation, obstructed your progress. All these were overcome by unceasing labor and unflagging energy. The 2,000 feet of bridging which was hastily improvised out of materials created on the spot, and over which you passed, must long be remembered as a marvel. Descending the Mississippi still lower, you were the first to cross the river at Bruin's Landing [Bruinsburg] and to plant our colors in the State of Mississippi below Warrenton. Resuming the advance the same day, you pushed on until you came up to the enemy near Port Gibson. Only restrained by the darkness of night, you hastened to attack him on the morning of May 1, and by vigorously pressing him at all points drove him from his position, taking a large number of prisoners and small-arms and five cannon. General [John A.] Logan's division came up in time to gallantly share in consummating the most valuable victory won since the capture of Fort Donelson.

Taking the lead on the morning of the 2d, you were the first to enter Port Gibson and to hasten the retreat of the enemy from the vicinity of that place. During the ensuing night, as a consequence of the victory at Port Gibson, the enemy spiked his guns at Grand Gulf and evacuated that place, retiring upon Vicksburg and Edwards Station. The fall of Grand Gulf was solely the result of the victory achieved by the land forces at Port Gibson. The armament and public stores captured there are but the just trophies of that victory. Hastening to bridge the South Branch of Bayou Pierre, at Port Gibson, you crossed on the morning of the 3d, and pushed on to Willow Springs, Big Sandy, and the main crossing of Fourteen-Mile Creek, 4 miles from Edwards Station. A detachment of the enemy was immediately driven away from the crossing, and you advanced, passed over, and rested during the night of the 12th within 3 miles of the enemy, in large force at the station.

On the morning of the 13th, the objective point of the army's movements having been changed from Edwards Station to Jackson, in pursuance of an order from the commander of the department, you moved on the north side of Fourteen-Mile Creek toward Raymond. This delicate and hazardous movement was executed by a portion of your number under cover of [Brig. Gen. Alvin P.] Hovey's division, which made a feint of attack in line of battle upon Edwards Station. Too late to harm you, the enemy attacked the rear of that division, but was promptly and decisively repulsed.

Resting near Raymond that night, on the morning of the 14th you entered that place, one division moving on to Mississippi Springs, near Jackson, in support of General [William T.] Sherman; another to Clinton, in support of General [James B.] McPherson; a third remaining at Raymond, and a fourth at Old Auburn, to bring up the army trains.

On the 15th, you again led the advance toward Edwards Station, which once more became the objective point. Expelling the enemy's pickets from Bolton the same day, you secured and held that important position.

On the 16th, you led the advance, in three columns upon three roads, against Edwards Station. Meeting the enemy on the way in strong force, you heavily engaged him near Champion's Hill, and after a sanguinary and obstate battle, with the assistance of

General McPherson's corps, beat and routed him, taking many prisoners and small-arms and several pieces of cannon. Continuing to lead the advance, you rapidly pursued the enemy to Edwards Station, capturing that place, a large quantity of public stores, and many prisoners. Night only stopped you.

At day-dawn on the 17th, you resumed the advance, and early coming upon the enemy strongly intrenched in elaborate works, both before and behind Big Black River, immediately opened with artillery upon him, followed by a daring and heroic charge at the point of the bayonet, which put him to rout, leaving eighteen pieces of cannon and more than 1,000 prisoners in your hands.

By an early hour on the 18th, you had constructed a bridge across the Big Black, and had commenced the advance upon Vicksburg.

On the 19th, 20th, and 21st you continued to reconnoiter and skirmish until you had gained a near approach to the enemy's work.

On the 22d, in pursuance of the order from the commander of the department, you assaulted the enemy's defenses in front at 10 a.m., and within thirty minutes had made a lodgment and planted your colors upon two of his bastions. This partial success called into exercise the highest heroism, and was only gained by a bloody and protracted struggle; yet it was gained, and was the first and largest success achieved anywhere along the whole line of our army. For nearly eight hours, under a scorching sun and destructive fire, you firmly held your footing, and only withdrew when the enemy had largely massed their forces and concentrated their attack upon you. How and why the general assault failed, it would be useless now to explain. The Thirteenth Army Corps, acknowledging the good intentions of all, would scorn indulgence in weak regrets and idle criminations. According justice to all, it would only defend itself. If, while the enemy was massing to crush it, assistance was asked for by a diversion at other points, or by re-enforcement, it only asked what in one case Major-General Grant had specifically and peremptorily ordered, namely simultaneous and persistent attack all along our lines until the enemy's outer works should be carried, and what, in the other, by massing a strong force in time upon a weakened point, would have probably insured success.

Comrades, you have done much, yet something more remains to be done. The enemy's odious defenses still block your access to Vicksburg. Treason still rules that rebellious city, and closes the Mississippi River against rightful use by the millions who inhabit its sources and the great Northwest. Shall not our flag float over Vicksburg? Shall not the great Father of Waters be opened to lawful commerce? Methinks the emphatic response of one and all of you is, "It shall be so." Then let us rise to the level of a crowning trial. Let our common sufferings and glories, while uniting as a band of brothers, rouse us to new and surpassing efforts. Let us resolve upon success, God helping us.

I join with you, comrades, in your sympathy for the wounded and sorrow for the dead. May we not trust, nay, is it not so, that history will associate the martyrs of this sacred struggle for law and order, liberty and justice, with the honored martyrs of Monmouth and Bunker Hill?

John A. McClernand
Major-General Commanding[26]

Within days, the order appeared in the pages of the *Memphis Evening Bulletin*, the *Missouri Democrat*, and other influential newspapers in the midwest, copies of which circulated throughout the Union camps around Vicksburg.

On the evening of June 16, following an inspection tour of the works at Snyder's Bluff, north of Vicksburg, Sherman was handed one such paper by Maj. Gen. Frank Blair with the request that "I should notice it, lest the statements of fact and inference contained therein might receive credence from an excited public." Sherman was incensed at what he read and the following day wrote at length to Grant, "It certainly gives me no pleasure or satisfaction to notice such a catalogue of nonsense—such an effusion of vain-glory and hypocrisy; nor can I believe General McClernand ever published such an order officially to his corps. I know too well that the brave and intelligent soldiers and officers who compose that corps will not be humbugged by such stuff."

The note reveals the level of contempt Sherman harbored against McClernand. Seeing the order for what it was, he lashed out, "If the order be a genuine production and not a forgery, it is manifestly addressed not to an army, but to the constituency in Illinois, so far distant from the scene of the events attempted to be described, who might innocently be induced to think General McClernand the sagacious leader and bold hero he so complacently paints himself."

In a rare display of vindictiveness, Sherman continued:

I beg to call [your] attention to the requirements of General Orders, No. 151, of 1862, which actually forbids the publication of all official letters and reports, and requires the name of the writer to be laid before the President of the United States for dismissal. The document under question is not technically a letter or report, and though styled an order, is not an order. It orders nothing, but is in the nature of an address to soldiers, manifestly designed for publication for ulterior political purposes. It perverts the truth to the ends of flattery and self-glorification, and contains many untruths, among which is one of monstrous falsehood. It accuses General McPherson and myself with disobeying orders of General Grant in not assaulting on May 19 and 22, and allowing on the latter day the enemy to mass his forces against the Thirteenth Army Corps alone.

To justify this egoism so unbecoming of Sherman, he explained:

I would never have revealed so unwelcome a truth had General McClernand, in his process of self-flattery, confined himself to facts in the reach of his own observation, and not gone out of the way to charge others for results which he seems not to comprehend.

He then patronized Grant:

With these remarks I leave the matter where it properly belongs, in the hands of the commanding general, who knows his plans and orders, sees with an eye single to success and his country's honor, and not from the narrow and contracted circle of a subordinate commander, who exaggerates the importance of the events that fall under his immediate notice, and is filled with an itching desire for 'fame not earned.'[27]

On June 18, McPherson read a copy of the congratulatory address in a newspaper and fired a note of complaint to Grant: "The whole tenor of the order is so ungenerous, and the insinuations and criminations against the other corps of your army are so manifestly at variance with the facts, that a sense of duty to my command, as well as the verbal protest of every one of my division and brigade commanders against allowing such an order to go forth to the public unanswered, require that I should call your attention to it." The junior corps commander commented:

After a careful perusal of the order, I cannot help arriving at the conclusion that it was written more to influence public sentiment at the North and impress the public mind with the magnificent strategy, superior tactics, and brilliant deeds of the major-general commanding the Thirteenth Army Corps than to congratulate his troops upon their well-merited successes. There is a vain-gloriousness about the order, an ingenious attempt to write himself down the hero, the master-mind, giving life and direction to military operations in this quarter, inconsistent with the high-toned principles of the soldier.[28]

Grant, however, had already taken measures to deal with McClernand and quiet the uproar among his subordinates. "Inclosed I send you what purports to be your congratulatory address to the Thirteenth Army Corps," Grant wrote McClernand on June 17. "I would respectfully ask if it is a true copy. If it is not a correct copy, furnish me one by bearer, as required both by regulations and existing orders of the Department." That evening McClernand responded, "The newspaper slip is a correct copy of my congratulatory order, No. 72. I am prepared to maintain its statements."[29]

Upon receipt of McClernand's admission, Grant issued General Orders No. 164 by which the unrepentant subordinate was relieved of command and replaced by Maj. Gen. Edward O. C. Ord. The order was delivered with great delight by Lt. Col. James H. Wilson. McClernand scanned the note and said "Well, sir! I am relieved," to which Wilson remarked gleefully, "By God, sir, we are both relieved!"[30]

Outraged by Grant's action, McClernand immediately protested his removal in characteristic tenor. In writing to Grant, the dismissed officer was quick to point out, "Having been appointed by the President to the command of that [XIII] corps, under a definite act of Congress, I might justly challenge your authority in the premises, but forbear to do so at present." Confident his actions would be vindicated by a court of inquiry, McClernand wrote, "I am quite willing that any statement of fact in my congratulatory [order] to the Thirteenth Army Corps, to which you think just exception may be taken, should be made the subject of investigation, not doubting the result."[31]

His protest notwithstanding, McClernand returned quietly to Illinois from where he waged a battle to regain his command. On June 27 he wrote to General Halleck, now general-in-chief, a long letter in which he identified a major component of the enmity against him and perhaps the reasons he was removed—jealousy and resentment. "The real motive for so unwarranted an act," he wrote, "was hostility—personal hostility—growing out of the early connection of my name with the Mississippi River expedition and your assignment of me to the command of it." Embellishing this claim, he continued, "This feeling subsequently became intensified by the contrast made by my personal success at Arkansas Post with General Grant's retreat from Oxford and his repulse at Chickasaw Bayou, and still, more intensified by the leadership and success of my corps during the advance from Milliken's Bend to Port Gibson, to Champion's Hill, and to Big Black." Seeking to shift the focus of attention, he requested an investigation into Grant's conduct as an officer and demanded "that I be restored to my command, at least until the fall of Vicksburg."[32]

While the noose around Vicksburg tightened, Illinois Governor Richard Yates came to the support of his political ally and friend. On June 30 the governor wrote Lincoln, "Major General McClernand arrived here on the 26th instant. He has been received by the people here with the greatest demonstrations of respect, all regretting that he is not now in the field. I desire to suggest that if General McClernand, with some Western troops, was put in command in Pennsylvania, it would inspire great hope and confidence in the Northwest, and perhaps throughout the country."

Fortunately, the president did not act on this suggestion and Lincoln remained quiet on the subject of McClernand until he received Grant's report of the campaign.[33]

On July 19, Grant forwarded a copy of McClernand's report to Washington with the following endorsement: "This report contains so many inaccuracies that to correct it, to make it a fair report to be handed down as historical, would require the rewriting of most of it. It is pretentious and egotistical, as is sufficiently shown by my own and all other reports" (which in the case of many of his subordinates were also "pretentious and egotistical").[34]

In light of Grant's victory at Vicksburg, Lincoln wanted to put the matter to rest. On August 29, McClernand was notified by Halleck that the president had declined to order a court of inquiry. The general-in-chief informed McClernand that, "the President . . . directs me to say that a court of inquiry . . . would necessarily withdraw from the field many officers whose presence with their commands is absolutely indispensable to the service, and whose absence might cause irreparable injury to the success of operations now in active progress."[35]

And so, the court was never convened. Although McClernand penned a lengthy defense to Halleck on September 28, it was ignored by officials at the War Department and the matter was closed.

* * *

In evaluating the case of John McClernand, one must ask this question: Did Grant have the authority to relieve McClernand? McClernand certainly argued the point, as have many historians and military professionals. In reference to Lincoln's appointment of him to command the Vicksburg expedition, historian Edwin C. Bearss asserts, "The President's decision thus constituted an independent command in Grant's department." Those who support McClernand argue that as the president appointed him, only the president could relieve him of his command responsibilities. Grant's actions were sustained by the administration, however, which make the issue a moot point.

Was such a petty offense as the issuance of General Orders No. 72 sufficient grounds to relieve McClernand of command of the XIII Corps? If not, were the statements made in General Orders No. 72 untrue or misleading? Regardless, such statements were certainly in keeping with McClernand's previous actions to which Sherman, McPherson, Grant, and the entire army should have been accustomed.[36]

We have yet to get to the underlying reason of why McClernand was relieved of command for which the issuance of General Orders No. 72 was simply the pretext. Why then did Grant relieve McClernand of command? Was it due to lack of confidence? Although Grant frequently expressed a lack of confidence in McClernand and later wrote that he "doubted" his fitness to command, his actions do not support those claims. Among the factors to consider is that McClernand commanded the largest corps in the army. It led the march down the west side of the river in the opening stage of the Vicksburg campaign. His troops were the first to cross the river and land on Mississippi soil, potentially requiring them to fight an engagement independent of the other corps still in Louisiana. Moreover, his corps was positioned on the left flank at the point of danger—that is closest to the enemy, as the army pushed deep into Mississippi. The XIII Corps maintained the longest section of the siege lines. And, Grant was on the verge of strengthening McClernand's command responsibilities by increasing the number of men under him and lengthening the sector of siege lines for which he was responsible, prior to removing him from command. A general does not entrust such vital assignments and level of command responsibilities as these to someone in whom he has no confidence.

Was it due to the professional jealousy that West Pointers harbored for volunteer officers? Perhaps, in part. It certainly appears that Sherman and McPherson at least were somewhat envious of McClernand's success during the Vicksburg campaign. Grant himself clearly preferred that his subordinates be West Pointers rather than volunteer officers.

In spite of his many shortcomings as an officer, declaring him to be "unmanageable and incompetent," Grant could and did tolerate McClernand's irascible nature and often insubordinate actions. He even tolerated McClernand's repeated efforts to secure political advantages in his "highly colored" after action reports. But when that tendency to embellish one's success appeared in communications on the field of battle and resulted in the useless effusion of blood, McClernand's integrity as a combat officer was compromised and Grant's trust and confidence in him shattered.[37]

Recall the note on May 22 in which McClernand stated he was in "part possession of two forts and the Stars and Stripes are floating over them," and asked that the assaults be renewed as a diversion in his favor. When Grant discovered the true extent of the Federal penetration at Railroad Redoubt and grasped the number of lives lost as a result of the afternoon assaults, he determined that someone would pay for the loss of those lives, and that someone would be John McClernand. With his integrity compromised and no longer trustworthy, Grant had no recourse but to relieve McClernand of command. Unfortunately, rather than make public the true reason, Grant used the issuance of General Orders No. 72 as the pretext for removal of McClernand from command of the XIII Corps and the issue boiled in controversy for months.[38]

Although McClernand returned to command of the XIII Corps briefly in 1864, his military career was over. Following service in the field, he returned to the arena of politics, but never again exercised the powerful influence he once held in Congress. However, he did serve as Chairman of the Democratic National Convention in 1876 which nominated Samuel J. Tilden for president. McClernand led a long and active life and finally succumbed to the effects of dysentery on

September 20, 1900. He was survived by his wife and four children from his first marriage.

*   *   *

An objective evaluation of McClernand's military performance reveals that he demonstrated many fine qualities of leadership. He had unshakable confidence in himself and always acted from his strengths. He knew his men and their abilities, and he did not care about what the enemy did; rather he focused on what he could do to the enemy. Most important, he was not afraid to fight which earned him the respect of his soldiers. "A personality that responded to the challenges and difficulties in the political arena was apt to accept those of the battlefield and respond similarly," writes McClernand biographer Richard Kiper. "Ambition, oratory, determination, confidence, and courage were the heart and soul of John McClernand's composition. Properly harnessed, those qualities could make a great politician or a great general. Unharnessed by self-control, they could lead to insubordination, inflexibility, and want of introspection."[39]

Unfortunately for both the Illinois general and the nation he served, McClernand never developed the qualities of leadership he lacked—chief among them being selflessness. Perhaps Ezra Warner summed it up best when he wrote, "McClernand's chief failing as a troop commander, aside from inexperience, was his fatal proclivity to display the fruits of victory, no matter how garnered, upon his own standards." That failing ushered him into obscurity, where he languishes to this day.[40]

McClernand lived long enough to see the field of his most stirring triumph and stinging defeat turned into a national military park. On these grounds the people of Illinois erected a magnificent equestrian statue in his honor. Ironically, there are no monuments on the hallowed ground at Vicksburg in honor of either James McPherson or William Sherman, the corps commanders Grant credited in securing the victory.

*   *   *

The tarnished image of the fighting politician is worthy of polishing to a luster more deserving of his service. Perhaps historians will someday reevaluate John Alexander McClernand and the significant role he played in the Civil War. Only through objective evaluation will the shroud that continues to veil him be lifted, enabling the portraiture of this historical figure to be completed.

CHAPTER FIVE

Companion to the Fishes:
The Saga of the Gunboat *Cincinnati*

A s the storm clouds gathered over John McClernand in the closing days of May 1863, the Union siege lines around Vicksburg were extended until they reached the river above and below the beleaguered city. Completing the encirclement of Vicksburg and assuring its capitulation were the vessels of R. Adm. David Dixon Porter's Mississippi Squadron. The fleet played a crucial role in the campaign for Vicksburg, and its service was recognized on July 4 when Grant entered the city, rode to the waterfront, and there personally thanked and congratulated Porter for the assistance rendered by the United States Navy. However, the squadron's record of achievement at Vicksburg was not earned without loss.

*   *   *

Although the North's industrial might was evidenced on the battlefield at Vicksburg and elsewhere, no where was its influence more decisive than on the inland waters where United States naval forces seized control of the Mississippi River and its tributaries, destroyed Confederate lines of communications and supply, and provided Northern armies with pathways of invasion into the Deep South.

The importance of the inland waters, and especially the Mississippi River, cannot be overstated. Newspaperman and biographer Lloyd Lewis accurately portrays the Mississippi River in the mid-nineteenth century as being "The spinal column of America"—the symbol of geographic unity. He refers to the great river as "the trunk of the American tree, with limbs and branches reaching to the Alleghenies, the Canadian border, the Rocky Mountains." For more than two thousand miles the river flows silently on its course to the sea providing a natural artery of commerce. Gliding along the Mississippi's muddy water were steamers and flatboats of all descriptions heavily laden with the rich agricultural produce of the nation en route to world markets. Indeed, the silent water of the river and its navigable tributaries was the single most-important economic feature of the continent, the very lifeblood of America. One contemporary wrote emphatically "The Valley of the Mississippi is America."[1]

The following statements support that assertion:

—Union Brig. Gen. Thomas Williams, who would lose his life in action at Baton Rouge in August 1862, stated unequivocally that possession of New Orleans and the Mississippi River was "a commercial and political necessity to the United States."[2]

—William T. Sherman, a man destined to play a prominent role in driving the South to its knees, wrote, "The Mississippi, source and mouth, must be controlled by one government." So firm was his belief that Sherman stated, "To secure the safety of the navigation of the Mississippi River I would slay millions. On that point I am not only insane, but mad."[3]

—General-in-Chief Henry W. Halleck wrote in similar, direct, albeit less eloquent terms, "In my opinion, the opening of the Mississippi River will be to us of more advantage than the capture of forty Richmonds."[4]

—President Abraham Lincoln himself referred to Vicksburg and control of the great river above which the city was built as "the key" and said "that the war can never be brought to a close until that key is in our pocket."[5]

—His counterpart, Confederate President Jefferson Davis, expressed his belief that a determined defense of the Mississippi River would "conduce more than in any other way to the perpetuation of the Confederacy and the success of the cause."[6]

—And, finally, even Mary Boykin Chesnut, the "Diarist of the Confederacy," recognized the importance of the Mississippi as she recorded of the river early in the war that "The Mississippi ruins us if it is lost."[7]

True though these statements were, the Confederacy was ill prepared to defend the strategic waterway. Writing early in the war, Gen. P.G.T. Beauregard referred to the Mississippi River as "our most vulnerable point" and urged the authorities to do more to ensure control of the river. The validity of his statement was never questioned, but with dozens of ports in need of heavy ordnance and troops for defense, and more than a score of water routes leading into the Confederacy that needed to be controlled to prevent invasion, the demands for human and material resources were far in excess of the government's ability to meet the needs imposed on the South by geography.[8]

In a vain effort to protect more than 3,500 miles of coastline and vital ports along the Atlantic and Gulf coasts, the Confederacy placed immediate reliance on an older generation of fortifications that were seized from the Federal government upon secession of the Southern states. Constructed following the War of 1812 many, if not most, of these massive masonry forts were not yet completed by the outbreak of the Civil War. Defense of the inland waters posed an equally daunting task as scores of navigable streams meandered throughout the Confederacy. Many of these streams, such as the Tennessee and Cumberland Rivers, cut across vital supply and communications lines and hampered the lateral movement of troops from one theater of operations to another.

Other than near the mouths of the Mississippi River below New Orleans, fortifications such as those along the coast did not exist anywhere on the great river or its tributaries. To provide a semblance of protection to this vast region and block these natural arteries of invasion, the Confederacy constructed earthen forts such as Henry and Donelson, Pillow, and De Russy, and, as the war progressed, erected batteries to command the rivers at places such as Columbus, Kentucky, New Madrid, Missouri, the Post of Arkansas, Vicksburg and Grand Gulf, Mississippi, and Port Hudson, Louisiana. But, in the final evaluation, these fortifications proved no match for the firepower and mobility of Northern naval forces.

To wrestle control of the great waterway from the Confederates, the Administration in Washington, acting initially through Secretary of War Simon Cameron and later through Secretary of the Navy Gideon Welles, began construction of a fleet of gunboats. The idea had been advanced by Lincoln's attorney general, Edward Bates of Missouri, famous river salvager and engineer James B. Eads, and others who understood the economic significance of the river and the vital role it could and would play militarily in bringing an end to the rebellion.

According to Eads, who outlined his plan for the Lincoln administration on April 29, 1861, "The effects of closing the Mississippi [River] . . . would be disastrous to the South because it would effectually block the main channel through which flowed her food supplies." The only avenues of commerce open to the Confederacy west of the Appalachians would thus be the Tennessee and Cumberland Rivers and the tracks of the Louisville and Nashville Railroad. The railroad, advanced Eads, could easily be sabotaged and the rivers, except in periods of high water, were navigable only by small steamers which could not possibly transport the quantities of food needed to sustain the Confederate armies in the field or feed the Southern populace. Once these routes, along with the Mississippi, were sealed, Eads concluded, "starvation [would be] inevitable in less than six months."[9]

Long reliant on river transportation and commerce to fuel its industrial development, the Northern states possessed facilities for construction of boats at Pittsburgh, Pennsylvania; Wheeling, West Virginia; Madison, Jeffersonville, and New Albany, Indiana; Cincinnati, Ohio; Louisville, Kentucky; Mound City, Illinois; and at St. Louis, Carondelet, and Cape Girardeau, Missouri. The operations at these yards were quickly converted to building warships. River steamers were transformed seemingly overnight into army transports and supply vessels, while others, armed with ordnance of various sizes, were converted into cottonclads or thinly armored tinclads. The contribution that these vessels made to ultimate Union victory was significant. However, it was the construction of a revolutionary fleet of gunboats designed specifically for use on the inland waters that would give the North the military capability to seize and maintain control of the strategic waterways and enable the Lincoln administration to pocket the key to victory—the ironclads.

Before John Ericsson began construction of the more famous *Monitor*, Eads laid the keels for seven boats that became known as the City Class. Each vessel measured approximately 175' long 52' wide and mounted thirteen big guns. The casemates of these vessels sloped thirty-five degrees and consisted of twenty-six inches of white oak covered with two and one half inches of armor plating. Powered by an enclosed paddlewheel to glide over the often-shallow rivers, the ironclads, which weighed more than 850 tons when fully loaded, drafted only six feet of water and had a maximum speed of six knots.

Eads contracted with the War Department to construct the fleet in the remarkably short period of only sixty-four days. To meet such an ambitious time frame, the famed engineer set about his task with vigor. He employed 800 men to work on the hulls paying $2 per ten-hour day with 25 cents per hour overtime. Thirteen sawmills in Missouri, Kentucky, Illinois, and Ohio worked exclusively for Eads to cut lumber for the boats that were constructed at the Carondelet and Mound City boatyards. Although he failed to meet the completion date set forth in the contract, the vessels were launched in a period equaled only by the "Liberty Ships" of World War II fame.

It was an historic moment when *Carondelet* was launched on October 12, 1861, as she was the first ironclad built in the Western Hemisphere and ushered in the modern era of naval warfare. Her six sisters soon followed and by mid-January 1862, all were commissioned. The vessels that slid down the ways were named in honor of cities on the Mississippi and its major tributaries: *Cairo, Carondelet, Cincinnati, Louisville, Mound City, Pittsburg,* and *St. Louis* (later renamed *Baron De Kalb*). Each manned by a crew of 175 officers and men, the City Class gunboats proved the backbone of Union naval operations on the inland waters and were the forerunner of the present-day battleship. Within a month all were steaming downriver to seize control of the inland waters and assume their place in history.

Cincinnati, which was built by Hambleton, Collier and Company in Mound City, was distinguished from her sisters only by the color bands that appeared at the top of her chimneys—which were blue. On January 1, 1862, Flag Officer Andrew Hull Foote ordered Cmdr. Roger N. Stembel of the gunboat *Lexington* to assume command of the ironclad. Stembel, who had acted as an agent of the Navy to inspect the newly constructed City Class gunboats, commissioned his vessel at Cairo on

Eads' ironclads under construction at the Carondelet boatyard near St.Louis. Although built in Mound City, *Cincinnati* would have looked much the same way at this stage of completion. *Vicksburg NMP*

January 16. Within days the newly-commissioned ironclad was steaming up the Tennessee River en route to its first encounter with enemy batteries as part of a combined land and naval force that moved against Forts Henry and Donelson to crack the shell of the Southern Confederacy.[10]

Guarding the pathways of invasion that were the Tennessee and Cumberland Rivers was a trilogy of earthen forts. Fort Heiman towered above the Tennessee on the west bank of the river while Fort Henry stood opposite it on the river's eastern shore. Twelve miles farther east was Fort Donelson, the largest and most formidable of the three, which stood guard over the Cumberland River and the water approach to Nashville.

As the Union flotilla slowly steamed up river on February 5, 1862, lookouts aboard the gunboat *Conestoga* spied a torpedo and fished it out of the water. (Unlike today's self-propelled devices, these were stationary, floating devices comparable to what we call mines.) The "infernal machine"—as they were soon to be called by the Federals, was placed on the fantail of *Cincinnati* where it was inspected by Foote and Brig. Gen. Ulysses S. Grant. The flag officer suggested that it be taken

USS *Cincinnati* and her crew looked very similar to ill-fated sister ship *Cairo*, which was sunk by a torpedo on December 12, 1862, in the Yazoo River above Vicksburg.

apart in the process of which it suddenly began making a hissing sound. While others threw themselves to the deck, Grant and Foote raced up a nearby ladder—much to the amusement of the crew, but the device failed to explode. Somewhat embarrassed, Foote asked "General, why the haste?" Although equally embarrassed, Grant replied, "That the Navy not get ahead of us."[11]

On February 6, Forts Heiman and Henry stood silent against the gray dawn as the Federal gunboats prepared for battle. Unbeknownst to Foote and Grant, the Confederates had abandoned Fort Heiman, which was incomplete, and thus posed no threat to Northern arms. Fort Henry, however, was a powerful bastion that mounted 17 guns—12 of which fronted the river. Due to faulty engineering, the fort was situated on low ground close to the river, and partially flooded. Realizing that the fort was untenable, the Confederate commander, Brig. Gen. Lloyd Tilghman, sent most of his men to Fort Donelson and remained behind with a handful of gunners to contest the Union fleet.

At 12:30 in the afternoon the Union flotilla steamed forward. The four ironclads: *Cincinnati* (which served as the flagship), *Carondelet*, *St. Louis*, and *Essex* formed a parallel line in front, while the older wooden gunboats (timber-clads) *Tyler*, *Conestoga*, and *Lexington* took position astern and inshore. The gunboats opened fire at a range of 1,700 yards and increased with rapidity and accuracy as the fleet closed on the fort. For an hour and fifteen minutes the deadly dual continued during which Confederate gunners disabled *Essex* as a shot ruptured her boilers scalding 29 officers and men. In a letter to his wife, Foote described his experience aboard *Cincinnati*: "We were struck with rifle and heavy shot and shell 30 times, I had the breadth, for several seconds, knocked out of me, as a shot struck opposite my chest, in the iron clad pilot house on deck."[12]

The gunboats, however, gave as good as they received and disabled a number of Confederate cannon. "Dismembered bodies lay beside shattered guns, fires had kindled combustibles in the fort, and demoralized officers and men milled about," is how one described the scene inside the fort. At 1:50 p.m., Tilghman ordered the colors struck. The ironclads had proved themselves formidable weapons of war.[13]

St. Louis raced toward the fort to accept its surrender when Foote bellowed from *Cincinnati* to hold back. The flag officer wanted the prize for himself. He then ordered Commander Stembel to take possession of the fort. A detail from *Cincinnati* lowered a rowboat that had not been splintered by enemy fire and, gliding over the calming water, moved up to a sallyport, rowed inside the fort, and came to rest on the parade ground. Returning with Tilghman to the gunboat, Stembel watched as the Confederate commander greeted Foote saying, "I am glad to surrender to so gallant an officer." The crusty Foote was less gracious in his reply: "You do perfectly right, sir, in surrendering, but you should have blown my boat out of the water before I would have surrendered to you."[14]

Although not blown out of the water, Stembel's boat lost 1 killed (Seaman Pringle Caradice), and 8 wounded in its first engagement. The gunboat's paddlewheel and two guns were also disabled during the fight and *Cincinnati* was put out of action for two weeks as she returned to Mound City for repairs.[15]

During her absence from the fleet, Foote's gunboats were roughly handled when they attempted to force the surrender of Fort Donelson on February 14. Unlike at Fort Henry, the guns at Donelson were elevated above the Cumberland River which gave them the advantage of plunging fire. Although the gunboats had armor plating on their casemates and pilot houses, they had wooden decks and the hurricane deck had skylights for interior illumination and ventilation. Confederate fire ripped through the vulnerable portions of the boats disabling some of the vessels and inflicting heavy casualties on their crews. (The gunboats would face a similar situation at Vicksburg in 1863.) Despite this setback, Federal forces secured surrender of the fort on the 16th and the Union commander was given the nom de guerre that combined his terms and initials—"Unconditional Surrender" Grant.

After effecting repairs, *Cincinnati* rejoined the fleet which was now operating in the Mississippi's muddy water below the confluence of the Ohio River. On March 2, Flag Officer Foote, once again aboard *Cincinnati*, made an armed reconnaissance within 3-4 miles of Columbus, Kentucky, the Confederate's northern-most citadel on the great river. He spied the enemy burning their winter quarters and removing guns from the bluff which commanded the river. (By indirect approach, Union victory at Forts Henry and Donelson also forced the Confederates to evacuate their works at Columbus and withdraw southward into Tennessee.) "Columbus is in our possession," Foote notified Gideon Welles two days later, "the rebels leaving quite a number of guns and carriages, ammunition, and large quantity of shot and shell, a considerable number of anchors, and the remnant of chain lately stretched across the river, with a large number of torpedoes. Most of the huts, tents, and quarters destroyed."[16]

Seeking to quickly clear the enemy from as much of the Mississippi River as possible, Foote's flotilla continued downriver. In March and April, the City Class ironclads participated in the long range bombardment of Island No. 10 (which formally surrendered on April 8) and Fort Pillow, the latter less than ninety-river miles above Memphis. Throughout the bombardment of Fort Pillow, *Cincinnati* and the other ironclads took turn guarding the mortar scows that hurled their thirteen-inch shells into the fort with horrifying regularity.

In order to remove this deadly nuisance, Capt. J. Ed Montgomery, commander of the Confederate River Defense Fleet, boldly attempted to destroy the scow and its escort which every day took station off Craighead Point, above the fort. On May 10, after escorting *Mortar Boat No. 16* to its firing station, *Cincinnati* was tied fast to a tree and Commander Stembel turned all hands to holystoning the deck—unaware of the danger steaming toward him.

Eight Confederate vessels, including the powerful ram *General Bragg*, rounded Plum Point Bend and closed to within three-quarters of a mile of *Cincinnati* before Stembel bellowed for his men to slip the cables. Without the necessary head of steam, the ironclad sluggishly moved out into the stream and slowly made its way to a bar where Stembel hoped the water would be too shallow for the deeper draft rams to follow. *General Bragg*, however, bore down on the lumbering ironclad with incredible speed and crashed into *Cincinnati*'s starboard beam tearing away a section amidships six feet deep and twelve feet long.

Taking on water in her forward shellroom, *Cincinnati* retreated upriver with the *Bragg* and its armored beak still embedded in her hull. A portion of the crew was detailed to bail her out while the remainder were ordered on deck and supplied with cutlasses, muskets, and hand grenades in anticipation of an attempt to board her. Stembel walked on deck among his crew encouraging the men. A lurch in the *General Bragg* exposed her pilot at the wheel whom Stembel shot and killed with his pistol. In turn, a man in the pilothouse drew a bead on the *Cincinnati*'s captain. Stembel attempted to reach safety behind his own pilothouse when he was hit—the ball entering his back near one of his shoulder blades, and came out under his chin. He was carried below deck, all believing him to be dead or mortally wounded. (Although Stembel recovered from his wounds, he saw no more action during the war.) Command fell upon Lt. William R. Hoel who said "My lads, if this ship goes down, she must do so with colors flying!" to which the crew responded with three hearty cheers.[17]

The Confederate ram backed water frantically and finally broke free of *Cincinnati*, but a second ram, *Sterling Price,* smashed into her starboard beam abaft amidships, tearing away the rudder, sternpost, and a large piece of the stern. Next *Sumter* plowed into her stern which forced the bows of *Cincinnati* under, drowned her fires, and flooded the magazines and shell rooms. The powerful ironclad slowly sank and settled on the bottom in two fathoms of water (12 feet). In addition to the vessel itself, the crew suffered the loss of Stembel, Fourth Master G. A. Reynolds, and one seaman, all wounded. Reynolds passed away two days later.[18]

Believing *Cincinnati*'s damage only slight, the crew hoped to refloat her within 24 hours, but instead they worked frantically for several days to pump water from the hull and raise the boat to no avail. On May 13, Flag Officer Charles H. Davis, who had replaced Foote as commander of the Western Flotilla just prior to the action off Craighead Point, wrote to Cmdr. Alexander M. Penncok at the Cairo Navy Yard: "It is of the last importance that the *Champion*, with her pumps, or the bell boat, should be here at the earliest possible moment. The river is falling rapidly, and the preservation of the *Cincinnati*, which is lying at the bank, depends upon having the means of freeing her from water at once." Finally on May 15 *Cincinnati* was raised and taken to Cairo for repairs. "The gunboat *Cincinnati* left for Cairo last evening," Davis reported to Secretary Welles the following morning. "The injury she sustained proved to be much more serious than at first reported."[19]

Indeed it was, for on May 21, after placing *Cincinnati* in drydock, Pennock reported to Davis the extent of the damage:

> I beg leave to report that she received a severe blow abaft the iron plating on her starboard quarter, which broke the tops of the head timbers for about 14 feet. She also received two blows on the stern, one on each side of the rudder, which did considerable damage. The work of taking out the crushed timbers consumes more time than it will require to put the new ones in place.

The bulkheads in the hold are down, and the greater portion of her stores, furniture, etc. is ruined, and she will require a new outfit. I am of the opinion that it will require two weeks constant work to put her in readiness for service.[20]

Pennock was an exacting task master who pushed his laborers around the clock to put the ironclad in serviceable condition. He notified Davis on June 1, "The *Cincinnati* has her planking on again, and an attempt was made yesterday to take her off the ways, but, on account of their having settled, it was unsuccessful.

Another trial was made to-day, which was attended with partial success, and I hope to have her at Cairo by this evening." However, it was not until June 3 that the commander of the navy yard was able to inform Davis, "We succeeded last evening in getting the *Cincinnati* off the ways. I am equipping and shall dispatch her as soon as possible."[21]

By the time *Cincinnati* returned to duty, she had a new commander. Lt. John P. Hall, who had been assigned to temporary command of the gunboat following Stembel's wounding, was replaced by Cmdr. John A. Winslow. (Winslow would later command the USS *Kersarge* which sank the CSS *Alabama* off the coast of Cherbourg, France, on June 19, 1864.) Winslow, however, commanded the boat for less than two months during which time his vessel did not participate in any significant action. The only service of note being the assistance *Cincinnati* provided in covering the withdrawal of several boats that had participated in a fatal expedition up the White River in Arkansas.[22]

On July 14, 1862, Winslow was relieved of command and ordered to take charge of the naval station at Memphis. He was replaced by Lt. Commanding Byron Wilson, whose vessel spent the remainder of the summer patrolling the Mississippi from its anchorage at Helena, Arkansas.[23]

In an effort to strengthen the City Class ironclads, the Navy Department ordered Wilson to steam to Cairo where his vessel would be retrofitted with additional armor plate, the sides extended, and additions made to the fantail and forecastle. Several of the older model cannon were also replaced with IX-inch guns mounted in the bow. Provided these improvements had the desired effect, *Cincinnati* would serve as a pattern for the other gunboats of the same class.[24]

The commander of the Mississippi Squadron, Acting R. Adm. David Dixon Porter, was the uncle of *Cincinnati*'s commander, Lt. George Mifflin Bache.

National Archives

In mid-October, while *Cincinnati* was at the Navy Yard in Cairo, a major change in operational command on the western waters was implemented. The inland water fleet, heretofore under army control, was placed under the direction of the Navy Department and Acting R. Adm. David Dixon Porter assumed command of the fleet, which he now called the Mississippi Squadron. On November 8, 1862, Lt. George Mifflin Bache received orders from Porter (who was his uncle) to take command of the *Cincinnati* "and fit her for sea without delay."[25]

Porter's squadron was destined to experience an active winter of operations, and the admiral wanted his powerful ironclads with him as Federal land and naval forces sought to eliminate all vestige of the enemy from the banks of the Mississippi River. Under Bache's command, *Cincinnati* participated in the actions at Chickasaw Bayou (December 27-29, 1862), the capture of Fort Hindman at Arkansas Post (January 9-11, 1863), and the nearly-disastrous Steele's Bayou expedition (March 14-27), during which the vessel suffered only slight damage.

The winter of frustration ushered in a spring of promise and Union forces now focused their efforts on Vicksburg. The city, situated atop 300-foot high bluffs with powerful batteries trained on the river, was known as the "Gibraltar of America," and would prove a tough nut to crack. On March 31, Grant boldly launched his Army of the Tennessee on a march south through Louisiana from his base camps at Milliken's

Bend and Young's Point in search of a favorable crossing point somewhere below the city.

As the Union infantry slowly made its way south, corduroying roads and building bridges practically each step of the way, Porter's fleet readied itself for a daring run by the batteries. On the dark, moonless night of April 16, the vessels raised anchor and, with running lights extinguished and engines muffled, moved downriver toward the citadel of Vicksburg. For more than an hour the fleet withstood the punishing fire that poured from Confederate batteries. When the shelling stopped, Porter tallied the damage to his fleet and recorded the loss of only one transport vessel. What had been deemed impossible by many was achieved. *Cincinnati*, however, did not participate in this daring run, but remained moored north of Vicksburg to await what fate held in store for her.

Once below the city, Porter's boats were able to ferry the army across the river and onto Mississippi soil on April 30-May 1. Over the next seventeen days, in what is often referred to as the blitzkrieg of the Vicksburg campaign, Grant's army battled its way deep into the interior of Mississippi, captured the state capital of Jackson, and drove Confederate forces into the Vicksburg fortifications. On May 19 and again on May 22, he hurled his army against the city's defenses only to be repulsed with heavy loss. Realizing he could not take the city by storm, Grant laid siege to Vicksburg.

On May 23, the Confederate commander, Lt. Gen. John C. Pemberton, sought to strengthen his position to withstand the rigors of siege by transferring several large guns from the river batteries to the rear defense line. Union lookouts caught sight of this movement and reported it up the chain of command where it was falsely assumed that the Confederates were abandoning the Water Battery—the northern most battery in the city's river defense line. Grant requested by use of signal flags that Admiral Porter send the *Cincinnati* to investigate the report. The Southerners, however, had broken the Union signal code and were thus expecting the gunboat when it rounded De Soto Point, north of the city, and ready to give it a warm reception.

Cincinnati was to move in conjunction with several vessels from the lower flotilla. In preparation for possible action, the unarmored sections of the ironclad were reinforced with logs and bales of hay. Bache and his crew worked feverishly to have the vessel ready for action on May 26, as scheduled, but the preparations proceeded slower than necessary and the planned attacked was postponed until 8:00 a.m. the following morning.

Aboard *Cincinnati* on Wednesday morning, May 27, acting assistant surgeon Richard D. Hall sat writing a letter to his mother and wife Anna back home in Fairfield, Indiana. "We have also to destroy a masked battery that holds General Sherman in check and shells our rifle pits that bar his progress," he wrote concerning their mission. "This masked battery has destroyed a great number of his brave boys; they have made two charges and both times have been repulsed. He says that if the *Cincinnati* will take the battery and shell the pits that he and his men will go into Vicksburg. Well, we will do it for him and give him a chance."[26]

Because *Cincinnati* had farther to go to get into position, the ironclad raised anchor at 7:00 a.m., cast-off lines, and moved downstream. Once his boat drew abreast of the mortar sows, Bache hove to in order to allow the vessels of the lower flotilla to engage the guns at South Fort—the southern anchor of the Confederate defense line around Vicksburg. This would also allow his firemen an opportunity to build-up a head of steam as it would be needed in case of trouble.

At 8 a.m., as *Cincinnati* waited near the head of De Soto Point, the lower flotilla commanded by Cmdr. Selim E. Woodworth headed up-stream from Bower's Landing. Consisting of the ironclads *Benton*, *Mound City*, and *Carondelet*, and the ram *General Price*, Woodworth's flotilla drew abreast of the lower entrance to Grant's Canal, below and opposite the city, and from there began shelling recently constructed earthworks below South Fort. Unfortunately, the works that were shelled were manned by Union soldiers who quickly displayed the "Stars and Stripes." Realizing their mistake, the tars shifted targets to South Fort and Battery Barnes (today known as Louisiana Circle).

Confederate artillerymen sprang to their pieces but replied slowly and methodically so as not to waste precious ammunition. The sounds of the big guns sparked panic among the town's civilian population. Hugh Moss, a Southern cannoneer noted, "There was great commotion in the city—women and children and even men ran for their rat holes [caves] thinking that there would be a general attack in front and indeed this was the opinion of officers and men."[27]

The sound of firing below Vicksburg was the cue for Lieutenant Bache to resume his movement downriver. Under a full head of steam *Cincinnati* moved out into the channel at 8:30 and rounded De Soto

Point. Bache and his crew watched with baited breath as the powerful ironclad approached the Water Battery. Contrary to his expectations, Confederate guns opened fire and blanketed the river with dense clouds of smoke. Shot and shell from rifled 32-pounders and a 10-inch columbiad slammed into the boat's armored casemate, but either simply glanced or tumbled harmlessly into the muddy water.

Cincinnati's guns also swung into action, but failed to score any telling shots. Continuing his course, Bache rounded his gunboat opposite the Wyman's Hill Battery to engage the shore batteries. As he did so, a shot from a rifled 32-pounder in the Water Battery crashed through the starboard beam and into a shell room knocking over all the boxes of ammunition on one side of the alley. *Cincinnati* responded with a broadside from her starboard battery. The heavy recoil of the boat's big guns, however, caused the vessel to list and exposed its soft underbelly—that portion of the boat below the armored knuckle. At that moment an iron bolt fired from a 7-inch Brooke rifle pierced the skin of the vessel and crashed into the shell room below the waterline. A second shell from the Brooke gun tore through the stern and entered the magazine, flooding that area. *Cincinnati* was badly wounded.

Plunging fire from the Confederate batteries sent solid shot and shell crashing into the stricken ironclad that drove through her decking and roof. Killed and wounded sailors littered the gundeck and 5 of the boat's 14 guns were knocked out of commission. The three jackstaffs were also shot away, taking the national colors down with them in response to which the Southerners raised a mighty cheer.

Seeing the treasured banner fall, Quartermaster Frank Bois raced out onto the hurricane deck. Amidst a shower of splinters he seized the colors and nailed them to the stump of the forward mast. In recognition of his bravery, Bois was awarded the Medal of Honor. His citation read: "Conspicuously cool in making signals throughout the battle, Bois, after all the *Cincinnati*'s staffs had been shot away, succeeded in nailing the flag to the stump of the forestaff to enable this proud ship to go down 'with her colors nailed to the mast.'" Five other crewmen were awarded the Medal of Honor for their actions in this fight: Landsman Thomas E. Corcoran, Boatswain's Mate Henry Dow, Quartermaster Thomas W. Hamilton, who was badly wounded while at the wheel, Seaman Thomas Jenkins, and Seaman Martin McHugh.[28]

With his boat shipping water badly, Bache called on his firemen to pile on the coal to build up speed and make good his escape. But moving upstream against the powerful current of the Mississippi and exposed to a murderous fire from Confederate batteries, *Cincinnati* had run out of luck. A 128-pound ball from a 10-inch columbiad ripped through the pilothouse that killed the helmsman and carried away the starboard tiller, which made the boat difficult to manage. Realizing that his vessel was sinking, Bache seized the wheel and ran his gunboat into the left bank about a mile north of Mint Spring Bayou where he ordered the crew to abandon ship. The ironclad sank in three fathoms of water and only its chimneys and part of the casemate remained above water.

In the action on May 27, Bache lost 5 men killed, 14 wounded, and 15 missing or approximately 20% of the boat's complement. It was later determined that of the missing all but one had drowned. The lone survivor was Seaman Thomas Smith who had been swept downstream clinging to a bale of hay and later pulled ashore by the Confederates. The frightened bluejacket gained the dubious distinction of being the only Union sailor captured during the siege.

Despite the loss of his vessel and heavy casualties among the crew, Lieutenant Bache received praise from Sherman and Porter for the manner in which he had fought his vessel. He even received commendation from Gideon Welles, who wrote on June 12 in a manner uncharacteristically generous: "Whilst regretting the loss of a ship that has so often successfully engaged the enemy, the sad casualties attending it, and the sorrows that have been brought to the hearts of the families of those who gave up their lives in the service of their country, it is gratifying to feel that the officers and crew of the *Cincinnati* performed their duty nobly and faithfully." In closing, the navy secretary penned: "It is with no ordinary pleasure that I express to you and the surviving officers and crew of the *Cincinnati* the Department's appreciation of your brave conduct."[29]

In Vicksburg, Sgt. William Tunnard of the Third Louisiana Infantry recorded, "This combat was witnessed by hundreds of ladies, who ascended on the summits of the most prominent hills in Vicksburg. There were loud cheers, the waving of handkerchiefs, amid general exultation, as the vessel went down." One of those ladies was the redoubtable Emma Balfour, a prominent Vicksburg socialite who, with her husband Dr. William Balfour, had hosted the gala Christmas Eve ball in 1862 that was so rudely interrupted by the arrival of Sherman's Expeditionary Force prior to the Battle of Chickasaw Bayou. From the heights of Sky Parlor Hill she witnessed the stirring episode and recorded her observations in her journal:

> Five boats from below and one a terrible monster from above engaged our batteries. In a very short time we perceived that the monster was disabled and a tug from above came to her relief. Later, men were seen to leave her side. There she drifted over to the Mississippi shore, and then arose the glad shout: 'She is sinking!' Sinking indeed she was and there she lies under water except her chimneys and her horn! Those from below retired when they saw this, so the battle is over for today and we are again victorious on water![30]

As the ironclad slowly settled on the bottom of the river, news of its sinking spread as wildfire among the city's defenders. Confederate artilleryman Hugh Moss scribbled with jubilation in the pages of his diary, "Cheer after cheer from the men above told us that some good had been done for the monster had become companion to the fishes under the waters of the great Mississippi." As the smoke of battle drifted away, Sergeant Tunnard of Louisiana boasted that, "A large number of articles from the sunken boat were picked up in the river, including hay, clothing, whiskey, a medical chest, letters, photographs, etc. We often wonder if the surgeon [Richard D. Hall] on the *Cincinnati*, who so comfortably penned a letter to his affectionate wife as the boat neared our batteries, escaped unhurt." (Perhaps Tunnard would be pleased to learn that he did.)[31]

J.M. Swords, editor of *The Daily Citizen*, offered words of praise in the pages of the city's leading newspaper that during the siege was printed on wallpaper. "It is a high honor to Colonel Ed Higgins [commander of the river batteries] and his command of heavy artillery as well as to the country generally that this giant, the boasted monster and terror of the western waters, is now a total wreck in view of both friend and foe," he penned. Swords then editorialized, "It is one of those achievements, and when fully detailed in history will be appreciated by futurity as well as it is at present."[32]

On May 28, Mrs. Balfour and her husband invited Colonel Higgins and General Pemberton to lunch in thanksgiving for the sinking of

Cincinnati. Although delighted to avail themselves of the hospitality and fine food, the two officers shared a growing concern about the ironclad.

Fearful lest falling waters would expose enough of the vessel to facilitate salvage, a call for volunteers went out to destroy *Cincinnati*. Capt. James W. Barclay and 47 soldiers from the First and Third Missouri Cavalry (dismounted) stepped forward. At 10:15 p.m. on May 30, the band assembled at the Vicksburg wharf and embarked in small boats. With muffled oars, the men rowed upstream several miles and reached the hulk of the ironclad that rested 30 yards from shore. Quickly examining the boat, Barclay was satisfied that the vessel was too badly damaged for immediate service if raised. He further noted that the boat's heavy ordnance was still submerged and that the hull was slowly moving farther out into the river with the falling waters.[33]

After removing the flag that was still nailed to the mast, the Southerners set fire to the boat and miraculously returned safely to Vicksburg. Barclay presented the flag to General Pemberton, who returned it to the Missourians as a tribute to their courage and daring. The fire, however, did little damage to the gunboat and the Confederates feared that the enemy would remove the boat's heavy ordnance under cover of darkness. Thus, cannoneers of the First Tennessee Heavy Artillery at the powerful Water Battery were ordered to fire several shells into the wreck each night to discourage such activities.

By the second week in June, as falling water exposed more and more of the boat, another force of volunteers was organized to blow up *Cincinnati*. On June 14 the raiding party slowly made its way upstream under cover of darkness. The Federals, however, would not be caught napping a second time. Col. Charles Woods, whose brigade manned the right flank of the besieging army, was notified that a small fleet of skiffs was moving upriver from the city. Woods dispatched a detachment of the Twenty-fifth Iowa into position along the riverbank near the boat.

As the Iowans waited, three large boats came into view. When challenged, a man aboard one of the skiffs replied that they belonged to the mortar boats that were then shelling Vicksburg from the opposite side of De Soto Point. Before the Federals could investigate, the boats turned about and fled toward Vicksburg. En route back to the city, the flotilla was fired upon by the guns of Company F, Second Missouri Light Artillery. Shot and shell landed around the boats and saturated the occupants with sprays of water, but in the darkness the guns could not register a hit and the expedition reached safety at the city wharf. No further attempts were made to destroy the vessel.

By the end of June the water had subsided sufficiently for work crews from Colonel Woods' brigade to begin removing the guns and other items from *Cincinnati*. Some of these guns were mounted in a land-based battery—known as Battery Selfridge (located near the base of the U.S. Navy Monument at Vicksburg National Military Park), and manned by tars for the duration of the siege.

Following the city's surrender on July 4, 1863, efforts were taken to raise the vessel, which throughout the siege had rested within range of Confederate guns. *Cincinnati* was finally raised in August, repaired, and eventually returned to service. Having served faithfully on the inland waters, the ironclad was transferred to the West Gulf Blockading Squadron in February 1865. Her final moment of glory came on May 10 of that year when she captured the CSS *Nashville* on the Tombigbee River above Mobile. At war's end, *Cincinnati* returned to the place of its birth, Mound City, where it was decommissioned on August 4, 1865. Deemed surplus property by the United States Navy, the once-proud gunboat that was the terror of the Mississippi River was ingloriously sold for scrap on May 27, 1866—ironically the anniversary of her second sinking. Perhaps refusing to go out quietly, before she could be moved, the old warrior hit a snag and sank one final time at the mouth of the Cache River.

Despite her heroic record of service and achievement, *Cincinnati* has the unenviable distinction of being one of the few vessels in the history of the United States Navy to be sunk twice in combat.

CHAPTER SIX

The Lords of Vicksburg

"My first knowledge of the siege of Vicksburg was gained in sitting all night on a pile of coal, which had been overspread with rugs and blankets in the cellar of Christ Church," wrote William W. Lord, Jr. "With the deep but muffled boom of the guns reaching us at intervals in our underground retreat, my mother and sisters huddled around me upon the coal-heap, my father, in clerical coat, and a red smoking-cap on his head, seated on an empty cask and looking delightedly like a pirate, our negro servants crouching terror-stricken, moaning and praying in subdued tones in a neighboring coal-bin, and all lighted by the fitful glow of two or three tallow candles, the war became to me for the first time a reality and not the fairy-tale it had hitherto seemed." Though penned more than forty years after his harrowing experience, these words reveal how vividly he recalled the events that had enveloped his family in the summer of 1863 when the city in which he lived was the focal point of military operations that decided the fate of a nation.[1]

* * *

Vicksburg was still in its infancy when the city's Episcopal community formed in 1828. The Rev. James Fox, a circuit riding preacher, ministered to their spiritual needs until the Rev. George Weller arrived in 1838 and became the resident rector of the parish named "Christ Church." Intermittent church services were held for several years in borrowed buildings while the congregation struggled to build an edifice of its own. It was a joyous occasion when the cornerstone of the church was dedicated on April 19, 1839, by then Bishop Leonidas Polk. (Polk, an 1827 graduate of the United States Military Academy, had resigned from the army six months after graduation to enter the ministry. At the outbreak of hostilities in 1861, his friend and fellow West Point classmate, Jefferson Davis, prevailed upon Polk to accept a commission in the Confederate service. Rising to the rank of lieutenant general, Polk was killed at Pine Mountain, Georgia, on June 14, 1864.) Construction efforts, however, were delayed when a fire destroyed most of the material they had assembled on site. A further and much sadder setback occurred on November 8, 1841, when Reverend Weller died from yellow fever. The popular pastor was soon replaced by Rev. W. Frederic Boyd who served as rector until June 1845, by which time the church was finished and consecrated.[2]

Situated on the northwest corner of Locust and Main Streets, the church was a simple rectangle that measured 60 feet long by 40 feet wide. The bell tower, constructed of 14" by 14" cypress timbers, and front entrance faced Main Street. The support beams and roof trusses were also cypress with wrought iron pins to hold the wood elements together. The flooring was pecan which added to the elegance and dignity of the sanctuary, and stained-glass windows from Germany completed this edifice to the glory of God.

This simple, yet beautiful new church and its congregation of worshipers next welcomed Rev. Stephen Patterson who served as their spiritual leader from 1845 until 1853. A kind-hearted, gentle man, the minister was beloved by his parishioners and people from all walks of life and faiths across the city. It was in keeping with his life of service to Christ and his fellow man that "he died at his post, a martyr" while attending to those afflicted during a fearful epidemic of yellow fever that raged throughout Vicksburg. As a sign of their love and admiration, Patterson's flock laid him to rest in the yard of the church he had served so well.[3]

Due to their love for Reverend Patterson, the members of Christ Church received their next pastor with polite skepticism. As the nation was already embroiled in sectional controversy due to congressional debate on the Kansas-Nebraska Act, it did not help matters that the new minister was of northern birth. The Rev. Dr. William Wilberforce Lord

Rev. Dr. William
Wilberforce Lord

Vicksburg NMP

was born in New York on October 28, 1818, but had lived most of his life in the slave states of the South. A graduate of the Princeton Theological Seminary, he was a tall man with thin, dark hair and full side whiskers. The good reverend had a broad face with deep set eyes and a pleasant smile that revealed much about his character. Lord was a gifted orator with a powerful voice that combined with a dignified bearing to make him an imposing figure in his priestly vestments. As members of the church would soon discover, they were fortunate indeed that he was destined to shepherd them through the trying ordeal of civil war and the horrors of siege.

Accompanying him to Vicksburg was his wife, Margaret, and their infant daughter Eliza, who they called Lida. Together, they set about to make the rectory their home. Maggie, as Reverend Lord called his wife, was almost twenty years his junior. A native of Maryland, she bore three more children following their arrival in Vicksburg. Sarah was born within the year. William (Willy), their only son, came into the world in 1855, and their youngest, Louisa (Loulie), arrived the same year that John Brown led his raid on Harpers Ferry.[4]

The Lord household included several black servants, probably slaves, though in their letters and diaries they were never referred to as such by members of the family. There was Minnie, the maid, Chloe, the cook, and Chloe's husband and their two little girls. According to Lida, Minnie was known throughout town as the "secesh darkey" as she was "an ardent defender of 'the cause.'" There was a close attachment between the Lords and their servants. "These faithful women served us cheerfully during the siege and stood by us stoutly afterward," noted

Lida. In fact, Minnie would follow the Lords back "into the Confederacy" after the surrender of Vicksburg.[5]

Reverend Lord and his growing family adapted quickly to life in the Deep South and came to consider Vicksburg their home. They watched with mounting anxiety the storm clouds that gathered over the land and earnestly prayed that a merciful God would prevent sectional differences from tearing the nation asunder and turn brother against brother. The minister, especially, was torn between love of his native state and his adopted home. But as the Good Shepard had led him to Vicksburg, William Lord would cast his lot with the flock entrusted to his care and place his trust in God.

Despite their prayers and those of thousands like the Lords, secession became a reality as South Carolina left the Union in December 1860. Mississippi quickly followed suit and the people of Vicksburg braced themselves for the inevitable clash of arms. By late spring of 1862, their city was the lone obstacle to Union domination of the Mississippi River and the citizens of Vicksburg were not surprised when enemy warships of Flag Officer David Glasgow Farragut's West Gulf Blockading Squadron arrived on May 18. In terse words demand for the city's surrender was refused by Lt. Col. James L. Autry, the post commander, who replied that "Mississippians don't know, and refuse to learn, how to surrender to an enemy." Incensed, the naval commander gave notice of his intentions to attack and on May 22 ordered his gun crews into action. [6]

As the shells whistled through the air and exploded in the streets, panic gripped the residents of Vicksburg. "Men, women and children, both black and white, went screaming through the streets," recalled one citizen. Reverend Lord hurried his family and servants into the basement of the church the thick walls of which afforded a greater degree of shelter than those of the rectory. There in the basement of their house of worship the Lords huddled in one another's arms and prayed for deliverance from the dreaded bombs.[7]

It was a long and terrifying night for the Lords and their servants, but their prayers were answered as morning light found them safe and unharmed. Not knowing how long the Federal fleet and its big guns would pose a threat to the city, Reverend Lord decided to evacuate his family. As with scores of others in Vicksburg, they secured as best they could their earthly possessions and prepared to leave their home. "The next day [Friday, May 23], taking advantage of a cessation in the bombardment," wrote Willy Lord, "our entire household, excepting only my father . . . departed for [Uriah] Flowers' plantation near the Big Black River where shelter and entertainment had been offered us in anticipation of the shelling of the city. Our most valued household effects, including my father's library, reputed to be the most scholarly and largest private collection in the Southwest, followed us in a canvas covered army wagon. The family silver . . . we buried under the grass-grown sod of the churchyard."[8]

The move was a great adventure for the children, especially young Willy. Years later he wrote in happy recollection: "Mr. Flowers—a patriarch of the old school—gave us a planter's cordial welcome. The suite of apartments placed at our disposal was on the first floor of the family mansion, opening upon the cool and roomy reception hall, and fronting on three sides upon a wide piazza which ran entirely around the house. Here we were most pleasantly domiciled, to remain undisturbed as my father hoped, as long as the siege should last." Mrs. Lord, however, agonized over her husband's safety and, against his opposition, returned to town to share with him the uncertainty of the summer.[9]

The naval siege of Vicksburg, as it came to be known, continued from late May, all through June, and into late July, but to no avail. The guns of the Union fleet could not be elevated properly to aim an effective fire against Confederate batteries atop the bluffs overlooking the river. Recognizing the futility of their action, Union gunners maintained only an intermittent bombardment during the siege and inflicted few casualties on the defenders of Vicksburg. Sadly one citizen, Mrs. Patience Gamble, fell victim to the bombardment when she was decapitated by a shell as she left her home on Mundy Street, on the north edge of town.

Willy Lord and his sisters, however, had remained safely ensconced at the Flowers' plantation throughout the summer where they were far removed from the anxieties of war. They had spent the summer running through the fields, playing with the farm animals, and wading in creeks that ran clear and cool. Their almost carefree existence finally came to a close when Farragut's warships withdrew from Vicksburg and they were summoned home by their mother. "On our return journey to Vicksburg we rode in state in the Flowers' family carriage," boasted Willy, who went on to lament, "but left behind us, alas! the priceless library, our household treasure of art and bric-a-brac, and the greater part of my mother's dainty wardrobe."[10]

Life slowly returned to a semblance of normalcy in Vicksburg, but the Lords and all other residents were ever mindful that their city was the continuing objective of enemy operations. The streets were crowded with soldiers who also filled the stores, restaurants, and public buildings. (They also packed the pews of Christ Church every Sunday, much to the minister's delight.) Additional pieces of heavy ordnance arrived by train and were placed in battery along the river. And, throughout the fall, the garrison and thousands of slaves pressed into service labored to construct fortifications, clear fields of fire, and form obstructions of felled trees called abatis (the nineteenth century equivalent of barbed wire). Vicksburg quickly became known as the "Gibraltar of the Confederacy" which lulled the citizens into a false sense of security.

During the uneasy winter of 1862-1863, Federal forces under the command of Maj. Gen. Ulysses S. Grant maneuvered to get at Vicksburg without success. The Bayou campaigns, or "experiments" as Grant called them, ended in failure and by late spring he determined on a bold course of action that would result in the fall of Vicksburg three months later. The plan was to march his army south through Louisiana and search for a favorable crossing point below Vicksburg. There the Union fleet would hurl his army across the mighty river enabling Grant's men to operate against Vicksburg from the south and east, the area where the Confederates least expected.

On the night of April 16, 1863, R. Adm. David Dixon Porter led a flotilla of gunboats and army transports past the batteries of Vicksburg to rendezvous with Grant below the city. For more than an hour the gunboats and shore batteries hammered one another with solid shot and shell. Frightened citizens, including the Lords, sought shelter in basements and caves as bricks tumbled in the city streets. Six nights later the scene was repeated as additional vessels raced past the batteries en route to Grant.

Although unaware of the plans in operation, Reverend Lord sensed increasing danger and once again decided to evacuate his family to a safer area. He sent Maggie and the children to *Oakland*, the home of Flemens Granger, near the Big Black River east of Vicksburg. As the campaign unfolded, however, Mrs. Lord soon found herself and the children in the path of Grant's army as it battled its was toward Vicksburg.[11]

Having crossed the Mississippi River on April 30-May 1, the Union Army of the Tennessee overcame stiff Confederate resistance near Port Gibson on May 1. Pushing inland, Grant's army headed northeast and on May 12 drove a lone Confederate brigade from Raymond. Two days later, the Federals captured Jackson, Mississippi's capital city, and scattered Southern forces that were assembling there under the command of Gen. Joseph E. Johnston. Turning west toward his objective, Grant directed his army to Edwards from where Lt. Gen. John C. Pemberton and his Vicksburg field army was marching to do him battle.

"On May 16," recorded Lida Lord, "a neighbor rode over to report the evacuation of Jackson and we were surprised and dismayed by the news that Pemberton was falling back, closely pressed by Grant, upon Big Black [River] and Bovina." The young girl could not comprehend the dire implications of such news. Rather, she remained ignorant of the rapidly deteriorating situation and expressed her confidence by writing: "We did not allow ourselves, however, to doubt either the valor or the wisdom of our generals, but felt confident that this ambiguous movement was but a part of a preconcerted plan of Pemberton and Joseph E. Johnston—a plan which would lead up to the speedy surrounding and utter annihilation of Grant's army."[12]

But on that fateful day, the armies were destined to clash violently at Champion Hill—only a few miles distant from *Oakland*, and Confederate forces were routed and driven from the field in panic and confusion. Mrs. Lord and the children shuddered at the sounds of the guns and could only imagine the horrors that were being enacted on the bloody field of battle. About sunset a soldier rode into the yard to inquire the road to Bovina. Maggie in turn asked him of news from the front. "I am ashamed to tell you," he said, controlling his emotions, "we have been terribly whipped and the enemy are pursuing us to the Big Black and to Bridgeport Ferry." The hopes she had harbored throughout the day were dashed as she listened to the news for she now realized the proximity of their danger.[13]

"All that night we were packing and watching," wrote Mrs. Lord, "and the next morning [May 17] by daylight the yard was thronged by our poor, tired, hungry soldiers – all with the same words on their lips 'We were sold by General Pemberton.' My heart sank within me at this and I had little hope of Vicksburg itself, if as I almost believed Pemberton was a traitor." Lida also heard such critical comments of Pemberton and shared her mother's fears for the safety of Vicksburg. But there were more important things to do as the family prepared to return to the city than question the loyalty of the commanding general. The Lord's servants were also busy attending to the needs of the soldiers clad in butternut and gray who fled before the advancing foe. Lida observed, "From early dawn the cook was busy boiling coffee and baking biscuits, which Minnie, our zealous mulatto maid, handed in buckets and big trays to the scores of dusty, ragged, and foot–sore men who pressed up to the front door."[14]

The family started for Vicksburg around 3 p.m. that Sunday, May 17. Maggie and the children rode in a carriage that was followed by the servants in a wagon full of provisions. Reverend Lord, who had come from town to escort the family back home, rode behind in a buggy accompanied by Washington, a male servant. "The roads, always bad, were simply frightful," complained Lida for they had been hideously rutted by the passage of ambulances, artillery, and army wagons en route to Vicksburg. "At almost every turn we looked around in apprehension of the Yankee cavalry," recalled Mrs. Lord whose fear for the safety of her family increased as those in the wagons lost sight of one another.[15]

The caravan of wagons that plodded toward town was overtaken by darkness and rumors of the enemy's approach which "redoubled our anxiety," confessed Mrs. Lord. It was not until 10:00 p.m. that the cupola of the Warren County Courthouse and the spires of the city's churches came into view that they breathed a collective sigh of relief. "From the time we met our pickets stationed about a mile or a mile and a half from town there was a constant succession of camps and the whole town and hills seemed all aglow with the fires of the camps," recorded Maggie. "It was a beautiful, even wonderful sight," that left a lasting impression on Lida who added, "but we did not linger long to admire it, for behind us on the dark road to Bovina crept closer and closer the awful shadow of— Grant."[16]

Those in the wagons soon found themselves in the midst of a vast armed camp where there were, "Soldiers, soldiers at every step," observed Mrs. Lord. When she finally reached the rectory on Main Street, Maggie "found our gallery filled to overflowing with sleeping soldiers and [the] street full of wagons and artillery." For the next couple of hours, she "waited in tears—threw myself upon my knees (by the four little ones lying altogether on the bed sleeping, hungry as they were) and prayed Oh! How earnestly that my husband might be saved from their hands." Her anxiety finally ended when Reverend Lord arrived at midnight and she raced into the comfort of his arms.[17]

But there was little comfort among the city's garrison which throughout the night toiled with ax and saw, pick and shovel to strengthen their fortifications and prepared to resist the onslaught they knew was fast approaching. Stragglers were rejoined with their regiments, arms were issued to those who had cast them aside on the flight to Vicksburg, and guns from the artillery reserve were brought forward and placed into battery.

Maggie could see reflected in the faces of the soldiers around her that they were "all so despondent, so distrustful of their General and many almost hopeless of success under him." The insightful Emma Balfour, who poured forth all she had to refresh the troops as they arrived in the city, also noticed their despondency and candidly confided to the pages of her diary, "from all I saw and heard that it was want of confidence in the General commanding that was the cause of our disaster." The criticism of John Pemberton was so widespread and loud that Maggie Lord shared in her journal the concern of many in Vicksburg as she wrote, "Not the fear that Gen. Pemberton was a traitor but, although loyal to the South and personally brave, he was yet wholly incapable to act as Gen. of an army and I am sorry to [say] that that is still our almost only fear. That when the time comes, as we hope it will in a few days, when it will become necessary for him to sally out and attack them in front, while Johnston fights on their rear, his inefficiency will again lose us the victory."[18]

Despite the situation in which they found themselves when the sun rose on May 18, the family was happy to be home and reunited. But their happiness was destined to be short-lived as the Union army crossed Big Black River that morning and pushed hard toward Vicksburg. A deathly silence settled over the city and the hours slowly passed as citizens and soldiers alike awaited the enemy's approach. It was not until late in the day that the sound of scattered musketry along the picket line heralded their arrival which stirred a flurry of activity among the city's defenders. But the day wore away with nothing more than a long-range artillery duel as the Federals gathered their forces in hand and reconnoitered the Confederate works in preparation for assault.

It was a tense evening in Vicksburg for all knew that battle was imminent on the morrow and everyone in the city prepared for it, each in their own way. In the rectory on Main Street the Lords prayed as a family that a merciful God would look favorably upon them and crown the city's garrison with success. In the trenches around Vicksburg, the soldiers also prayed that they would be spared once the guns opened fire while others wrote letters home—for some of whom it would be their last. And throughout the night the bell on the courthouse chimed as if to announce that for many the sands of time were about to run out.

At 9:45 a.m. Union cannon roared into action on May 19 and for hours pounded the earthen forts around Vicksburg with solid shot and shell. That afternoon, when the guns fell silent, Grant hurled a portion of his army against the city's defenses along Graveyard Road, northeast of Vicksburg. Although the Federals planted several stands of colors on the exterior slope of Stockade Redan, they were driven back with heavy loss. "All day the cannonading was terrific and the air was full of conflicting rumors," wrote Lida Lord, "but toward the evening the news was brought that in three tremendous charges the enemy had been repulsed with great slaughter." The enemy's failure pleased her. "Then began the moral reconstruction of our army," she boasted. "Men who had been gloomy, depressed, and distrustful now cheerfully and bravely looked the future in the face. After that day's victory but one spirit seemed to animate the whole army, the determination never to give up."[19]

Anxious as he was for a quick victory, Grant realized that perhaps he had been too hasty in making the assault. Of his three corps, only one—Sherman's had been in proper position to attack. He decided to place his entire army in line and make a more thorough reconnaissance in preparation for a second strike. In the meantime, Porter's fleet continued to hammer away at the city's river defenses that placed the citizens of Vicksburg in harm's way.

"Our own trials began on Thursday [May 21], when the gunboats opened fire," recalled Lida. The day began delightfully for, "The sky was blue, and free from the familiar battle-smoke; the smell of the roses came in through the open windows." But the peace was soon shattered when the "bombs," initially concentrated against Confederate shore batteries, began exploding indiscriminately throughout town. The young girl remembered that the family was about to sit down for dinner, "On the table were glass and silver and dainty china, delicate rolls and steaming coffee." Suddenly "a bombshell burst in the very center of that pretty dinning room, blowing out the roof and one side, crushing the well-spread teatable like an eggshell, and making a great yawning hole in the floor, into which disappeared supper, china, furniture, and the safe [food chest] containing our entire stock of butter and eggs." The hole in the floor was six feet deep and twelve feet in circumference claimed her brother Willy, who declared, "Not a vestige of the table or its contents was ever found." Almost at that same instant, a solid shot came crashing through the side wall of the house, directly above a settee in the library. "As it happened, my father, with two of his friends among the officers, was seated upon this settee, discussing the folly of dodging while under fire, when this particular cannon ball crashed through the wall just above their heads and caused them all to dodge and fall upon their hands and knees. None was hurt, though all were powdered with splintered wood and crumbled plaster."[20]

Grateful to be alive, the Lords and their servants fled to a nearby cave where a neighbor, Gerard Stites, offered them refuge. "All that Thursday night the shelling never ceased," noted Lida. "Candles were forbidden, and we could only see one another's faces by the lurid, lightning-like flashes of the bursting bombs." The cave was hot, crowded, and the air stifling. "Frightened women sobbed, babies cried, tired and hungry children fretted, and poor soldiers groaned; and a little girl, crushed by a fall of earth from the side of one of the caves, moaned incessantly and piteously." Lida later learned that there were at least 65 people crowded into the cave that night. (Another occupant claimed there were as many as 200.) "No wonder," she exclaimed, "that the blessed daylight came like heaven."[21]

But even with the rising sun there was no respite for those huddled in the cave as on May 22 Union land batteries opened fire preparatory to Grant's next strike. For fours hours Federal guns bombarded the city's defenses and tore large holes in the earth forts that guarded Vicksburg. Then, in even greater numbers than before, blue-clad soldiers surged across the field and clawed their way up the slopes toward the Confederate fortifications. Though they succeeded in planting their colors on the exterior slopes at several locations along the line, and even penetrated the works at Railroad Redoubt, the attack was checked and finally repulsed. His nose bloodied twice, Grant decided to lay siege to the city and force the garrison of Vicksburg into submission through attrition.

Saturday, May 23, dawned overcast and raining and firing along the line stopped as Grant contemplated his next move. The quiet that settled over Vicksburg gave the Lords, and those with them, an opportunity to venture forth from the cave. While the others sought a breath of fresh air, Willy explored his new surroundings and provided us with a description of the cave:

> It was shaped like the prongs of a garden rake, the five excavations from the street or road all terminating in a long central gallery, so that in case any one of them should collapse escape could be made through the inner cave and its other branches. The entrance galleries at either end were reserved for servants and cooking purposes, and the intervening galleries and inner central gallery were occupied as family dormitories, separated from each other by such flimsy partition boards, screens, and hangings as could be devised.

According to Lida, in the Lord's family dormitory there were quartered "eleven of us—three white adults and four children, with our maid Minnie and cook Chloe and Chloe's two little girls."[22]

In addition to the Lords, six or eight families lived in these tight quarters, among them were those of Sheriff William McRae, grocery and commission merchant Duff Green, and Annie Lake, the widow of Judge William Lake. (Judge Lake had served in Congress prior to the Civil War. In 1861, while campaigning for a seat in the Confederate Congress, he was killed in a duel by his opponent, Henry C. Chambers, who went on to serve in Richmond.) A number of single people and "innumerable servants" also occupied the cave. Willy Lord observed that in these large communal caves, "a common danger abolished the unwritten law of cast. The families of planters, overseers, slave-dealers, tradespeople, and professional men dwelt side by side, in peace if not harmony."[23]

In the early days of the siege, those in the caves, not knowing how long they might be forced to live underground, returned home when firing permitted to secure the necessities of life and even a few luxuries. Beds, chairs, carpets, mirrors, and washstands were among the items taken into the caves. Some caves even had libraries and wine cellars. Though there is no record as to the items the Lords may have taken into

Lucy McRae

Vicksburg NMP

this cave for their comfort, it is assumed they took mostly bedding, clothing, and food, which was in keeping with the other occupants of this large communal cave. One of the "rats," as they called themselves, was Lucy McRae, the teenage daughter of Sheriff William McRae. She recalled that, "Mother took pillows, comforts, provisions, and clothing into the cave with her. All along on the ground of this cave planks were laid, that our beds might be made as comfortable as possible under the circumstances."[24]

Life underground however comfortable it was made, held no charms for the Lords or those with them and provided them with only the hope of safety. In reality, there was no safe place anywhere inside Vicksburg, above or below ground, as every inch of town was within range of Union cannon or heavy mortars. "The mortars, which were planted just opposite the city on the Louisiana side [of the river], kept up a continual fire upon us," noted Lucy McRae. She and her fellow citizens came to fear them especially as the mortars hurled 218-pound projectiles that at the height of their trajectory blocked out the sun. When these "bombs" came crashing to earth and exploded the resulting craters measured more than six feet deep. Only the deepest of caves could withstand a direct hit.[25]

The Lords remained in this cave through the end of May and into June. Though within sight of their home, it was much too dangerous to venture far from the cave, even during periods of relative calm, for no one dared be on the streets not knowing when or where the "bombs" might fall. Only the brave or foolhardy chanced walking the streets, one of whom was the indomitable Emma Balfour. A devout Christian and member of Christ Church, Mrs. Balfour recorded in her diary of Sunday, May 31: "This morning it is comparatively quiet—Trinity Sunday—how like and yet unlike Sunday. All nature wears a Sabbath calm, but the thunder of artillery reminds us that man knows no Sabbath—Yankee man at least." Starved for spiritual sustenance she boldly went in search of Reverend Lord and implored him to hold services. "On Sunday Mr. Lord at the particular request of Alice Lake and myself held service," she later wrote. "There was not much firing and though the ringing of the bell only announced services, there were thirty persons. I walked there and back, but was glad to do so for the sake of worshipping once more. The church has been considerably injured and was so filled with bricks, mortar and glass that it was difficult to find a place to sit."[26]

Just as for Mrs. Balfour, the Eucharist was a tonic for the minister and from that day on for the duration of the siege, regardless of the danger, Reverend Lord held true to his calling and ministered to his people by holding daily services. "Daily, in the absence of sexton and vestry, the rector opened the church, rang the bell, robed himself in priestly garb, and took his place behind the chancel rail," Willy proudly wrote of his father years later. "Then, with the deep boom of cannon taking the place of organ notes and the shells of the besieging fleet bursting around the sacred edifice, he preached the gospel of eternal peace to an assemblage of powder-grimed and often blood-stained soldiery, than whom I have ever heard him say, there never were a more devout or attentive audience."[27]

While attending to these duties in late May or early June, Reverend Lord was injured as evidenced by an entry in Lucy McRae's journal that noted the minister "was suffering with a sore foot and leg, which was all bandaged and propped on a chair for comfort." Perhaps the injury was caused by a shell fragment, or in a fall as he rushed from the cave to the church and back, or while clearing rubble from inside the vestibule of the church. Either way, the injury pained him for the remainder of the siege and at times almost incapacitated him.[28]

On June 9, the Lords and their companions realized just how vulnerable they were to the scepter of death that ruled over Vicksburg. That evening, as the children prepared for bed, Lucy McRae recorded that Mr. Lord said, "Come here, Lucy, and lie down on this plank," and commented that "Dr. Lord was almost helpless [due to his leg injury], but assisted me to arrange my bed, my head being just at his feet." Within seconds pandemonium erupted inside the cave and Lucy captured the moments of horror for posterity:

> The mortars were sending over their shells hot and heavy; they seemed to have range of the hill, due, it was said, to some fires that a few soldiers had made on the hill beyond us. Every one in the cave seemed to be dreadfully alarmed and excited, when suddenly a shell came down on the top of the hill, buried itself about six feet in the earth, and exploded. This caused a large mass of earth to slide from the side of the archway in a solid piece, catching me under it. Dr. Lord, whose leg was caught and held by it, gave the alarm that a child was buried. Mother reached me first, and a Mrs. Sites [probably Mrs. Gerard Stites whose cave they were in], who was partially paralyzed, with the assistance that Dr. Lord, who was in agony, could give, succeeded in getting my head out first. . . . The blood was gushing from my nose, eyes, ears, and mouth. A physician who was then in the cave was called, and said there were no bones broken, but he could not tell what my internal injuries were.[29]

As the mortar rounds continued to fall in frightful proximity, the mouth of one of the entrance caves collapsed when a large shell exploded and separated the Lords from their father. Willy recalled that his father's "powerful voice was audible above the roaring avalanche of earth, as he shouted, 'All right! Nobody hurt!'" Lida Lord asserted, "But for this timely check there must have been a disastrous crush; for many were rushing for the openings, while others, blinded and terrified, were plunging farther back into the hill. For, truly, though there were horrors enough within, where else could the poor souls go?"[30]

(Strange as it may sound, in the midst of all this terror and fright, there was cause for joy. Lucy McRae noted the reason: "during all this excitement there was a little baby boy born in the room dug out at the back of the cave; he was called William Siege Green."[31])

"Following these narrow escapes there was no longer a feeling of security even in the more deeply excavated portions of the cave," wrote Willy Lord, who expressed the belief shared by all in the underground dwelling. "These discomforts, supplemented by the odor of stale food in the heavy, earth laden atmosphere of the overcrowded caves so offended my mother's sensibilities that, persuaded by her, my father caused a private cave for the exclusive use of his own family to be constructed in one of the hills behind the Military Hospital. Here, under the shadow of the yellow hospital flag . . . it was believed we should be comparatively safe."[32]

The hospital of which he wrote was known as City Hospital. Located on the Jackson Road, on the edge of town, the hospital was less than one-half mile from the rectory that was their home. Behind the hospital the ground dropped off sharply to the east to a tributary of Stout's Bayou, which would provide the family with its drinking water. Excavated by Reverend Lord and members of Col. Francis Cockrell's Missouri Brigade, the family's new home was shaped like the letter "L." Willy wrote that it consisted of "an entrance cave of considerable length connected by an inner gallery with a shorter cut in the hill side which served as an exit or rear entrance and was open to the sky." His mother provided greater detail in her journal:

> Imagine to yourself in the first place a good-sized parapet, about six feet high, a path cut through, and then the entrance to the cave. . . . Secured strongly with boards, it is dug the height of a man and about forty feet under the hill. It communicates with the other cave which is about the same length opening out on the other side of the hill—this gives us a good circulation of air. . . . I have a little closet dug for provisions, and niches for flowers, lights, and books— inside just by the little walk is our eating-table with an arbor over it and back of that our fireplace and kitchen with table, &c. In the valley beneath is our tent and back of it the tents of the generals. This is quite picturesque to look at, but Oh! how wearisome to live!

"When finished," declared young Lida Lord, "it was the coziest cave in all Vicksburg, and the pride of our hearts from that day until the fatal Fourth of July."[33]

Although it was beyond the reach of the mortars and their dreaded bombs, the Lords' new cave was within range of enemy batteries along the siege lines around Vicksburg. (The land based batteries mounted mostly smaller field guns, i.e. 3-inch Ordnance Rifles, 12-pdr. Napoleons, 10-pdr. Parrott Rifles, etc., that were augmented by a scattering of larger siege guns.) Willy observed, "Fortunately a majority of these shells were of the smaller sort, with their force fairly spent before they reached us. If one of the huge bomb shells from the mortar boats had fallen and exploded on the summit of our little hill, it would probably have put an end both to our cave dwelling and to ourselves." The young boy went on to say, however, that, "We soon became familiar with the sound of those shells that gave warning of their approach, and expert in seeking the shelter of the cave when we heard them coming through the air. The cone-shaped Parrott shell, our most frequent visitor fortunately could be heard a long distance off, and so gave time for flight to our underground home."[34]

Their new cave was also within sight of the city's defenses and, to the family's great delight, close to the camp of Colonel Cockrell's Missouri Brigade. The Lords developed a close attachment to the soldiers, especially the children who found the Missourians to be "clever, merry gentlemen." Eleven-year-old Lida was infatuated with the soldiers of whom she wrote, "They were gallant, handsome fellows, whose jokes and genial camaraderie lent a charm even to those dark hours. From that time on they were identified with our daily life, shared our few pleasures and many anxieties, and gave us in return heart and hope and the benefit of all the thousand incidents and rumors of trench and camp." "They spent most of their leisure in the cave," recalled Willy, "making its gloomy recesses echo with songs and laughter." By candle light the battle-hardened soldiers even "carved silhouettes of our faces and their

Vicksburg NMP

Life underground during the siege was a harrowing experience for the Lord family and other residents of the beleaguered city.

own in the soft clay walls, and made artistic niches and shrine-like shelves in which to place candles, books, or vases of flowers."[35]

Although far more comfortable and infinitely safer than the communal cave, the Lords longed to return to their home, the dream of which seemed luxurious beyond imagination. Pleased by comparison to their previous cave, Lida still complained, "We were almost eaten up by mosquitoes, and were in hourly dread of snakes. The vines and thickets were full of them, and a large rattlesnake was found one morning under a mattress on which some of us had slept all night."

Danger was still ever-present, and they all knew that death could come in an instant. "My own little brother, stooping to pick up a minie ball, barely escaped being cut in two before our eyes," tearfully recalled Lida, "a Parrott shell passing over his back so close that it scorched his jacket." Though terribly frightened by his brush with death, Willy later noted with pride, "The unexploded shell, after the charge had been carefully withdrawn by my friends the Missourians, was added to my juvenile war collection."[36]

Despite the dangers and the shadow of death that was everywhere to be seen, Reverend Lord remained ever-faithful to his calling and the needs of his parishioners in Vicksburg. "Every day, as long as the siege continued, he crossed that hospital ridge and passed over the most exposed streets on his way to the church," wrote Lida in admiration of her father, "always carrying with him his pocket communion service, apparently standing an even chance of burying the dead, comforting the dying, or being himself brought home maimed, or cold in death." Daily, the family agonized over his safety for, as little Willy observed, "we only knew him to be safe when he returned at night."[37]

Sometimes at night the hardier residents of the city assembled at Sky Parlor Hill or one of the other high points in Vicksburg to watch the mortar rounds in flight. The trajectory of the bombs was easier to follow at night due to their burning fuses. "They come gradually making their way higher and higher, tracked by their firing fuse till they reach their greatest altitude," noted the redoubtable Emma Balfour in her diary, "then with a rush and a whiz they come down furiously, their own weight added to the impetus given by the powder. Then look out, for if they explode before reaching the ground which they generally do, the pieces fly in all directions—the very least of which will kill one and most of them of sufficient weight to tear through a house from top to bottom!"[38]

Dr. Lord and others who walked the city streets at night by choice or necessity kept their eyes on the sky in search of burning fuses, the telltale sign of the dreaded bombs. One night in June, the minister returned safely to the cave—to his family's relief, and with laughter in his voice told of a humorous incident that Lida recorded:

> One evening, coming back in the dusk, he saw a burly wagoner slip off his horse and get under it in a hurry. His head appeared, bobbing out first from one side, then from the other. Above him in the air, bobbing too, and with a quick, uneasy motion, was a luminous spark. After a full minute spent in vigorous dodging, the man came out to prospect. The supposed fuse was still there, burning brilliantly. "Darn the thing!" he grunted. "Why don't it bust?" He had been playing hide-and-seek for sixty seconds with a fine specimen of our Southern lightning-bug, or firefly![39]

The resulting laughter which filled the cave was but a moment's respite from the fear that gripped Maggie and the children as they struggled daily to survive. By late June their only hope was in the person of General Johnston and the Army of Relief, rumored to be advancing to their rescue. As with the weary soldiers who stood to the trenches and all other residents of Vicksburg, Lida's ears "were always strained to catch the first sound of Johnston's guns. Every extra-heavy cannonading [heard from the direction of the battlefield] was a message of hope." But their hope turned to despondency as with each passing day there was no relief in hearing. Mrs. Lord wrote in despair: "Sunday, June 28th, Still in this dreary cave. Who would have believed that we could have borne such a life for five weeks? The siege has lasted 42 days and yet no relief—every day this week we have waited for the sound of Gen. Johnston's guns, but in vain." [40]

The only guns they heard were those of the enemy whose forces were slowly strangling them into submission. During a period of intense shelling Maggie held her youngest child, Loulie, who sobbed uncontrollably. "Don't cry, my darling. God will protect us." In response to which Loulie expressed a growing sentiment of those in Vicksburg, "But, momma, I'm so afraid God's killed too." Although God had not abandoned them, their "Angel of Deliverance," Joseph E. Johnston, certainly had and Lida lamented, "alas!, we were never even to touch the hem of his robe."[41]

By July 3, Pemberton had also given up on General Johnston and met with Grant between the lines and inquired as to the terms on which the Union commander would accept the surrender of Vicksburg and its garrison. Although no terms were reached at this meeting, word quickly spread throughout town that surrender had been decided upon which filled Mrs. Lord with "a sickening dread and anxiety." Her worst fears were confirmed the following morning, July 4, when "About half past 8 o'clock, before I was dressed, Mr. Lord came into the cave, pale as death and with such a look of agony on his face as I would wish never to see again, said 'Maggie take the children home directly, the town is surrendered and the Yankee army will enter at 10 o'clock.'" "Judge my feelings," the stunned woman later wrote. "I was speechless with grief, no one spoke, even the poor children were silent."[42]

Gathering up their earthly belongings, the Lords left their cave for the final time and clamored up the hill past the hospital, the yellow flag of which had afforded them a degree of protection during the long days of siege. "As I started up the hill with Flora [another servant] and the children, the tears began to flow," wrote Maggie unashamedly, "and all the weary way home I wept incessantly, meeting first one group of soldiers and then another, many of them with tears streaming down their faces." As Mrs. Lord and her children reached the Jackson Road and turned toward home, Lida recalled that we "met group after group of soldiers and stopped to shake hands with all of them. We were crying like babies, while tears rolled down their dusty cheeks, and eyes that had fearlessly looked into the cannon's mouth fell before our heartbroken glances. 'Ladies, we would have fought for you forever. Nothing but starvation whipped us,' muttered the poor fellows."[43]

The steeple of Christ Church soon came into view standing tall amidst the rubble as firmly as the God it honors. Continuing down Main Street, past the church, their hearts sank even farther upon the sight of their once happy home. "We found the rectory in deplorable condition," commented Willy. His mother, however, provided greater detail of the destructive nature of war when she sadly declared, "such a scene of desolation you can hardly imagine. The dressing room was in ruins, the end where the fireplace had been was blown entirely out. The nursery uninhabitable a hole deep almost as a cistern in the middle of the floor, every room in the house injured and scarcely a window left whole." Yet despite the overwhelming sense of loss, as she gazed into the eyes of her husband and their children, Mrs. Lord was grateful for the protection afforded by a merciful God who had sheltered them through the siege. Even in this hour of strife, Maggie, mindful of her blessings, bravely admitted that the damage to their home was "a small matter."[44]

The city streets soon filled with the thousands of dirty, ragged soldiers that had comprised the once-proud Army of Vicksburg. They were everywhere to be seen desperately searching for food, clothing, or medical treatment. Their eyes were glazed over, their cheeks were hollow, and you could count their every bone. "Our poor soldiers came in a continuous stream past the house," noted Mrs. Lord who observed that the city's valiant defenders were "so pale, so emaciated, and so grief stricken, panting with the heat and Oh! saddest of all, without their colors and arms."[45]

Late in the morning the strains of martial music were heard as the Federal army entered Vicksburg. With a lively gait a long column of soldiers clad in blue, led by Maj. Gen. Ulysses S. Grant, marched past the rectory and down to the Warren County Courthouse. There the Stars and Bars of the Confederacy were lowered and replaced by the Stars and Stripes symbolic of Union victory. "You can imagine our feelings when the U.S. army entered, their banners flying and their hateful tunes sounding in our ears," entrusted Mrs. Lord to her journal. "Every house was closed and filled with weeping inmates and mourning hearts. You may be sure that none of us raised our eyes to see the flag of the enemy, in the place where our own had so proudly and so defiantly waved so long."[46]

Later that day, as Mrs. Lord attempted to save what she could from the rubble of their home and clear space enough in the house for the family to sleep, she was startled to find a group of ten Union soldiers on her back porch rummaging through a basket of clean clothes. "What do you mean by such a liberty?" she asked indignantly. "I should think soldiers would have too much feeling in this hour of distress to intrude even to the privacy of a lady's home." "Do you call this a lady's home?" they replied, "You ought to keep it in better order." Of the unwelcomed visitors, Mrs. Lord complained, "All day they were streaming through town and in and out of my yard and *so* drunk."[47]

Along with most others in Vicksburg, the Lords found themselves to be a "family in destitute circumstances," which enabled them to receive rations from the Union army. Although a proud woman, Maggie had no difficulty in accepting rations for her family from the army that now occupied Vicksburg for "the U.S. army robbed me of far more than their rations could ever repay." The week after July 4, Mrs. Lord called on General Grant, whom she found to be "a kindly gentleman . . . anxious to aid the people all he could," to obtain permission to leave the city. Grant expressed his admiration of the women of Vicksburg, whom he said "cannot be conquered," and granted the Lords passage on a transport carrying sick and wounded Confederates to New Orleans.[48]

Having survived the horrors of siege and life underground, the Lords left Vicksburg a few weeks after the surrender going first to Mobile, Alabama, and then to Charleston, South Carolina, where Reverend Lord continued his ministry in service to man and God. "As we stepped aboard the boat which was to bear us on toward the unknown experiences that awaited us during the death struggles of the Confederacy," lamented Willy Lord, "we became without realizing all the hardships and bitterness the word implied, refugees adrift upon the hopeless current of a losing cause."[49]

CHAPTER SEVEN

"I Am Too Late": Joseph E. Johnston and the Army of Relief

A cold hard rain fell on the evening of May 13, 1863, as the wheels of the train slowed to a stop at Jackson. Stepping out onto the platform was a slender figure immaculately clad in the gray uniform of a Confederate general. Yet, in the frenzied exodus of civilians from the city, few took notice of Joseph E. Johnston as he mounted his horse and rode several blocks north along State Street, past the capitol with its stately columns shrouded in darkness and, without fanfare, established his headquarters at the Bowman House Hotel. Without reconnoitering the city's defenses or inspecting its troops, he was content to listen to the reports of his subordinates after which he wired the authorities in far off Richmond, "I am too late." Rather than fight to defend Mississippi's capital, he ordered the archives of the state to be removed and the city evacuated. It was an inauspicious entrance for Johnston into the unfolding drama that focused on Vicksburg—the Confederate fortress on the Mississippi River, defense of which was vital to a people struggling to establish their independence.[1]

Considered by many to be the Confederacy's second ablest general, Joseph E. Johnston was a man of stark contrasts. While acknowledging that he was a man of remarkable talent and ability, this essay seeks to demonstrate that during the Vicksburg campaign, with his own destiny in

Gen.
Joseph E. Johnston

National Archives

the balance, Johnston failed to rise to the occasion and seize the opportunity to save his nation and thus secure his place among the great military captains of history.

*   *   *

The Virginian graduated from West Point in 1829, standing 13th in a class of 46 cadets. Going on to fight against the Seminole Indians and later in Mexico, Johnston earned a reputation as a brave and competent officer. He rose steadily through the ranks as the nation drifted to the brink of civil war and, in 1860, was elevated to brigadier general and appointed quartermaster general of the army. When hostilities between the states erupted, Johnston resigned his commission and offered his sword first to Virginia, then to the Confederacy. As the highest-ranking officer in the United States Army to resign his commission to fight for the South, he fully expected to be named top general in the Confederacy. It was a blow to his rather large and extremely sensitive ego when three men he considered his junior were placed above him in seniority. This rankled Johnston whose jealousy and resentment could not be disguised and, during the war, he fomented a bitter and acrimonious relationship with President Jefferson Davis.[2]

Despite the obvious strained relations resulting from Johnston's bruised ego, Davis appointed him to command the Southern forces that assembled at Harpers Ferry. What in retrospect could have been construed as an omen, Johnston concluded that Harpers Ferry could not be held and evacuated the strategic town at the confluence of the

Shenandoah and Potomac Rivers before it was seriously threatened by Federal forces. This pattern of operations would be followed throughout the war and affect a string of cities and towns in Virginia, Mississippi, and Georgia; for Johnston believed in sacrificing geography to mass available manpower to form large armies with which to do battle and win independence by force of arms.

The tarnish to his reputation suffered at Harpers Ferry was somewhat erased in the excitement of victory at Manassas, but was not forgotten by Davis. Although Johnston basked in the glory gained at First Manassas, the president's confidence in his abilities continued to wane as the spring of 1862 witnessed his army's steady retreat up the Peninsula toward Richmond. It proved fortunate for Davis and the Confederacy that Johnston was badly wounded at the Battle of Seven Pines on May 31. Incapacitated, he was thus replaced by Robert E. Lee and Johnston would never again command the principal Confederate army in Virginia.

National Archives

President Jefferson Davis

While recuperating from his wound, Johnston continued his attacks against Davis and fell in with those who opposed the president politically. Due to these attacks against him, Davis only reluctantly appointed the general to a command when he reported fit for duty in November. Johnston was assigned to command the Department of the West, a broad area between the Appalachian Mountains and the Mississippi River. It was hoped that Johnston could coordinate the movements of the armies of Gen. Braxton Bragg in Tennessee and those of Lt. Gen. John C. Pemberton in Mississippi.

Contrary to statements relative to his condition to return to duty, Johnston was still not fully recovered physically and was confined to his bed for lengthy periods in the winter of 1862-1863. This writer submits that he was not well mentally either for as desperate a wound as he had received at Seven Pines was bound to take some fight out of anyone. And, as the general was unwilling to support the president's strategic plan for the department, it is clear that Johnston's heart was never in this role. His actions while in command of this department would be to everyone's dissatisfaction (except his own).

In December 1862, President Davis, responding to a request from Governor John J. Pettus that he visit Mississippi to help bolster the flagging morale of the people, traveled to his home state. In order to help familiarize Johnston with his new department, Davis requested that the general accompany him on this trip. The presidential party arrived in Vicksburg on the evening of December 19 and was greeted by polite cheers. The two men spent the next couple of days examining the city's fortifications then went on to inspect Pemberton's army which at that time was at Grenada, in north Mississippi, contesting the overland advance of Union forces led by Maj. Gen. Ulysses S. Grant.

Returning to Jackson, Davis addressed the legislature in the House chamber of the capitol the day after Christmas. The legislators listened intently for any indication of how the government and, especially Davis himself, planned to assist the people of Mississippi in their hour of need. But only rhetoric flowed from his lips. His grand and flowery phrases were meaningless and the hopes of his listeners faded. The only statement of substance was a pledge to order additional pieces of heavy ordnance to Vicksburg, which all knew was not enough. The president concluded his remarks with a statement hardly worthy of confidence, "I shall go away from you with a lighter heart . . . anxious, but hopeful."

Although his speech was received with polite applause it failed to assuage the fears of Mississippians who braced themselves for what was to follow.[3]

As the applause slowly ebbed, shouts of "Johnston, Johnston" rang out. The general, who normally shied from public appearances, slowly approached the podium and addressed the audience in his customary manner. "Fellow citizens, my only regret is that I have done so little to merit such a greeting," he said, and proclaimed, "I promise you, however, that hereafter I shall be watchful, energetic, and indefatigable in your defense." Events would prove otherwise.[4]

What made the inspection tour so significant were the impressions it left in the mind of each man. Davis was impressed by the scope and strength of the fortifications that ringed Vicksburg and declared them strong, formidable. Indeed, he thought they could never be taken. Thus, during the course of the campaign and especially throughout the period of siege, despite increasingly gloomy reports emanating from Mississippi the Confederate president harbored little fear of the loss of Vicksburg. A Davis biographer wrote that the president was "strangely uninvolved" in the affairs centered on Vicksburg. Believing the city to be an impregnable fortress and that time was on his side, Davis failed to heed the warnings, sent few reinforcements, and concentrated his attention on the campaigns in the East. In fact, Davis was shocked in July when he received word of the city's surrender. Incredulous, he asked repeatedly of those around him, "How could this be possible?"[5]

Unlike Davis, Johnston was unimpressed by the fortifications and disturbed that they embraced, what he termed, "the usual error of Confederate engineering." He expressed fears that, at Vicksburg, "An immense intrenched camp, requiring an army to hold it, had been made, instead of a fort requiring only a small garrison." He compared Vicksburg to Fort Donelson stating that it was nothing but an elaborate trap that would ensnare its defenders. The general warned that if an army fell back into these defenses and was allowed to be besieged, you could write it off. It was as good as lost.[6]

* * *

As the spring of 1863 burst forth in all its beauty upon the land, events in the lower Mississippi River valley signaled trouble for the

Confederacy. The Union Army of the Tennessee, commanded by Grant, launched a bold campaign against Vicksburg in which the Federal troops marched down the west side of the Mississippi and were hurled across the great river at Bruinsburg. On May 1, in the opening clash on Mississippi soil, Confederate forces fought with grim determination to drive the Federal invaders back into the river, but were overwhelmed by superior numbers and driven from the field. "A furious battle has been going on since daylight just below Port Gibson," Pemberton wired Davis that evening. "Large reinforcements should be sent from other departments. Enemy's movement threatens Jackson, and, if successful, cuts off Vicksburg and Port Hudson from the east." The news frightened the most stout Southern heart. The consequences of Confederate reaction, politically and militarily, to the deteriorating situation in Mississippi would determine the fate of the Southern nation and her people.[7]

The gaseliers at the president's house in Richmond burned late into the night that first week of May as a small group of men stood around a table examining a map of the region. Jefferson Davis paced the floor as he directed that troops from as far away as the Atlantic coast be rushed to Mississippi. But more than troops were needed if Mississippi was to be saved and the vital connection to the vast Trans-Mississippi region secured. Leadership—aggressive leadership—was essential, and that leadership had to come from someone with the authority to act and the ability to communicate with other Confederate forces in the region as well as the authorities in Richmond. This was doubly important because if Pemberton was bottled up in Vicksburg, he would not have the ability to communicate as necessary to conduct operations throughout this department. To meet this pressing need, the president turned to Johnston who, at that point in time, was the only full general available for such duty.

On May 9, 1863, Secretary of War James A. Seddon sent a note to Johnston, who was then at Tullahoma, Tennessee. "Proceed at once to Mississippi and take chief command of the forces, giving to those in the field, as far as practicable, the encouragement and benefit of your personal direction," ordered the secretary. The Virginian replied, "I shall go immediately, although unfit for field service." The next morning Johnston and his staff boarded a train for the long circuitous trip to Mississippi. The route carried him from Tullahoma through Chattanooga to Atlanta, then on to Montgomery, Mobile, and Meridian to Jackson.

Secretary of War
James A. Seddon

National Archives

The jostling of the cars taxed him physically and he was in ill humor when he arrived in Jackson on the 13th, amidst a driving rain.[8]

Once he arrived in the capital city, Johnston met with Brig. Gen. John Gregg, the commander of the Jackson defenses. When he was appraised that four enemy divisions were at Clinton—between Jackson and Vicksburg—the Virginian wired Pemberton, "It is important to reestablish communications, that you may be re-enforced. If practicable, come up on his rear at once. To beat such a detachment, would be of immense value. The troops here could cooperate. All the strength you can quickly assemble should be brought. Time is all-important."[9]

Despite the aggressive tenor of the note and the keen perception of the situation it revealed, Johnston had no intention of cooperating in an attack on the Federals. Rather, his previous note to Seddon in which he informed the secretary of war, "I am too late," more accurately expressed his assessment of the situation. Vicksburg Historian Edwin C. Bearss writes, "Johnston seemed to think that disaster was inevitable, and he desired to clear himself in advance of any responsibility for it, rather than bend his energy to avert it." Instead of marching into battle, the Confederate commander decided to evacuate the capital and move northeast, toward Canton, away from both the enemy *and* Pemberton. According to historian Bearss, the general's decision was evidence that: "Johnston decided to retreat before any pressure was exerted and, in fact, before he could possibly be sure that the Union buildup was aimed at Jackson."[10]

In the general's defense, it must be said that at the time of the evacuation, he only had 6,000 men in Jackson. However, Confederate reinforcements were en route to the capital, a fact of which he was aware, and by late afternoon his numbers would have increased to 10,000, with an additional 3,000 men expected on May 16. These expected reinforcements meant Johnston would have fought at only a 2-1 disadvantage. As such, it is difficult to fathom why Johnston failed to man the city's defenses and prolong the fight for Jackson. As events would soon prove, his evacuation of the city effectively removed him and his entire army from the campaign.

On May 14, as Confederate soldiers withdrew north along the New Orleans, Jackson & Great Northern Railroad toward Canton, two Federal corps, commanded by Maj. Gens. William T. Sherman and James B. McPherson attacked the city and drove Johnston's rear guard from Jackson. Federal troops immediately began neutralizing the capital with the torch. Machine shops and factories were set afire, railroad tracks and telegraph lines were cut, and anything of military value was destroyed. Grant then turned his army west toward his objective—Vicksburg. En route from Jackson to Vicksburg, the Union army met Pemberton's force at Champion Hill on May 16. In the largest, bloodiest, and most significant action of the Vicksburg campaign, Confederate soldiers were driven from the field in panic and confusion. The next day, along the line of the Big Black River, Pemberton's army was again routed and driven from the field and fled to the safety of the Vicksburg defenses.

When informed that the army under Pemberton's command had fallen back into Vicksburg, Johnston sent the Pennsylvanian in gray a note by courier. "If Haynes' Bluff is untenable, Vicksburg is of no value, and cannot be held. If, therefore, you are invested in Vicksburg, you must ultimately surrender. Under such circumstances, instead of losing both troops and place, we must if possible, save the troops." Johnston directed, "If it is not too late, evacuate Vicksburg and its dependencies, and march to the northeast." But Pemberton, with orders from Davis to hold Vicksburg, decided to remain inside the city's defenses and await relief from Johnston. The soldiers under his command were thus destined to experience war in all its horrors during the long 47-day siege of the city, trapped in a terrifying quest for survival.[11]

Although the Virginian was deeply angered by Pemberton's decision, he informed the Vicksburg commander, "I am trying to gather a force which may attempt to relieve you. Hold out." Thus relief operations became his focus and Johnston set his energies to assemble in the Jackson/Canton area what became known as the Army of Relief. On May 18, he wired Adjutant General Samuel Cooper from Vernon: "to make it possible to relieve Vicksburg, very large re-enforcements will be necessary. I hope that the Government will send without delay all that can possibly be spared from other points." From Richmond came this response: "All aids and facilities in the power of the Department to render you will be promptly and heartily given." Secretary Seddon, however, added a caveat of ominous proportion, "but they are felt to be far less adequate than we would gladly furnish. Guns and artillery have been forwarded from the nearest points we could find them." Thus Johnston was put on notice not to expect much in the way of reinforcements—what could be sent was being sent. Consequently, upon their arrival, it was absolutely essential that he move quickly to succor Vicksburg lest Grant too be reinforced and render the failure of relief operations a mathematical certainty.[12]

As promised, reinforcements were sent to Jackson. Troops from Tennessee, the Gulf coast, and the Atlantic seaboard arrived by the thousands. On May 27, writing from Mississippi's fire-gutted capital city, Johnston acknowledged their arrival to Seddon: "On the 20th and 21st instant, the brigades of Generals [States Rights] Gist, [Matthew] Ector, and [Evander] McNair joined my command. The last troops of Brigadier-General [Nathan] Evans' brigade arrived on the day before yesterday. Major-General [William W.] Loring, with his command, arrived here about the 19th instant, and Brigadier-General [Samuel] Maxey's brigade on the 23d instant." In tallying his force, Johnston notified the secretary of war, "The troops above mentioned, with General [John C.] Breckinridge's division [then en route from Bragg's army in Tennessee] . . . will make a force of about 23,000 effective men." The following morning he wired the president, "Unless you can promise more troops, we must try with that number." Davis replied, "The rein-forcements sent to you exceed by, say, 7,000 the estimate of your dispatch. We have withheld nothing which it was practicable to give," " he emphasized. "We cannot hope for numerical equality, and time will probably increase the disparity."[13]

Despite the urgency of the situation and the inability of the government to do more for Johnston, the debate over numbers intensified as May turned into June. Davis and Seddon insisted that the Army of Relief was larger than Johnston claimed, believing his force to number "34,000, exclusive of state militia," while the general gave his strength as considerably fewer men. The truth was somewhere in between. (Edwin C. Bearss claims that Johnston's force numbered 31,000.) From Canton, on June 1, Johnston yielded a slight adjustment to his numbers claiming that he had 24,100 men. However, this number did not include his cavalry, which numbered 1,600, nor the five field batteries then present that mustered 400 men. This raised his total to more than 26,000. His note further states "These are numbers of effectives," which means that even more men were in Jackson and possibly could be called upon for field service.[14]

Regardless of numbers, by June 4, Johnston had received his final reinforcement and it was clear to all that not another man or gun could be spared from elsewhere in the Confederacy. In anguish, Seddon wrote to Johnston, "I regret inability to promise more troops, as we have drained resources even to the danger of several points. You know best about Bragg's army, but I fear to withdraw more. We are too far outnumbered in Virginia to spare any. *You must rely on what you have* [emphasis added]." He again impressed upon the general, "With the facilities and resources of the enemy, time works against us."[15]

In Vicksburg, although Pemberton's garrison had easily and bloodily repulsed Grant's attacks against the city on May 19 and again on the 22nd, Union forces had settled into a war of attrition. By the end of May Federal troops had encircled Vicksburg and now worked to starve the garrison into submission. In order to conserve what food supplies were on hand, Pemberton ordered the daily ration cut to three quarters, then to half, and then to quarter. Throughout the month of June rations were cut again, and yet again, and yet again. By the end of June the garrison was issued only a handful of peas and rice per man per day. It was not much to maintain their strength upon, but it was all they had. Even their water was eventually rationed to one cup per day. The limited quantity of food and water fueled the spread of disease and weakened the valiant defenders of Vicksburg day by weary day.

To the citizens and soldiers trapped in Vicksburg, Johnston became viewed as a savior. On June 1, Lt. William A. Drennan, a member of the garrison, confided to the pages of his diary the hope of many in Vicksburg when he wrote, "I have every reason to believe that ten days will bring relief in the person of Gen'l Johnson, with fifty thousand men. God send him quickly—is the prayer of thousands daily offered up." Such hope was reinforced when a courier from Johnston arrived in the city with a note dated June 7 that read in part, "We are nearly ready to move." But the days continued to pass. "I had fixed on the 10th of the month for Genl. Johnson to come to our relief," lamented Lieutenant Drennan, "but the day has come and gone and no relief in hearing as yet. I do not despair by any means yet I confess that I feel disheartened."[16]

"When might I expect you to move, and in what direction?" Pemberton queried of Johnston on June 7. A few days later he informed the Virginian, "The enemy is landing troops in large numbers on Louisiana shore, above Vicksburg. . . . On the Graveyard road the enemy has run his saps to within 25 yards of our works. He will probably attempt to sink a mine. I shall try to thwart him." He then implored, "I am anxiously expecting to hear from you, to arrange cooperation."[17]

Johnston's replies bolstered his subordinate's morale with repeated assurance that salvation was coming: (May 25) "Bragg is sending a division [Breckinridge's]; when it comes, I will move to you;" (June 7) "We are nearly ready to move;" and (June 22) "I will have the means of moving in a day or two." He emphasized to Pemberton that he "could do no more than attempt to save you and the garrison," but to do so required "exact co-operation." Toward that end he inquired of the Vicksburg commander, "Which is the best route? Where is the enemy encamped?" (That he asked such questions leads one to wonder what Johnston's scouts were doing.)[18]

Pemberton and his officers worked diligently to plan a coordinated movement against Grant in a desperate attempt to break free of the siege and save the garrison. But despair spread as wildfire throughout the ranks of his army and infected the men with a sense of hopelessness. "Another Sabbath morning, and yet, no relief from Gen'l Johnson," Lieutenant Drennan recorded in his diary on June 21. "He knows his business and I am willing to believe that it is for the best. I have put off his coming until Wednesday. . . . The men are becoming impatient and although they have borne it with remarkable fortitude, yet they are worn out and desponding. Another week will render many of them in poor condition to remain in the trenches, and their present rations will make them still more discontented." By the end of June, even the resolute Drennan would give up on Johnston.[19]

Throughout the month of June as the Union vice closed ever tighter, communications between Pemberton and Johnston relative to coordinated movements to save the garrison became less frequent. Growing difficulty in exchanging messages between the two generals led to delay that further reduced effective communications. The breakdown in communications would have proved fatal to coordination, had coordination truly been the objective. Although Pemberton was desperate to be saved, the records clearly evidence that Johnston was equally desperate to avoid action.

Nothing could spur the Virginian into action. Davis and members of his cabinet urged Johnston to move quickly, but none more forcefully than Secretary of War Seddon, who admonished, "Vicksburg must not be lost without a desperate struggle. The interest and honor of the Confederacy forbid it." And yet, to the urging of his superiors and pleading by Pemberton, Johnston would only reply, "I am too weak to save Vicksburg."[20]

Whether he was or not we will never know, but the window of opportunity closed by mid-June as tens of thousands of Federal reinforcements arrived in the Vicksburg area and sealed the doom of the beleaguered city. (On June 7, the combined armies of Pemberton and Johnston numbered approximately 60,000 men compared to Grant's, whose army was positioned between the two Confederate forces, at 56,000 strong. Ten days later those numbers were dramatically different as Grant's troop strength swelled by 21,000. The increase in numbers gave the Union commander a sizeable numeric superiority and enabled him to transform his position to an advantage. It is important to further note that Pemberton's numbers decreased on a daily basis due to the attrition of siege operations and that the authorities in Richmond could not augment Johnston's strength.) Grant placed these reinforcements to guard the strategic Mechanicsburg Corridor that formed the watershed between the Yazoo and Big Black Rivers, and provided an avenue of approach to Vicksburg from the northeast. It was believed that any Confederate relief operations would be launched down the Mechanicsburg Corridor from Yazoo City or Benton.

The "Exterior Line," as it came to be called, was situated to protect the rear of Union forces besieging Vicksburg. It ran east from Haynes'-Snyder's Bluffs, on the Yazoo River north of Vicksburg, over Oak Ridge, then south through Tiffentown to the Big Black River. The line was anchored on the south where the tracks of the Southern Railroad of Mississippi crossed the river, east of Vicksburg. The troops that manned the "Exterior Line" were placed under the command of Grant's most-trusted subordinate, William T. Sherman, and equaled in size any force that Johnston could possibly bring to bear against them. Once this line was fully formed, what chance Johnston may have had to relieve Vicksburg was gone.

In despair, the Vicksburg commander on June 23 sent a communication to Johnston suggesting that the Virginian propose terms for surrender of the city to Grant. Pemberton added, "I will strain every nerve to hold out, if there is hope of our ultimate relief, for fifteen days longer." Johnston replied on June 27, four precious days later, "Negotiations with Grant for relief of the garrison, should they become necessary, must be made by you. It would be a confession of weakness on my part, which I ought not to make, to propose them. When it becomes necessary to make terms, they may be considered as made under my authority." Yet, despite knowing of the dire situation in Vicksburg, Johnston delayed another four days before he finally set his Jackson force in motion on July 1 toward the Confederate Gibraltar on the Mississippi River. By then, it was too late.[21]

On July 3, as his advance units neared the Big Black River, an eerie silence settled over the area as the sound of cannonade from Vicksburg ceased. Although only twelve days had passed, rather than the fifteen Pemberton had pledged when he penned the dire warning of imminent catastrophe, Johnston knew beyond doubt that the silence indicated the valiant defenders of Vicksburg had reached the limits of human endurance. In fact, at that very moment, Pemberton and Grant sat between the lines in the shade of a stunted oak and the Confederate commander requested of his opponent the terms by which he would receive the surrender of the city and garrison of Vicksburg, which was consummated the following day.

(It is interesting to note that in his After Action Report, Johnston states that the army marched out of Jackson on June 29 and that he reached the Big Black River on July 1. Yet the orders to commence the march were not issued until June 30 with instructions to move at sunrise on July 1. Johnston further attempted to cover his actions by sending Pemberton a note on July 3 that read in part: "I hope to attack the enemy in your front about the 7th, and your co-operation will be necessary." By the time the letter, which was never received, was sent, the firing in Vicksburg had already ceased.)[22]

Johnston knew all too well what the silence meant. Fearing that Grant would now turn on him, he fell back to Jackson where his army was in turn besieged from July 10-17. Compelled to evacuate the capital city, the Confederates fled across the Pearl River and marched east through Brandon to Morton where they remained into August. One day, as Johnston sat rocking on the porch of his headquarters, a solitary horseman arrived. As he dismounted, Johnston recognized John Pemberton and sprang to his feet. Descending the steps, he walked toward Pemberton, extended his hand and said, "Jack, I am glad to see you." Pemberton saluted coldly and replied, "General Johnston, by the terms of my parole I am required to report to you. I have done so." He closed his salute, turned on his heels, mounted his horse, and rode off. For the remainder of their lives, the two men never again met. (Although unsubstantiated, Pemberton biographer Ballard, notes "if the incident occurred, it probably happened just as described.")[23]

Recriminations and finger pointing for the loss of Vicksburg continue to this day, and probably will for as long as this campaign is studied. One thing, however, is certain: Johnston's failure to rescue Pemberton and save Vicksburg was a staggering blow to the Confederacy from which the Southern nation never recovered. Chief of Ordnance Josiah Gorgas commented to President Davis that Vicksburg fell from want of food. "Yes," answered Davis, "from want of provisions inside, and a general outside who wouldn't fight."[24]

For Joseph E. Johnston, the general who failed to try, such has been his legacy.

CHAPTER EIGHT

"No Longer a Point of Danger":
The Siege of Jackson

66 Glory hallelujah!" declared William T. Sherman on July 3 when notified by Grant that Vicksburg would surrender the following morning. "The best Fourth of July since 1776," he stated emphatically. Both generals desired to press the advantage and turned their attention to Joe Johnston whose Army of Relief was at that moment slowly approaching Big Black River north of the Southern Railroad. "I want Johnston broken up as effectually as possible, and roads destroyed," directed Grant. Eager to take to the field, Sherman replied, "telegraph me the moment you have Vicksburg in possession, and I will secure all the crossings of [Big] Black River, and move on Jackson or Canton, as you may advise."[1]

The quiet of the morning on July 4 was ominous to the soldiers of Johnston's army, the vanguard of which was less than twenty miles from Vicksburg. So close and yet the men of the so-called Army of Relief must have sensed that they were too late to rescue Pemberton's garrison and reverse the waning tide of Southern fortunes. Especially knowing that the Federals usually marked Independence Day with an artillery salute, the men in gray wondered at the silence and many expressed criticism of their commander for failure to march on Vicksburg at an earlier date.

Johnston himself, however, was keenly aware of what the silence meant for in his last communication from Pemberton, dated June 23, the

Maj. Gen.
William T. Sherman

National Archives

Vicksburg commander had suggested the Virginian propose terms for surrender of the city to Grant. Pemberton added, "I will strain every nerve to hold out, if there is hope of our ultimate relief, for fifteen days longer." Although only twelve days, rather than fifteen, had passed since Pemberton penned the dire warning of imminent catastrophe, Johnston knew beyond doubt that the silence indicated the valiant defenders of Vicksburg had reached the limits of human endurance.[2]

Johnston spent much of July 4 examining the reports sent in by scouts while his men remained in camp. It was futile, he expressed to his subordinates, to attempt a crossing of the Big Black River north of the railroad in the face of an entrenched enemy, and reasoned that there might be a soft spot in the Union fortifications somewhere below the tracks. Johnston, therefore, resolved to explore the region south of the railroad; but before his troops took up the line of march on July 5 the fears of all were confirmed with the news of Vicksburg's surrender. Fearing that Grant would now turn on him, Johnston determined to fall back to Jackson.

Morale within the army sank as the gray columns headed east back to the capital city. The sun beat down unmercifully on the tightly packed ranks and the thick clouds of dust that swirled around the men made it difficult to breathe. Adding to their misery was an acute shortage of water that prevented the soldiers from soothing parched throats. Despite the hardships suffered on the march, the columns moved quickly aware that the enemy would soon be snapping at their heels.

It took Johnston's army two days to reach the capital and, on the evening of July 7, his weary soldiers filed into the Jackson defenses. "These intrenchments were very badly located and constructed," noted Johnston, "and offered very slight obstacle to a vigorous assault." The following morning large fatigue parties were detailed to strengthen the fortifications. Under a blazing sun the soldiers worked alongside impressed slaves and toiled to enlarge the earthworks and extend the line so that it was anchored on the Pearl River above and below Jackson.[3]

These preparations were completed not a moment too soon for the sound of artillery fire in the distance announced the approach of Sherman's blue-clad legions. To inspire his men, Johnston issued an address to his army that was read to the soldiers on July 9:

Fellow Soldiers:

An insolent foe, flushed with hope by his recent successes at Vicksburg, confronts you, threatening the people, whose homes and liberties you are here to protect, with plunder and conquest. Their guns may even now be heard at intervals as they advance.

This enemy it is at once the mission and duty of you brave men to chastise and expel from the soil of Mississippi.

The commanding general confidently relies on you to sustain this pledge he makes in advance, and will be with you in your good work unto the end.

In closing, Johnston admonished, "The country expects in this, the great crisis of its destiny, that every man will do his duty."[4]

The enemy force closing in on Jackson consisted of thirteen divisions. For the drive against Johnston, the seven divisions that had been with Sherman on the Exterior Line were reinforced by six divisions from the XIII and XV Corps that swelled the numbers of his Expeditionary Army to 46,000 men. Sherman's infantry crossed Big Black River at three locations. From south to north they were the railroad bridge, Messinger's Ford, and Birdsong's Ferry. The cavalry brigade commanded by Col. Cyrus Bussey crossed the river at the mouth of Bear Creek between Messinger's Ford and Birdsong's Ferry. By July 7 Sherman had concentrated his force near Bolton, less than 20 miles west of Jackson.

Just as with the Southerners, Sherman's troops suffered terribly from the heat and drought as they marched along under the blistering

Mississippi sun. Their suffering became almost unbearable due to the scarcity of fresh water. The retreating Confederates had poisoned the water by tossing the carcasses of dead animals in all the ponds and lakes along the route. Thus the Federals had to haul their drinking water from the Big Black River. To ease their plight, Sherman limited marching to the morning and late afternoon and early evening.

The Northern soldiers closed in on Jackson on July 10 and the head of each column came under artillery fire as it neared the city's defenses. Hearing the cannonade, Sherman rode to the front to reconnoiter. What he saw convinced him that Johnston had taken refuge in Jackson and that the Confederates had strengthened the capital's fortifications. Cautiously Sherman halted his troops and informed Grant "that everything betokens a strong resistance." Not wishing to assault the works Sherman issued orders for his corps commanders "to form lines of circumvallation about 1,500 yards from the enemy's parapet, with skirmishers close up, and their supports within 500 yards." He further instructed that each corps construct covered batteries for its guns and trenches for the men. The Siege of Jackson had begun.[5]

Throughout the day on July 11, Sherman's corps moved into position around the capital and extended their lines to the Pearl River on both flanks. On the Union right, astride the Raymond road, was the corps commanded by Maj. Gen. Edward O. C. Ord. Operating along the

Clinton road, in the center, were the men led by Maj. Gen. Frederick Steele, while out on the Canton road, the left flank was manned by the XI Corps veterans under the command of Maj. Gen. John G. Parke. While the infantrymen

Maj. Gen.
Edward O. C. Ord

National Archives

Maj. Gen.
John G. Parke

National Archives

labored with picks and shovels to throw up their earthworks, the artillerymen constructed battery position on commanding ground and dragged their cannon into position. By day's end, Sherman was satisfied with the way the siege was progressing and ordered his guns to open at seven o'clock the next morning.

A siege was necessitated in part due to the limited quantity of artillery ammunition carried to Jackson in Sherman's supply train. Staff officers were sent dashing westward with instructions for the reserve supply train, that had been left at Messinger's Ford, to come forward. Until the train arrived it would be necessary to conserve artillery ammunition. On the morning of July 12, the Union guns opened a bombardment that was less than one hour in duration. "Each gun will fire not to exceed thirty rounds, solid shot and shell in proper proportions," Sherman's order commanded. "The shots will be directed against any groups of the enemy's troops, or in direction of the town of Jackson." More than 3,000 projectiles were fired and depleted the army's supply of shells.[6]

After the guns fell silent, Ord pushed the division of Brig. Gen. Alvin P. Hovey closer to the enemy to perfect his alignment and ordered it to dig in. Hovey in turn notified Brig. Gen. Jacob Lauman, whose division was to move into position on his right, of his intentions. Lauman, however, was still operating under orders that were a day old. Although the orders directed him to connect with Hovey, they further instructed Lauman that, "As the enemy may have some force on the [New Orleans,

Jackson & Great Northern] railroad, should they show an infantry line in force (which is hardly probable), make a reconnaissance, and, if it is necessary to form line and attack to drive the force in front, do so, so as to keep your connection with General Hovey." The failure to update his orders soon led to confusion and the death of many soldiers in blue.[7]

Swinging his division into position east of the railroad, Lauman formed his troops into line on the forward slope of Bailey Hill. The lead brigade, commanded by Col. Isaac Pugh, moved forward with its left flank anchored on the railroad. Wading Lynch Creek, Pugh's men pulled abreast of Hovey's but then continued the advance through a thick stand of timber. Steadily closing on the Confederate works, Pugh's rugged soldiers poured out of the woods into a cornfield, 500 yards across, at the opposite end of which was a dense abatis of felled trees.

Reluctant to advance any farther, Pugh halted his men and requested that Lauman come to the front. After surveying the field, Lauman ordered Pugh to push forward his skirmishers and resume the advance. With a mighty cheer the troops moved into the cornfield. "As soon as the line had crossed the field and had got fairly into the timber," reported Pugh, "the enemy opened a murderous fire on my whole line." Musketry and canister tore through their ranks and yet the Federals closed to within 80 yards of the enemy works. "The fire was murderous" at this point, wrote Pugh, "that what officers and men were left fell back." Not all, however, raced to the rear through the gauntlet of fire. Scores of men simply fastened handkerchiefs to their ramrods and waved them as a sign of surrender. In this ill-fated action, Pugh lost more than one-half of his brigade as he left behind 465 men killed, wounded, and missing on the bloody field of battle. Confederate casualties were only seven men, of whom two had been killed.[8]

Ord had not witnessed the assault and was shocked to learn of Lauman's debacle. Riding with his staff to Lauman's headquarters, Ord found confusion among the troops who were scattered about the area and ordered that the men be placed under cover and the rolls called. Stunned by the turn of events, Lauman himself was confused and failed to carry out the orders. Believing that his subordinate was mentally incapacitated for command and fearful lest the Confederates follow up their success, Ord relieved Lauman and directed that he report back to Vicksburg.

The Northern dead and wounded lay upon the field for two days, during which time many of the wounded died from exposure and the bodies of the dead began to bloat. The stench was offensive to those on both sides of the battle lines. At noon on July 14 there was a cessation of hostilities to enable the Confederates to bury the dead for the bodies, badly decomposed by the sun, could not be removed for burial within Union lines.

There would be no more assaults against the Jackson defenses and Sherman bided his time waiting for the reserve train to arrive with artillery ammunition. Once the ammunition arrived, Sherman planned to "make the town too hot to hold him [Johnston]." The Confederate commander knew that a crossfire of shot and shell from the enemy guns could reach all parts of the town and would make Jackson untenable. He informed the Richmond authorities on July 11, "If the position and works were not bad, want of stores (which could not be collected) would make it impossible to stand a siege. If the enemy will not attack, we must, or at the last moment withdraw. We cannot attack seriously without risking the army." Four days later he telegraphed President Davis, "The enemy is evidently making a siege which we cannot resist." Knowing how Davis would respond, Johnston added, "It would be madness to attack him." Johnston's only hope of remaining in Jackson was to intercept the supply train with Sherman's artillery ammunition. For once the Union guns opened there would be no alternative but evacuation. It was a gamble worth taking.[9]

On the 14th, Johnston learned that the supply train had crossed Big Black River and was en route to Sherman. He summoned the commander of his cavalry division, Brig. Gen. William H. Jackson, to his headquarters and outlined the task at hand. The Tennessean, nicknamed "Red" due to the color of his hair, was an 1856 graduate of West Point who had commanded a cavalry brigade in Earl Van Dorn's Holly Springs raid in 1862. Noted for his leadership qualities, Jackson was an aggressive fighter who quickly prepared his raiding party.

As the sun slowly faded in the western sky Jackson's troopers pulled out of their camp east of the Pearl River. The horse soldiers rode up the left side of the river to a point opposite Madisonville and crossed on a pontoon bridge. The next morning they were joined by two regiments of Mississippi cavalry and, passing around the left flank of Sherman's army, rode westward. Riding through Battle Springs, nine miles northwest of the capital city, the column turned south toward Clinton where Red Jackson planned to capture and destroy the supply train.

On July 15, as the Southerners moved into position to strike the train, a deserter told Federal officers that Jackson had crossed Pearl River and informed them of his objective. Sherman advised Grant by telegraph of this development and requested that a brigade stationed near Champion Hill, midway between Vicksburg and Clinton, escort the train to Clinton. Fearful that the Southerners would strike at Clinton, Sherman also sent a brigade from Jackson to reinforce the lone regiment then stationed there.

At daybreak on July 16, Jackson's mounted men advanced in two columns and converged on the town. Rather than surprise the Northerners, the horse soldiers found the enemy ready and waiting for them. Union pickets contested the advance and compelled Jackson to deploy his troopers into line of battle. The Confederates drove forward and forced the pickets back; but the troopers were soon brought to a halt by a powerful battleline that proved more than their match. After an hour of brisk skirmishing, Jackson had to content himself with cutting the telegraph line then withdrew to the northwest toward Brownsville.

Later that day a combat patrol sent out by Red Jackson swept down on Bolton and captured eight wagons that belonged to the XIII Corps. The main prize, the supply train with Sherman's artillery ammunition, was just coming into sight from the west. Although tempted to strike, the leader of the Confederate patrol took notice of the brigade-size escort of

infantry that accompanied the wagons and decided not to press his luck. The supply train rumbled through the afternoon and successfully reached Sherman's army late that evening.

Johnston was sorely disappointed to learn on the

Brig. Gen.
William Hicks "Red" Jackson

National Archives

afternoon of July 16 of Jackson's failure. The Confederate commander realized that Sherman would open with all his guns in the morning that would rain solid shot and shell down upon his men. With his only hope of holding the capital now gone, Johnston ordered his army to evacuate the city. After dark the wily Virginian began the movement by removing his guns from their emplacements. An hour later, the weary infantrymen began filing out of their works, formed column, and crossed the bridges that spanned the Pearl River. The last to leave Jackson were the skirmishers and those on outpost. Once the men were safely across the river, the bridges were then fired behind them and Jackson was open for Sherman.

On through the long night Johnston's dispirited army marched eastward in an effort to distance itself from expected pursuit. The rising sun on July 17 found the gray column still in motion. Tired and hungry, the soldiers pushed steadily over the dusty road and finally went into bivouac in the fields near Brandon that night. The following morning the march east resumed during which thundershowers settled the dust, but made the road difficult for wagons and artillery to pass. On the 20th, Johnston's men reached Morton, forty miles from Jackson, and there the retreat halted. The Siege of Jackson and its aftermath were an inglorious end to the Army of Relief.

Meanwhile in Jackson, Union soldiers spotted the glow from the burning bridges on the night of July 16. Coupled with the sounds of wagons, many of the Northern pickets were convinced that Johnston was evacuating the city. Sherman, however, mistakenly believed that the Southerners were strengthening their position and this gave the Confederates the time needed to safely evacuate Jackson. It was not until the morning of the 17th that the Federals suspected something was up. Skirmishers cautiously advanced at various points along the line. On the Canton road they spotted a white flag being waived by a jubilant black man who informed the soldiers that the enemy was gone.

Word quickly spread throughout the army. "I have just made the circuit of Jackson," Sherman notified Grant. "We are in full possession, and Johnston is retreating east, with 30,000 men, who will perish by heat, thirst, and disappointment." The Stars and Stripes were soon floating in victory atop the state house where Mississippi's Ordinance of Secession had been passed on January 9, 1861. Although Sherman sent a small force across Pearl River, due to the "intense heat, dust, and fatigue of the men," he did not launch a vigorous pursuit of Johnston's retreating army.[10]

Flushed with victory, Sherman established his headquarters in the governor's mansion and on the evening of the 18th hosted a victory dinner with his generals. He had every reason to celebrate for, in addition to driving Johnston from Jackson and capturing the capital of Mississippi, his army took possession of the abandoned public property. The Federals seized 3 cannon, 1,396 rifle-muskets, and 23,245 rounds of artillery ammunition. The Northerners also fired 4,000 bales of cotton the Confederates used in the construction of their fortifications. All this was accomplished with the loss of approximately 1,000 men.

"I will perfect the work of destruction," Sherman promised Grant. "I propose to break railroad 10 miles, south, east, and north, and out for 40 and 60 miles in spots." Union soldiers set about the task of destruction with a vengeance. Machine shops and factories were burned, Confederate artillery ammunition was cast into Pearl River, and the railroads that radiated from Jackson were effectively destroyed. Eugene Beauge of the Forty-fifth Pennsylvania Infantry, IX Corps, described the work of railroad destruction: "A good way to dispose of the ties and rails at the same time, after tearing up the track, was to pile up the ties, set them afire, then lay the rails crosswise on top; the rails in this way, when red hot, ending and warping themselves out of shape while the ties went up in smoke." Beauge noted that another method "was to take a rail, red hot in the middle, and bend it around a tree." Rails destroyed in the method were referred to as "Sherman's neckties."[11]

The work of destruction continued until July 23. So complete were the Federals in neutralizing the city militarily that Sherman boasted to Grant, "Jackson will no longer be a point of danger." Much of the city was a smoldering ruin and Jackson was given the sobriquet of "Chimneyville." The destruction of Mississippi's capital evidenced that the war was taking a new turn and foreshadowed the implementation of total war that would lay Georgia and the Carolinas to waste in 1864-1865. However, Sherman did not leave the citizens of Jackson destitute. The mayor and a citizens' committee appealed to the Union commander for help in feeding people. Sherman agreed, and provided 200 barrels of flour and 100 barrels of salt pork.[12]

On July 20, with their work of destruction at Jackson almost finished, elements of Sherman's army began the return march to Vicksburg. Three days later Sherman himself and the last vestige of the Union Expeditionary Force left Jackson. The heat and humidity continued to plague the troops, who straggled badly. By the 25th, however, the last of Sherman's men had crossed the Big Black River and went into bivouac at their designated staging areas. There for the remainder of the summer they enjoyed some much needed rest following the long and tiring, yet highly successful campaign season.

Vicksburg was in Union hands and Confederate forces in Mississippi would never again pose a threat to free navigation of the great river. Sherman summed up the Jackson campaign by writing, "It seems to me a fit supplement to the re-conquest of the Mississippi River itself, and makes that perfect which otherwise would have been imperfect."[13]

CHAPTER NINE

Crucial to the Outcome: Vicksburg and the Trans-Mississippi Supply Line

Church bells rang in joyous chorus throughout the North as news of the fall of Vicksburg spread as an electric shock across the nation and, in towns large and small, bells in county courthouses and city halls joined in glorious refrain. In the states of the Old Northwest, the farmers of which region depended on unfettered navigation of the Mississippi River to send their crops to world markets, the news of Vicksburg's surrender was especially well received. The success of Union arms was hailed in banner headlines from St. Louis to Cincinnati, Des Moines to Indianapolis, and Chicago to St. Paul. The victory was all the more dear to the citizens of that region for it was primarily soldiers from their states who had shed their blood on battlefields from Ft. Donelson to Shiloh, Chickasaw Bayou to Arkansas Post, and from Port Gibson to Champion Hill who had triumphed at Vicksburg.

To place Vicksburg and the campaign for control of the Mississippi River in proper perspective, modern students of the Civil War *must* understand the significance of the city and the river to the war efforts of the North and South—a significance that was clearly understood and fully grasped by Union and Confederate leaders once hostilities began. Yet, an article in *North & South* magazine (Volume 6, Number 7) mocked the significance of Vicksburg and the Mississippi River as "myths by authors obviously oblivious to its realities."[1]

This essay will examine the significance of the Mississippi River, of Vicksburg in particular, and the vast Trans-Mississippi region, and allow you to determine if its importance to the Confederacy is myth or reality.

* * *

Shortly after the outbreak of the Civil War, President Abraham Lincoln had gathered his civil and military leaders to discuss strategy for opening the Mississippi River and ending what he termed a rebellion in the Southern states. Seated around a large table examining a map of the nation, Lincoln made a sweeping gesture with his hand then placed his finger on the map at Vicksburg and said, "See what a lot of land these fellows control of which Vicksburg is the key. . . . The war can never be brought to a close until that key is in our pocket."[2]

William T. Sherman, the Union general destined to play such a prominent role in the campaign for control of the great river, echoed the president's sentiments relative to Vicksburg and the Mississippi River. "The Mississippi, source and mouth, must be controlled by one government," wrote Sherman emphatically, who confessed, "To secure the safety of the navigation of the Mississippi River I would slay millions. On that point I am not only insane, but mad." General-in-Chief Henry W. Halleck wrote of the campaign to capture Vicksburg in similar, direct, albeit less eloquent terms, "In my opinion, this is the most important operation of the war. To open the Mississippi River will be to us of more advantage than the capture of forty Richmonds."[3]

Confederate President Jefferson Davis equally recognized the importance of the Mississippi River. Long a resident of Warren County, of which Vicksburg is the county seat, Davis was uniquely qualified to understand and appreciate the river's strategic significance to a people struggling to establish their independence. The depth of his understanding was best expressed in a letter written after the fall of Vicksburg to Lt. Gen. John C. Pemberton, the general responsible for defense of the city. "I thought and still think you did right to risk an army for the purpose of keeping command of even a section of the Mississippi River," penned Davis of his conviction. "Had you succeeded, none would have blamed, had you not made the attempt few would have defended your course."[4]

Surrender of the Confederate Gibraltar on July 4, 1863, was the culmination of the largest and most complex combined land and naval operation undertaken in American military history up to that time. The campaign lasted eighteen months and involved almost 200,000 soldiers and the inland water fleets of the Union and Confederate navies. Such massive commitment of men and material devoted to this single objective, and the duration of the campaign itself, evidence that Vicksburg was a city of unparalleled military, economic, and political significance to the leaders of the North and the South—a significance that was greatly enhanced after New Orleans and Memphis fell to Union forces. Vicksburg, in the words of Jefferson Davis, was left as the "nailhead that held the South's two halves together."[5]

"Thank God," sighed Lincoln from the depths of his soul when word reached him of Vicksburg's surrender. "The Father of Waters again goes unvexed to the sea." The eloquence of his simplicity was equaled only by the exuberance of those in the combined army/navy force that compelled surrender of the city. Perhaps none expressed their sentiments better than Sherman who boldly and justifiably proclaimed, "Glory Hallelujah! The best Fourth of July since 1776." His declaration could not have been more fitting had he known at that time of the battle of Gettysburg fought on July 1-3, which, when combined with the results at Vicksburg, marked the turning point of the war. That turning point was as obvious in Washington as it was in Richmond, where Col. Josiah Gorgas, chief of the Confederate Ordnance Department, lamented of the twin disasters: "Yesterday we rode on the pinnacle of success—today absolute ruin seems to be our portion. The Confederacy totters to its destruction."[6]

Myth or reality aside, statements such as these provide ample evidence that Vicksburg was significant, if for no other reason than simply because the leaders of the warring sides said it was, and the people of the time period accepted that significance, whether real or imagined, and acted according to that level of significance through force of arms with violent execution.

Northern jubilation, however, was soon overshadowed by the casualty lists from Gettysburg that appeared in newspapers from Boston to New York and Philadelphia to Pittsburgh; while Southern hopes were further crushed as similar lists were published in papers from Richmond to Atlanta and Charleston to Jackson. The harvest of death in Pennsylvania was staggering and directly impacted more families on both sides of the Mason-Dixon Line than did the 20,000 Union and Confederate casualties suffered at Vicksburg. In the depth of such widespread sorrow, recognition of Vicksburg's significance began to fade almost immediately.

Vicksburg's short-lived hold on prominence had been undermined during the campaign itself by the lack of newspaper coverage that failed to rivet the nation's attention on what proved to be the most decisive campaign of the war. Siege operations were dull, mundane, boring, and resulted in far fewer casualties than the actions at Chancellorsville and Gettysburg that occurred during the same time period. Battle action and casualties sold newspapers and editors sent their reporters to more active areas of operations, whether significant or not. Photographers as well focused their lenses on scenes of death and destruction. Thus in the rich photographic history of the war there are numerous photographs of Gettysburg dead, but precious few of Vicksburg, and none from the battlefields of Port Gibson, Raymond, Jackson, Champion Hill, or Big Black River Bridge—actions which lead up to the siege of the river city.

Although the second largest city in Mississippi in 1860, Vicksburg was far removed from the population centers of the North and South and drew little attention from people in the large eastern cities. It was also far removed from the centers of political power in Washington and Richmond and did not attract the same level of attention from elected officials who lived with the constant threat of enemy attack. These same officials viewed on a daily basis the sick and wounded of their respective nation's principle army and failed to conceive of the suffering and sacrifice of their armies in the West.

Further eroding Vicksburg's stature over time has been the lack of regimental histories and published diaries of those who participated in the campaign that attract the modern researcher/writer. Few western soldiers were as literate as their eastern counterparts and the paucity of letters, diaries, and memoirs dim our understanding of the complexities of the war west of the Appalachian Mountains. The small number of modern works on the war in the West is a direct result of the lack of primary source material.

However, the most influential factor for Vicksburg being relegated to secondary status in the minds of modern students of the Civil War is the immortal Gettysburg Address. Had Abraham Lincoln not accepted the invitation to give a "few appropriate remarks" at the dedication of the soldiers' national cemetery at Gettysburg, or had he delivered a "Vicksburg Address" instead, the small town in Pennsylvania and the battle that it witnessed would be more like Sharpsburg, Maryland, than the American Mecca it is today.

These factors, and many others, all contribute to Vicksburg standing in the shadow of the far bloodier, but less significant action at Gettysburg. It is all too easy for the general reader, popular historians, and students of the Civil War to accept the popular version of history. Even some academics who are intimidated by the complexities of the campaign and fail to take the time to properly evaluate the operations that focused on Vicksburg subscribe to popular belief. Further diluting our understanding and appreciation for the Vicksburg campaign are television shows and epic films that are long on romance but skimp on historical accuracy.

But the facts themselves remain. Though often ignored, they cannot be denied. Whereas two armies, badly bruised and bleeding, marched away from Gettysburg to fight another day, Union victory at Vicksburg was complete. In addition to taking the city and capturing a garrison of 29,500 officers and men, the Union Army of the Tennessee under Maj. Gen. Ulysses S. Grant seized a huge amount of military stores. Among the public property captured were 172 pieces of artillery, 38,000 artillery projectiles (mostly fixed), 58,000 pounds of black powder, 50,000 shoulder weapons (mostly British Enfield rifle muskets, arguably the finest infantry weapons of the time period), 600,000 rounds of ammunition, and 350,000 percussion caps—resources in men and materiel that the South could ill afford to lose. In addition to this tally must be added the 7,000 casualties inflicted on Southern forces during the inland phase of the campaign leading up to the siege and 82 cannon captured as Grant's army pushed deep into the interior of Mississippi and compelled the evacuation of Southern strongholds that centered on Snyder's Bluff, north of Vicksburg, and Warrenton and Grand Gulf, south of the city.[7]

In terms of artillery alone, 254 cannon were captured by Federal forces during the Vicksburg campaign. (For the sake of comparison, not a single Confederate cannon was lost at Gettysburg.) This figure represents more than 11% of the total number of cannon cast by the Confederacy

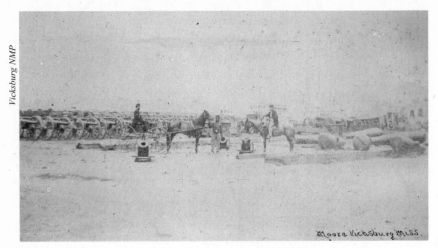

Captured Confederate artillery ready for shipment north
following the siege of Vicksburg.

from 1861-1865. Of this figure 85 were heavy siege guns. In their work on Confederate cannon foundries, Larry Daniel and Riley Gunter state, "Even under the best of circumstances it took some 400-500 hours of labor to complete a 10-inch columbiad weighing 19,000 pounds. It took the Tredegar Iron Works [which produced one-half of all the cannon cast by the Confederacy] a minimum of one month to cast, finish, and mount such a weapon. For the larger Brooke guns it took the Selma Naval Ordnance Works in the neighborhood of 1000 hours for completion." At such a rate it would take four years for Southern foundries to replace the heavy ordnance alone that was lost at Vicksburg.

Although Confederate foundries produced field guns at a more rapid rate, it would take one full year for iron workers at Tredegar, Bellona, and a score of smaller foundries across the South to replace the 169 light guns captured by the Federals during the campaign for Vicksburg. (This does not include the corresponding number of limbers, caissons, forge wagons, implements, harnesses, saddles, bridles, and the myriad of other accouterments associated with artillery that were also lost during the campaign.) Thus, rather than produce weapons to strengthen the armies in the field, Southern foundries were simply working to replenish diminished supply. As events proved in the wake of the disasters of 1863 at Gettysburg, Vicksburg, and Chattanooga, the Confederacy did not have the luxury of time to replenish this tremendous loss.[8]

In addition to the guns themselves, the Southern nation was deprived—in part, of the means by which to replace its lost artillery for there were two foundries in Vicksburg the smelters of which turned forever cold for the Confederacy when the city surrendered on July 4, 1863. The A. M. Paxton Foundry and the A. B. Reading Foundry, the later of which had produced 45 cannon for the Confederacy, had been a mainstay of the Vicksburg economy prior to the war and a vital part of Southern manufacturing during the conflict itself. In addition to cannon and munitions for artillery, these foundries produced iron for rails, boilers and steam gauges for steamboats and railroad engines, circular saw mills, water and gas pipes, farm tools, and implements of all kinds for agricultural, commercial, and residential use. The loss of these foundries further compounded the shortage of these items throughout the Confederacy and, though minimally, affected industrial output, the production of lumber, and even the cultivation of foodstuffs at a time of desperate need.[9]

*   *   *

Vicksburg NMP

Captured Confederate munitions ready to be turned over to Federal artillery batteries following the siege of Vicksburg.

From the outset of the war, the importance of the great river as a line of supply, communications, and operations was apparent to all. Although "too thick to drink and too thin to plow," the Mississippi River was regarded as "the spinal column of America." Indeed, the silent water of the mighty river was the single most-important economic feature of the continent, the very lifeblood of America. One contemporary wrote emphatically that, "The Valley of the Mississippi is America," reflecting the depth of significance, nay, near religious fixation, in which citizens North and South held the river.

The Mississippi River and its tributaries were the interstate highways of the nineteenth century. These streams drain half the continent and along their waters steamers, flatboats, and vessels of all description heavily laden with the agricultural and industrial produce of the land moved downstream to New Orleans. The Crescent City was the second busiest port in America in 1860. Only New York City surpassed New Orleans in the number of vessels entering and leaving its docks.[10]

Upon the secession of the Southern states, especially Louisiana and Mississippi, the river was closed to unfettered navigation which threatened to strangle Northern commercial interests. It was imperative for the administration in Washington to regain control of the lower Mississippi River and thereby open that avenue of commerce to allow the rich agricultural produce of the Northwest to reach world markets. In America then as now, economic importance translated to political importance and it was of agonizing concern to Abraham Lincoln that the great waterway be open to navigation as quickly as possible. Despite early successes, when that goal was not achieved by late 1862, the administration's anxiety reached new heights. Union General John McClernand, a former Democratic member of Congress who had represented the Springfield region of Illinois, wrote to Secretary of War Edwin Stanton on November 10: "I am conscious that if something is not soon done to reopen that great highway that a new party will spring into existence, which will favor the recognition of the independence of the so called Confederate States, with the view to eventual arrangements, either by treaty or union, for the purpose of effecting that object."[11]

McClernand's statement accurately assessed the political climate of the region, which reflected that of the nation as a whole. The climate of defeatism gave rise to the Copperheads and Peace Democrats who grew in strength and numbers in key northwestern states. Their influence on the national level and the extent of dissatisfaction with the Lincoln government was revealed in dramatic fashion as the fall elections went against the administration. The Republican Party lost 23 seats in the House of Representatives where its 59% margin of control dropped to 46% forcing the administration to form a coalition government until the elections of 1864.

Political importance thus translated to military importance and control of the Mississippi River became a cornerstone of the Anaconda Plan which sought to split the Confederacy in two along the line of the Mississippi River and sever a major Confederate supply route that ran east-west through Vicksburg—a line of supply on which the armies of Robert E. Lee and Braxton Bragg relied on for supplies of food, clothing, and reinforcement of fresh troops. Ulysses S. Grant later wrote of the political considerations that influenced the development of his operations along the Mississippi River: "The campaign of Vicksburg was suggested and developed by circumstances. The elections of 1862 had gone against the prosecution of the war: voluntary enlistments had nearly ceased, and the draft had been resorted to; this was resisted, and a defeat, or backward movement, would have made its execution impossible. A forward movement to a decisive victory was necessary."[12]

As important as the river was to the North, it was equally important to the South. In his biography *Jefferson Davis the Man and His Hour*, Jack Davis notes the Confederate president's strategic dilemma of defending the vast circumference of the Southern nation and its largest city—New Orleans. He emphasized that the "most vital region that demanded immediate attention was the rest of the Mississippi [River], from the Mississippi state line near Woodville north to the Kentucky and Missouri borders. This would be the lifeline by which men and materiel from the interior of the Confederacy would be moved to New Orleans or equally critical imports sent upriver to railheads [i.e., Vicksburg and Memphis] for dispersal. At the same time the river had to be held to keep open communications between the Confederacy east of the stream and to the west."[13]

Although New Orleans fell in April 1862, and Memphis in June of that same year, Confederate leaders sought desperately to retain control over as many miles of the river as possible to maintain the connection between the Trans-Mississippi (that vast region west of the river) and Cis-Mississippi (the heartland of the Confederacy east of the river) by concentrating their forces at defensible areas along the Mississippi. Among the sites selected, Port Hudson, Louisiana, and Grand Gulf and Vicksburg in Mississippi became the most powerful bastions. Vicksburg was the largest and most important of these posts.

In a December 1862, letter to Lt. Gen. Theophilus H. Holmes, Jefferson Davis presented a keen appraisal of the military situation that his government faced. "There are two prominent objects in the programme of the enemy," noted Davis. "One is to get possession of the Mississippi river and to open it to navigation. . . . The other is to seize upon the capital of the Confederacy, and hold this out as a proof that the Confederacy has no existence." Of the two objectives, he candidly admitted that the river was of greater importance, and in reference to Vicksburg, termed the city's possible loss "to be a much greater calamity than would be the loss of Richmond." In his letter to Holmes, the Confederate president explained the river's value: "But the control of the Mississippi River will be not only indirectly valuable to the enemy by the injury which its loss would inflict upon the Confederate States, but directly by furnishing the best possible base for operations in the valley both on the East and West side of the River, by answering the exigent demand of the North Western States for the restoration to them of the unrestricted use of that river, and by utilizing the heretofore fruitless possession of New Orleans."[14]

Davis echoed these sentiments in a speech to the Mississippi legislature on December 26, 1862, when he traveled to the Magnolia State to make a first-hand inspection of the Department of Mississippi and East Louisiana and assuage the fears of its populace as Federal forces were in motion throughout the region. He stated that defense of Vicksburg and Port Hudson was vital to the Confederacy as a successful defense of the Mississippi River would "conduce more than in any other way to the perpetuation of the Confederacy and the success of the cause." Defense of the twin bastions was indeed paramount as they formed the connection between the Trans-Mississippi and Cis-Mississippi, which provided for the passage across the great river of vital supplies, especially food, that were desperately needed by Confederate armies in the field and increasingly so by a civilian population in want of sustenance.[15]

Following the loss of New Orleans and Memphis, Vicksburg became the major conduit through which supplies passed from one side of the river to the other as it was the only city with rail links to the rest of the

Confederacy. From Vicksburg, the Southern Railroad of Mississippi connected the city with Jackson and, via Jackson, points elsewhere in the Confederacy. West of the river, the tracks of the Vicksburg, Shreveport, and Texas Railroad stretched to Monroe and the Ouachita River. In his work *Confederate Neckties: Louisiana Railroads in the Civil War*, Larry Estaville wrote, "For two years the V.S. & T. formed an essential part of the supply line that stretched from the Mexican border to Virginia. To help support the war-torn eastern areas of the Confederacy, the Vicksburg, Shreveport and Texas carried over its rails English rifles and ammunition that the Rebels landed in Mexico and smuggled across the border, Texas beef and grain, Louisiana sugar, salt, and molasses, and much more."[16]

Indeed, the vast Trans-Mississippi region was a land of milk and honey, the fertile soils of which produced foodstuffs in abundance for the Confederacy. The following information is taken from the Preliminary Report on the Eighth Census 1860. The states ranked as follows:

Arkansas:

7th in molasses
10th in asses & mules

Louisiana:

1st in cane sugar
1st in cane molasses (about 7/8 of all produced in the United States)

Texas:

1st in working oxen
1st in "Neat cattle" (meaning domestic cattle)
1st in sheep
3rd in horses
4th in milch cows
4th in asses & mules
7th in swine

These three states combined annually to produce more than 50 million bushels of Indian corn, two million bushels of wheat, five million bushels of sweet potatoes, and 11 million pounds of butter. The facts alone suggest it was the Trans-Mississippi, and not the Shenandoah Valley, that was the true breadbasket of the Confederacy.[17]

It is important to further note that the region also produced 2 million pounds of wool and processed more than 1.5 million bales of cotton. Lead was also an essential item for Confederate armies that fought with increased desperation as the conflict continued into 1864, and most of the Southern lead fired on battlefields across the nation came from the Trans-Mississippi region. With large quantities of these desperately needed supplies being funneled through Vicksburg from the states of the far South, we can readily understand, as Peter Walker observed in his classic study *Vicksburg A People at War, 1861-1865*, that "the single line of iron running eastward from Vicksburg and the sorry little spur of track stuck out into Louisiana loomed larger and larger in military planning," both in Washington and Richmond. The military might of two nations would focus on the iron rails radiating from Vicksburg, and over which flowed the lifeblood of the Confederacy. The campaign they waged for control of the city determined the outcome of a war.[18]

But throughout the antebellum period and during the war years, Southern railroads could not compete in importance to the rivers that flowed silently to sea, nor the steamboats that plied their muddy water. In Vicksburg, the heartbeat of the town emanated from the docks along the waterfront. Prior to the Civil War, "Steamboats from New Orleans, Memphis, St. Louis, and Louisville arrived daily" in Vicksburg. Vessels from Cincinnati, Wheeling, and Pittsburgh arrived there on a less regular basis. "Three times a week boats left Vicksburg for Memphis and New Orleans, and the Yazoo boat, which went deep into the delta to Greenwood, made its run four times a week. Every half hour a ferry crossed the river to De Soto City, Louisiana, the eastern terminal of the Vicksburg, Shreveport, and Texas Railroad."[19]

With the advent of Civil War, the amount of boat traffic on the Mississippi and the number of vessels that tied up at Vicksburg fell dramatically. Yet the city continued to serve as an important port for the Confederacy and its docks were generally piled high with "white gold" in its various forms that was of such vital need to the Southern nation, its armies, and people. The forms of "white gold" were, of course, cotton, salt, and sugar. Let us examine these commodities and their significance during the war and to the Confederacy in particular.

In 1861, the South produced 4.5 million bales of cotton, or two-thirds of the world supply, and much of this was raised in the fertile lower Mississippi River valley. (The agricultural region serviced by Vicksburg alone produced 250,000 bales that were shipped downriver to New Orleans.) Confederate foreign policy was based on cotton and was referred to as "King Cotton Diplomacy." Southern leaders were convinced that the key to success lay in gaining foreign recognition and they viewed cotton as the great leverage. More than three-fourths of the cotton used in the textile mills of Great Britain and France came from the American South. Almost one-fourth of Great Britain's population depended in some way on the textile industry. The authorities in Richmond believed the need for cotton would compel Great Britain and France to intervene in the war and raise the Union blockade of Southern ports in order to save their own economies. "Although the South never succeeded in convincing the foreign powers to intervene against the North," write Orville Burton, "cotton diplomacy was successful in obtaining financial help from abroad." In all, the Confederacy realized almost eight million dollars in foreign exchange based on cotton that was used to purchase an array of war materiel from arms and equipment to warships.[20]

As important as they were to the Confederacy, the cotton lands of the lower Mississippi River valley were equally important to the North, and New England in particular. In 1860, there had been almost five million spindles in operation in New England that employed tens of thousands of people. That same year, more than two million bales of cotton, processed through the port of New Orleans, supplied those spindles with enough cotton to produce $100 million worth of cloth. By 1862, only 25% of those spindles were active and the cry for Southern cotton was heard loud and clear in Washington. New England had played a vital role in Abraham Lincoln's ascension to the presidency in 1860 as evidenced in part by his selection of Hannibal Hamlin of Maine as his running mate. Lincoln realized that he had to keep New England pacified and alleviate the cotton shortage if he were to be re-elected in 1864 in order to continue to direct the war to a successful conclusion. Thus it was imperative for the administration in Washington to reestablish control over the Mississippi River and its tributaries and open the flow of cotton from the states of Mississippi, Louisiana, and Texas. To do so, his land and naval forces had to silence the Confederate river batteries at Vicksburg.[21]

Salt was another form of "white gold" that was of equal importance to the supplies of lead, corn, beef, pork, horses, and other essential items funneled through Vicksburg from the Trans-Mississippi region. It is important to note that the Preliminary Report on the Eighth Census 1860 lists only eight states as producing salt, which is essential in the curing and preservation of meat. Of these, only two were Southern states, Virginia and Texas. (Salt was discovered in Louisiana during the Civil War and the Bayou State became the largest supplier of salt in the Confederacy.) Although figures are not available for Louisiana and Virginia, Texas alone produced 120,000 bushels of salt.[22]

Due to the increased demand for salt caused by the mobilization of troops and the need to feed Confederate armies in the field, the scarcity of this vital commodity quickly grew acute. On December 20, 1862, in a joint address to the Mississippi legislature, Gov. John J. Pettus informed his listeners, who included Jefferson Davis, "The most pressing want of our people at the present time is a supply of salt." Less than seven months later, upon the fall of Vicksburg, the supply of salt from the mines in Texas and at New Iberia, Louisiana, was cut. (To give you an idea of the quantity of salt that passed through Vicksburg, a single steamer, the *T. D. Hine*, arrived at the city's docks on January 20, 1863, it carried 248,927 pounds of subsistence stores, of which 107,467 pounds were salt.) Salt rose dramatically in price and soon became worth its weight in gold. By 1864 the single largest expenditure of the states of Mississippi and Alabama was for salt to stave off imminent starvation among the civilian populace. Other Southern states made hefty appropriations for salt, but there was little to be had at any price. Without salt to cure and preserve meat, the beef necessary to feed the armies had to be shipped on the hoof. This further taxed the already strained and rapidly deteriorating Confederate transportation system, which ultimately broke under the pressure.[23]

This brings us to the third form of "white gold"—sugar. Along with molasses, sugar was not only used as a physical substitute for meat, but as commodity money with which to purchase meat. (Remember that Louisiana ranked first in the production of cane sugar and first in the quantity of cane molasses produced in the United States in 1860, the latter accounting for 7/8 of the nation's total production.) The author of the article in *North & South* states that "attempts by commissary officers in 1863 to send Texas cattle to Virginia had to be abandoned because of poor grazing east of the river and the high cost of forage." He went on to write, "Also, throughout the war the Confederate army in Virginia obtained most of its beef-on-the-hoof from Florida, which then produced nearly as much cattle as Texas, and until the summer of 1863 Tennessee amply provided the Southern army that bore its name with red meat." But such meat had to be procured at a cost to the Confederate government, a cost that increasingly had to be paid in something other than script as the nation's paper currency plummeted in value. By 1863, exchanging sugar for meat was "one of the Confederacy's principal methods of procuring meat," states Michael Wright in his article "Vicksburg and the Trans-Mississippi Supply Line, 1861-1863."[24]

Contrary to the statements made in the *North & South* article, meat was not so plentiful in 1863, and Southern armies across the broad spectrum of war were in need of beef, pork, and mutton. On March 12, 1863, Gen. Joseph E. Johnston telegraphed Lt. Gen. John C. Pemberton in Mississippi: "The supplies of sugar and molasses for the troops here [Alabama] and in Tennessee come through Vicksburg. I need not tell you how important those supplies are to the troops in these times of scarcity of meat." He emphasized, "Other departments have greater difficulty in obtaining food than yours." That same day Secretary of War James A. Seddon directed Pemberton to send eastward as much sugar and molasses that was not absolutely necessary for subsistence of the Vicksburg garrison. Three days later, on March 15, Johnston again wired Pemberton urging him to increase and expedite the shipment of sugar and molasses from Vicksburg. "It is very important," wrote the Virginian, "for with these articles meat can be purchased, which is to be obtained in no other way. You are aware that it is very scarce in all our armies now." Pemberton complained in reply that most of the boats on the Mississippi were already "engaged in carrying sugar, molasses, and salt either for private parties or for the government," much to the detriment of his own efforts to stockpile supplies of other items in Vicksburg.[25]

Sugar as a commodity money came to be used throughout the Confederacy and was exchanged pound for pound for meat—and "at prices less than half the market value." One illustration of this means of procurement comes from the pen of Maj. A. D. Banks, Johnston's A.A.G. in Alabama. On May 5, 1863, he wrote to the general, "The commissary arrangements in this department look well. They have about 250,000 pounds of salt meat in depot, and about 2,000 head of cattle either herded or engaged. This meat has been secured chiefly by exchange for sugar and molasses, and is still accumulating. I am in hopes that enough will be gathered to justify sending forward some to the Tennessee army." Thanks to Banks' tireless efforts, by May 15 he was able to inform Johnston that "between 500,000 and 600,000 pounds of salt meat and 2,000 to 3,000 head of cattle could be sent forward on very short notice." He again reported, "This meat has been secured chiefly by exchange for sugar and molasses."[26]

Although the exact quantity of sugar passing through Vicksburg cannot be determined, it was very large as evidenced by the records of the Southern Railroad. According to one railroad official, "private freight could be shipped from Vicksburg only one day a week, the rolling stock being devoted the rest of the week to government sugar." The railroad had a freight capacity of some 200 tons daily, each way, but the line was subject to accidents and was temporarily cut during the Vicksburg campaign by Union cavalry under Col. Benjamin Grierson. Still, it carried enormous quantities of sugar that benefited Confederate armies across the South.[27]

"Assuming that the railroad operated half the time, and then at only 50 percent of its capacity, about 300 tons of sugar per week could have been transported," estimated Mike Wright in his study on the Southern Railroad. At the rate of trade, 300 tons of sugar could be exchanged for 600,000 pounds of meat. Thus, in the course of a year, notes Wright, "This quantity of meat was enough to supply about 260,000 men for the entire 12 months, at the 1864 monthly meat ration," which was 10 pounds per man. This was enough meat to feed the combined manpower of the Confederacy's principal armies. But with the surrender of Vicksburg to Ulysses S. Grant on July 4, 1863, "The demise of the Trans-Mississippi line cut off the flow of sugar permanently, which deprived the South of an apparently most effective means of subsisting its troops."[28]

In light of this evidence, can we conclude that the Trans-Mississippi supply line that ran through Vicksburg was important? Can we assert that its loss had a profound effect on the outcome of the war? Can we claim that rather than myth, the significance of the Mississippi River, of Vicksburg in particular, and the vast Trans-Mississippi region beyond, was in fact reality?

There is more to consider. For example, with the loss of Vicksburg and Port Hudson, not only was the river now under Union control, but hundreds of square miles of land changed hands. This land provided President Lincoln with a vast region in which to test his Reconstruction policies and address the needs of the freed blacks. Further, the Union victory at Vicksburg led to a dramatic increase in the enlistment of blacks from Louisiana and Mississippi into the army and navy of the United States. These recruits enabled the Union to use black troops in the occupation of Vicksburg, Grand Gulf, Natchez, Baton Rouge, and elsewhere rather than white soldiers—combat veterans, who were thus freed to fight elsewhere.

With Pemberton's army gone and Johnston's army no longer a threat, a large portion of Grant's army was able to move to Memphis. From the Queen City it partially reconstructed the Memphis & Charleston Railroad en route to Chattanooga, where it helped raise the siege and thus opened the door to the Deep South, which the author of the article in *North & South* suggests was "the true path to Northern victory in the West."[29]

"We must go back to the campaigns of Napoleon to find equally brilliant results accomplished in the same space of time with such a small loss," wrote Francis V. Greene of the Union effort to take Vicksburg. The results of the campaign established Ulysses S. Grant as one of the great captains in history and identified him in the mind of Abraham Lincoln as the general who could lead the Union armies to victory. Eight months later Grant was elevated to the rank of lieutenant general and given command of all Union forces. Thirteen months later he accepted the surrender of the vaunted Army of Northern Virginia that for all practical purpose signaled the end of the war.[30]

Grant's campaign for Vicksburg remains the subject of examination and evaluation by modern soldiers and is required study at the United States Military Academy. In its May 1986 version of FM 100-5 (field manual on operations), the United States Army boldly proclaims this of U. S. Grant: "His operations south of Vicksburg fought in the Spring of 1863 has been called the most brilliant campaign ever fought on American soil. It exemplifies the qualities of a well conceived, violently executed offensive plan." The Army assessment continues: "The same speed, surprise, maneuver, and decisive action will be required in the campaigns of the future." Indeed, for although replaced in the June 1993 version of FM 100-5 by an evaluation of Operation Desert Storm, as the campaign conducted by Gen. Norman Schwarzkopf was a mirror image of the Vicksburg campaign the Army's assertion has been validated.[31]

One year after Pemberton and Grant met to discuss the surrender of Vicksburg, Union occupation forces erected and dedicated a stone obelisk on the site in recognition of its significance in American history. It was one of the earliest monuments erected on any battlefield of the Civil War and the first of many to be erected at Vicksburg. Today, Vicksburg National Military Park boasts of 1,330 monuments, markers, tablets, and plaques that make it one of the more heavily monumented battlefields in the world. The exquisite statues of stone and bronze that were executed by the most renowned sculptors of the late Nineteenth and early Twentieth centuries make Vicksburg, in the words of one Civil War veteran, the "art park of the world." Each year the national military park at Vicksburg attracts more than one million visitors from around the world, further attesting to its significance on a world scale, and that number continues to grow.

But, as the article in *North & South* indicates, Vicksburg still has a long way to go before it finally settles into its well deserved place in history. Thanks to the efforts of several stalwart historians, including Edwin C. Bearss, whose trilogy *The Vicksburg Campaign* sets the standard for campaign studies; Warren Grabau, author of *Ninety-eight Days: A Geographer's View of the Vicksburg Campaign*; Michael Ballard, author of *Pemberton: A Biography*; Timothy Smith, author of *Champion Hill: Decisive Battle for Vicksburg*, and others whose writing efforts will soon come to light, the Vicksburg campaign is finally receiving the just recognition it so richly deserves in the historiography of the Civil War.

Someday it will reclaim the level of significance it was accorded during the struggle for national identity.

CHAPTER TEN

Stephen D. Lee and the
Making of an American Shrine

On the hot afternoon of May 22, 1863, Brig. Gen. Stephen D. Lee watched in awe as Union troops poured out of a ravine only 400 yards away and deployed into line of battle on a ridge opposite his lines. One Confederate soldier who gazed over the parapets of earth and log recorded for posterity that the Federals deployed into line of battle with man touching man, rank pressing rank, and line supporting line. He could see Union officers riding up and down the lines giving encouragement to their men, making sure that all was set for the advance. He watched as the colors were uncased and caught the breeze above the lines. He listened to the sound of cold steel as the enemy affixed their bayonets in final preparation for the charge. To him, this pageantry of war was grim, irresistible, and yet magnificent in the extreme.

But there was little time for admiration as the blue lines swept across the fields. With a mighty cheer the Federals swarmed up the slopes and into the ditches fronting the Vicksburg defenses. Planting several stands of colors atop the Confederate fortifications, a handful of Union troops entered Railroad Redoubt on Lee's left—the city's defenses had been pierced.

With calm determination, Lee rode to the point of danger. Exhorting his men to stand their ground in the face of overwhelming numbers, he gathered reinforcements and led the counterattack that drove the Federals

Brig. Gen.
Stephen Dill Lee

National Archives

back and sealed the breach. It was the most sublime moment of his distinguished military career. A moment that would connect him indelibly with Vicksburg and define the essence of his very soul in the closing years of his life.

The South Carolina native was born and bred for a life of service. His years as a cadet at the United States Military Academy at West Point and his service in the armies of two nations defined and polished the man and prepared the soldier for the destiny awaiting him.[1]

The purpose of this essay is not to address the military career of this gallant soldier, or the political career of this noble statesman. It is not to describe his role as a devoted husband or father; nor is it to evaluate his exceptional career as an educator. Rather, it is to review and honor his efforts to establish an American shrine, one that would stand as a tribute to a generation which fought in defense of ideals held dear and remind generations yet to come of the sacrifices that have been made to forge a nation and make us unique among the peoples of the world.

Life in the postwar era at *Devereaux* in Noxubee County was a difficult period for Lee. Although he enjoyed the pleasant side of life as a farmer, especially the time spent with his wife Regina, whom he affectionately called Lily, and their son Blewett, there was a void in his being, a hollow feeling which grew more intense as the years passed. The need to fill that void became more urgent with age, especially in light of his deep religious beliefs that called him to follow the teachings of Christ and lead a life of service to his fellow man.[2]

Such calling led him first to the field of politics and then to education. Although both were personally rewarding, Lee was drawn by the Muse of History to service in a field more in keeping with his life's experience, one for which he was uniquely qualified. He slowly became interested in honoring his fellow veterans. His efforts to serve them soon became a passion that would dominate his life for the last twenty years.[3]

In 1887, he was invited to attend the unveiling of a monument in Vicksburg honoring soldiers from Louisiana who had served in defense of that city in 1863. Lee had led Louisiana troops in the Battle of Chickasaw Bayou, near Vicksburg, in 1862 and wanted to honor the men of his command, but pressing duties at Mississippi Agricultural and Mechanical College, of which he was then president, prevented his attendance. The following year, with the situation at the college steadily improving, he began to devote limited time to veterans' affairs and delivered a number of speeches commemorating the service of Confederate soldiers.[4]

In 1889, Camp 32 of the United Confederate Veterans and Grand Army of the Republic Post 7, both of Vicksburg, invited the national membership of the G.A.R. to attend a grand reunion of former soldiers of both armies in the Hill City. The Blue & Gray Association, which was formed to oversee the reunion, invited General Lee to attend and to present an address to the veterans who assembled in Vicksburg in May 1890. In his speech, Lee praised the men in blue and gray who had shown both bravery and devotion to duty during the war, and hailed the efforts made for reunification of the North and South. His remarks were well-received by those in attendance and reported favorably in newspapers across the nation. His speech, and those that followed which he delivered with increasing frequency, attracted national attention and Lee quickly rose to become a leader among Southern veterans.

Many veterans who had attended the Blue & Gray Reunion, including Lee, were saddened to see the battlefield at Vicksburg all but forgotten. Although many of the forts and long lines of trenches that played such a significant role in the 47-day-long siege of the city were still visible, no effort to preserve them was evident. The former soldiers left Vicksburg convinced that the fields on which they had fought and thousands of their comrades had died "deserved more and must be properly marked and preserved by our government." It was an idea that strongly appealed to Lee.[5]

In these closing years of the Nineteenth Century, as the generation that fought the great war departed to answer the final roll call in response to Gabriel's trumpet, veterans of the blue and gray banded together and moved to preserve the fields of battle on which they had fought. As statehouses and legislatures across the nation were still dominated by Civil War veterans, as was Congress and the White House, such noble sentiment was quickly acted upon. In 1890, Congress set aside the battlefields around Chattanooga, Tennessee, as the nation's first national military park. Establishment of Antietam National Battlefield in Maryland, site of the single bloodiest day of combat in American military history, quickly followed. Congress set aside the battlefield at Shiloh in 1894, and the land at Gettysburg in 1895.

Stephen D. Lee supported these efforts in recognition of which he was elected vice-president of the Shiloh Battlefield Association in 1893. Although an honorary position that he shared with a dozen other prominent Union and Confederate veterans, it was an honor of which he was immensely proud. It also illustrates Lee's embrace of the New South philosophy and his willingness to work with former enemies for the interests of a unified nation.[6]

Lee wrote to a friend that "while I will remain forever loyal to the tender memories of the past, I will continue to be loyal also to our great country." Such sentiment made him popular with both Confederate veterans and Southern women and invitations for him to speak at monument dedications and other veteran related events arrived frequently at the homes he had in Starkville and Columbus.[7]

On April 26, 1893, he traveled to Vicksburg to dedicate the Confederate monument at Cedar Hill Cemetery where Southern soldiers who died during the siege of the city are interred. Lee rode the train from Jackson with Gov. John M. Stone and former governor Robert Lowry, both of whom were Confederate veterans. In his speech Lee "hailed the private soldier as needing no better monument than his record, extolled the South's untarnished honor, and closed with a flowery tribute to southern women." An editorial in one of the Vicksburg newspapers that afternoon echoed Lee's remarks. "Too much honor cannot be paid to the memory of the dead Confederate soldiers," it read. "They were the highest exemplars of bravery, self-sacrifice, and devotion. No greater praise can be awarded to any man than to say that he was a good

Confederate soldier." These remarks established him as the spokesman for Confederate veterans.[8]

The following year, the Governor's Greys from Iowa, led by former Union Captain John F. Merry, visited Vicksburg. Although a goodwill visit, Merry's principal objective was to sound out Southern veterans and the people of the Hill City as to their views on the establishment of a national military park at Vicksburg. Locally, a man named Tom Lewis was urging city officials to appropriate funding for the purchase and preservation of the forts that ringed the town. His efforts, however, failed to stir the elected officials into action. It was obvious to Merry that congressional action was necessary and that only the veterans themselves could succeed in this effort. To do so would require the support of former Confederate soldiers, not just those in Mississippi, but across the South. To Captain Merry, Lee's participation was deemed vital to gain Southern support for the park idea.[9]

Lee was enthusiastic about the idea. Although defeat at Vicksburg had helped seal the doom of the Confederacy, the general believed that the Southern soldiers who had fought so valiantly at Vicksburg deserved to be honored rather than shadowed by shame. He promised both his support and energies on behalf of the enterprise and agreed to the formation of the Vicksburg National Military Park Association.

On October 22, 1895, a preliminary meeting of the Association, called by Captain Merry, was held in the Club Room of the New Pacific House (commonly called the Piazza Hotel). Lee was elected chairman and addresses were made by Lee, Merry and others, and plans were outlined for a permanent organization. The purpose of the Association was to petition Congress to establish a national military park at Vicksburg. Lee was elected president of the new organization. The other officers were Charles Davidson, formerly of the Twenty-fifth Iowa Infantry, vice-president, William T. Rigby, former captain in the Twenty-fourth Iowa Infantry, secretary, and Charles C. Flowerree, of Mississippi (former colonel of the Seventh Virginia Infantry), treasurer. The Board of Directors included such prominent men as William D. Hoard, former governor of Wisconsin, John M. Stone, governor of Mississippi, Frederick D. Grant, son of Ulysses, Thomas N. Waul of Waul's Texas Legion, Lucius Fairchild, governor of Wisconsin, Russell Alger, secretary of war, John B. Gordon, commander of the United Confederate Veterans, and Edmund Pettus, former Confederate colonel and U.S. senator from Alabama. Capital Stock was sold for $5.00 per share, the proceeds of which would cover the expenses of the Association, and the veterans moved quickly to initiate their noble work.[10]

On November 18, 1895, Governor Stone signed the Charter of Incorporation and the secretary of state issued it the following day. Anticipating that the charter would be approved, on November 20 a train carrying 100 directors and members of the Association representing the Northwest left Chicago bound for Vicksburg. The *Vicksburg Evening Post* recorded their arrival:

> Capt. Merry's party reached the city at 7:30 o'clock, at which hour a vast throng assembled at the depot to greet its arrival. A detachment of the Warren Light Artillery was already on the ground for the purpose of firing the salute, but the Volunteer Southrons and band, and the resident veterans of both armies, acting as a guard of honor, escorted Gov. Stone, Gen. S. D. Lee and other distinguished gentlemen to the platform where they awaited the coming of the visitors. As the train came in the guns of the Warren Light Artillery signaled its approach and seventeen rounds were fired—the Governor's salute.

Following a series of welcoming remarks, the visitors were escorted to the Carroll Hotel "by a procession which would have done honor to a President or Emperor."[11]

The following morning, November 22, the incorporators held a meeting in the parlors of the Hotel Carroll at 10:00 a.m. and the articles of incorporation were read and adopted. Those in attendance subscribed for an additional 100 shares of capital stock at the cost of $5.00 per share.[12]

Lee called the first meeting of the board to order. Former Union general Lucius Fairchild of Wisconsin rose and recommended "that the proposed Park should include the lines of the earthworks of the opposing armies and the land included within these lines, with such additions as are necessary to include the Headquarters of Generals Grant and Pemberton. Such of the water batteries as it may be desirable to designate, and other historical spots, the whole not to exceed four thousand acres." The recommendation met with universal approbation and the Executive Committee was instructed to urge Congress to establish a park along the lines Fairchild proposed.[13]

That afternoon, Lee called into session the first meeting of the Executive Committee of the Board of Directors. A committee consisting of Lee, Davidson, Rigby, Flowerree, and Edward Scott Butts of Mississippi was constituted and charged with preparing a bill for the establishment of a park at Vicksburg, presenting the bill to Congress, and providing information as to the cost of land. The Committee was to have full power on behalf of the Association. The Committee immediately arranged for a survey of desired land to be made and a map produced of the proposed park. Options on the land were secured over the next few weeks illustrative of the sentiment throughout Vicksburg and Warren County which genuinely favored the establishment of a park.[14]

Members of the Executive Committee spoke at length with the Hon. Thomas C. Catchings, U.S. Representative from Mississippi's 3rd Congressional District which encompassed Vicksburg. A former Confederate soldier who had served in Congress since 1885, Catchings cautioned that the plan was too ambitious, that due to the desired size of the park it would meet with opposition in Congress, especially from the tight-fisted speaker Thomas B. Reed of Maine. It was recommended that the proposed size of the park be cut down to the bare minimum needed to protect the key features of the battlefield.

Seven weeks later, on January 10, 1896, General Lee called a second meeting of the Executive Committee to order in the parlors of the Hotel Carroll. Rigby made a motion outlining the size and location of the proposed park. The park would encompass only 1,200 acres, consisting of a main body, two Confederate wings and two Union wings, the average costs of which was $35 per acre.[15]

Members of the Association were startled by both the proposed limited size of the park and the asking price for the land. James K. P. Thompson of Iowa expressed a concern shared by many when he observed, "I am fearful the average price of land is so high that Congress will not deem it wise at this time to purchase, although I hope I may be in error. It shows that the greed of man is not confined to any ositermal lines, but they are just as likely to be found in a warm and a cold climate." Despite disappointments and concerns the recommendation was freely discussed and passed. Lee, Davidson, Rigby, and Flowerree were instructed to go to Washington and have Representative Catchings present the bill.[16]

Lee, however, did not travel to Washington due to an outbreak of smallpox at the college, but the others did go and there met John Merry, James G. Everest, member of the Association and commander of the Society of the Army of the Tennessee, and Representative Catchings. They remained in Washington for two weeks and Catchings' bill (H.R. 4339) was referred to the Committee on Military Affairs, chaired by Congressman John A. T. Hull from Iowa.[17]

Eleven days later the bill was released from Committee and referred to the Committee on the Whole House on the State of the Union. No action, however, was taken and the Association members returned to Vicksburg sorely disappointed. Representative Catchings later presented a memorial from Mississippi, while Henry Cabot Lodge presented one from Massachusetts, and a third was presented by Warren O. Arnold from Rhode Island. Despite such widespread support for the park, Speaker Reed, referred to by members of the House of Representatives as "The Czar," refused to allow the bill to reach the floor.

During the congressional recess, joint resolutions were passed by the legislatures in Mississippi, Iowa, New York, Massachusetts, and Rhode Island endorsing the park bill. Yet, despite such encouraging actions, it was a winter of frustration for both Lee and Rigby. Adding to the general's worries, Regina Lee's health took a turn for the worse. Concerning an inquiry from Rigby as to when the next meeting of the Association should be called, Lee replied:

> I hardly know how to answer your letter. I hope to go to New York or Chicago with Mrs. Lee to have an operation performed which may involve her life, in all probability. My first duty is to her. I hope to take her if she will go somewhere . . . and, if the operation is successful, I will probably remain with her a month. So have the meeting at the time that will suit the other members of the governing board, and I will be present if I can.[18]

During the winter, Merry, Rigby, and others planned their strategy for the next session of Congress. Rep. David Henderson of Iowa advised, "We have got to take [Speaker] Reed by the throat at this session." Fred Grant, then police commissioner for New York City, wrote to Rigby on November 9, 1896, offering words of both solace and encouragement:

What you say with reference to getting the appropriation for the Park at Vicksburg, is the usual experience, and I am not at all surprised at Speaker Reed not desiring the matter to come up in the last session of congress, owing to the financial condition of the country. However, the outlook for the coming year is much better, and I presume his objections will be less serious. .

Supporters of the bill on Capitol Hill were persistent in their entreats to "Czar" Reed to no avail. On December 14, Congressman David B. Henderson of Iowa assured his friend Rigby, "I have been pushing the Speaker, but much work is needed in that quarter."[19]

On December 16, Lee called a meeting of the Board of Directors of the Association in the parlors of the Carroll Hotel in Vicksburg. Lee, Rigby, and others were instructed to travel to Washington in January to push the park bill. Accompanied by Fred Grant, James Everest, and members of the Society of the Army of the Tennessee, Lee and Rigby visited with Speaker Reed and urged his support of the park bill. The speaker, although not opposed to the park idea, was not sympathetic to the appropriation necessary for its establishment.[20]

Reflecting on the meeting weeks later, Lee lamented, "I feel all has been done that could be done for the Park Bill. The trouble is, the empty treasury—and Mr. Reed has 8000 arguments on his side." Knowing that his frustration was shared by Rigby, Lee attempted to buoy the spirit of his new friend. "You have certainly done your duty in the premises, and covered every chance," he wrote. "Mr. Reed is a man after his own mould, and I don't believe any one can influence him against his decision when he has deliberately made up his mind." But, Lee, too, despaired. "Although I think the bill may pass in the next Congress, yet the options will all have expired & we can never renew then as favorably again," he wrote. With deep emotion, he expressed a fear shared by Rigby and those in the Association when he wrote, "In the mean time many an old veteran in both armies will have 'crossed over the river.'"[21]

When Congress reconvened, memorials "Praying" for establishment of the park that had been passed by the legislatures of Illinois, Indiana, Michigan, Minnesota, Pennsylvania, and Wisconsin were introduced on the floor of the House of Representatives by members from those states. The speaker ignored the pressure and H.R. 4339 died when the 54th Congress adjourned in March 1897.

"The failure of Congress to act on the Vicksburg Park Bill, makes it necessary to make a new start with the next Congress," wrote Lee to Rigby on October 29, 1897. "All preliminary work has already been done of course, but I want to consult with you as to what is now necessary for us to do." In a vein of desperation he implored, "What can we do? When can we do it? Where will we get the funds to further prosecute our efforts?"[22]

Despite the pall of gloom, members of the Association persevered and Representative Catchings bided his time. It was the 2nd Session of the 55th Congress before he again determined to act. On December 9, 1897, he introduced H.R. 4382 "to establish a national military park to commemorate the campaign, siege, and defense of Vicksburg." As before, the proposed legislation was referred by Speaker Reed to the House Committee on Military Affairs.

Rigby urged Lee to accompany him to Washington in January to push for support of the park measure. Frustration with events and concern over his wife's continued poor health influenced Lee to write:

> Ex-Gov. Hull & Genl. Catchings both were of opinion that neither Col. Flowerree nor myself would avail anything by again appearing before Speaker Reed. I have already addressed him on the Park Bill in his private office. The members of the Mil'ty Comtee have seen the park ground & have all information possible. The speaker is the only obstacle & if his comrades in the G.A.R. and other organizations cannot reach him, certainly I cannot . . . I hope the Speaker will yield this time, but I must confess I do not imagine that he will.

He went on to suggest that they attempt to get the bill passed in the Senate then go to the House.[23]

The general did not accompany his comrades to Washington. Perhaps it was well that he did not for although the measure was reported out of committee on March 1, 1898, before the proposal could be voted on the nation found itself at war with Spain. (The battleship *Maine* had been blown up in Havana on February 15, and war erupted in April.) War measures engrossed the legislators' attention for the next six months. Lee's frustration reached new depths.

At year's end, the general called to order a meeting of the Association in Vicksburg during which he reviewed the efforts thus far made on behalf of the park bill. Again, he and Rigby and others were appointed a committee to go to Washington and push for passage of the measure. Lee was unable to go and so Rigby traveled to the capital where he again met with Fred Grant and James Everest. They spoke at length to dozens of congressmen and secured a private meeting with Speaker Reed whose reluctance to call up the bill for a vote appeared to waiver.[24]

The Treaty of Paris had been signed on December 11th. With the war against Spain over, veterans' issues were again of interest to Congress. Even the tight-fisted Reed seemed anxious to fund projects and programs of interests to veterans and dropped his opposition to the park measure. The opportune moment had finally arrived and, as the measure had been reported favorably out of committee in March 1898, Rep. John A. T. Hull of Iowa asked on February 6, 1899, that Speaker Reed suspend the rules and pass the Vicksburg Park Bill. As soon as H.R. 4382 was read by the clerk, it was voted on and passed unanimously.

The *Vicksburg Evening Post* announced passage of the bill on February 7 stating that, "No matter ever brought before the Congress has been more faithfully presented and worked for in the past three years, than the bill which passed the House yesterday under a suspensions of the rules for the establishment of a National Military Park at Vicksburg."[25]

Two days later, Senator Ed Pettus of Alabama, a member of the Senate Committee on Military Affairs who had served under Lee's command at Vicksburg, sent to the floor a companion bill, S.4382. On February 10, Mississippi senator Hernando De Soto Money asked for "unanimous consent" to call up the measure. After a reading, the measure was passed. On February 21, 1899, President William McKinley affixed his signature to the bill making Vicksburg the fifth battlefield from the Civil War to be set aside in perpetuity as a national military park or national battlefield.

Elation hardly describes the reaction of General Lee, Captain Rigby, and the others who for years had devoted their time and energies to the park effort. Their devotion was now to be rewarded. The legislation by which the park was established called for the appointment of three commissioners to oversee the park. All three had to be veterans of the Vicksburg campaign, one Confederate representative and two Union representatives. Lee was clearly the logical choice for the Confederate representative and Captains Rigby of Iowa and Everest of Illinois were named the Union representatives.

Stephen D. Lee, seated at right, was elected by his fellow commissioners as chairman of the Vicksburg National Military Park Commission.

The Commission held its first meeting in Washington on March 1, 1899, during which Lee was elected chairman, and thus first superintendent of the park. He was also the first former Confederate to become chairman of a national military park. The general was much pleased by his appointment, especially as the $300 per month salary enabled him to resign as president of the college and to spend more time with Mrs. Lee. To a friend he wrote, "I got the place all right, a better place than I thought it was and duties apparently light." Such was not to be the case and Chairman Lee devoted long hours to correspondence and other park matters that first year in office.[26]

After receiving their commissions the three men traveled to Vicksburg where they arrived on March 14 to establish the park office and start their new duties. A topographical survey was ordered of the lands to be acquired, tracts were purchased, and exhaustive correspondence was entered into with veterans of the siege to amass information necessary to accurately mark the battlefield with tablets. The commissioners worked to construct roads and bridges and secure the placement of monuments by the various states represented by troops during the siege and defense of Vicksburg.

Lee was desirous that both sides be treated fairly in the presentation being formed by the Commission through its pattern and placement of tablets. He also worked to secure the identical number and kinds of cannon used by both armies during the siege for he wanted to demonstrate that the North's artillery superiority was a major factor leading to the Confederate defeat at Vicksburg. His actions quickly placed his stamp on the park that is still evident one hundred years later.

The furious pace required of the commissioners, and of Lee and Rigby in particular, soon exhausted the general. On December 20, he wrote to Secretary of War Elihu Root asking to be temporarily relieved from his duties as chairman of the park commission. Citing Mrs. Lee's long and continued illness and the restrictions it thus placed upon his ability to travel on park business, he recommended that Captain Rigby be named acting chairman. The secretary of war approved both the request and recommendation. Lee never resumed his duties as chairman.[27]

Mrs. Lee's health continued to deteriorate over the next two years requiring the general's constant attention. His own health too began to decline and Lee was forced to conduct less and less park business. He reluctantly accepted the limitations that age and health were forcing upon him and on November 21, 1901, tendered his resignation as chairman of the Commission to Captain Rigby. In a touching letter written from the heart he expressed his admiration for his fellow commissioner:

> I felt at the time when Colonel Everest and yourself by your votes made me your Chairman that it was an act of delicate courtesy extended to me by former antagonists, but now ever dear friends. From the very inception of the park movement, you have been the

most active and industrious person connected with the enterprise. You have done more work and put more thought on the great enterprise than any member or person connected with the park. From this fact I have never failed to agree with you in almost every suggestion or act connected with your management, and I really feel from association and work you are now the most competent member to be the permanent Chairman of the Commission. I, therefore, tender to you my resignation as Chairman of the Commission and request that you assume all the duties of the office as permanent Chairman.

Lee, however, remained on the Commission as the Confederate representative and continued to work on behalf of the park until his death.[28]

On October 3, 1903, Regina passed away. Her loss was unbearable for Lee whose heart would never recover. Sensing more strongly than ever his own mortality, the general devoted his remaining energies entirely to honor the veterans who had fought in the Civil War, especially those who wore the gray. In 1904 he replaced the late John Brown Gordon of Georgia as commander of the United Confederate Veterans, a post in which he would serve until his own death four years later.

In May 1908, veterans of Michael Lawler's Union brigade, the very unit which pierced the lines at Railroad Redoubt on May 22, 1863, assembled in Vicksburg for a reunion and invited General Lee to attend. Although his health was broken, Lee traveled to Vicksburg where he arrived on Thursday, May 21, and stayed at the home of his friend and fellow commissioner Captain Rigby. The general spent Friday in the company of Union veterans and that afternoon delivered a "fervid and patriotic" address in which he praised the bravery of his former enemies and extolled the spirit of nationalism which characterized America in the early twentieth century.[29]

Having spoke with energy and passion, he was emotionally and physically drained by day's end. Still, Lee agreed to pose for a picture, but urged the photographer to hurry as he "felt badly" and wanted to return to the city. That evening, following a light dinner, a severe attack of indigestion crippled the general who was placed in bed and Dr. J. A. K. Birchett was called to the Rigby home on Cherry Street.[30]

Upon examination, the doctor realized that Lee was a very sick man and administered medication. The patient responded to the treatment and appeared to improve over the next few days. Scores of people visited with the general during this time to wish him well and offered their prayers for his rapid recovery. But the Angel of Death came. On Tuesday, May 26, his condition grew worse and deteriorated rapidly. That night he slipped into a coma from which he never awoke. At 6 a.m. on Thursday, May 28, the gallant warrior breathed his last. The Vicksburg paper lamented his loss in headlines which read "General S.D. Lee's Great Heart Beats No More. Commander-in-Chief U.C.V. Is Dead."[31]

"Everywhere the death of Gen. Lee is the sole topic of conversation in Vicksburg today," noted the paper. "All are united that the loss of the great and good man is irreparable." Schools and business throughout the city closed, buildings were draped in black, flags were lowered to half-staff, and everywhere men, women, and children, even those who knew him not, cried over the loss of this "simple, large-hearted, modest, God-fearing man." The Vicksburg paper eulogized, "It was another great man, Robert E. Lee, who said that the word 'duty' was the greatest in the language. General Stephen D. Lee lived up to that word in the very highest degree. His whole life, and it was a long life, was one of unceasing devotion to duty, and he performed what ever duty was allotted to him with his whole heart, and mind and soul concentrated in the performance."[32]

The body of General Lee, dressed in civilian clothes and placed in a black coffin that was covered by the Stars and Bars of the Confederacy, was made available for public display at the park office at 100 North Cherry Street where it laid in state until Friday morning. Hundreds of mourners, many of whom were veterans of the Blue and Gray paraded by his coffin as if on review and paid their final respects to a man who was in every respect their friend. Reflective of the outpouring of grief was the announcement of florists throughout Vicksburg that "they had sold all available flowers and could fill no more orders."[33]

At 7:20 a.m. on Friday, May 29, three extra cars attached to the regular train left Vicksburg and carried the remains of General Lee trough Jackson to Meridian and on to Columbus. Along the route the tracks were covered with flowers and everywhere people from across the state gathered to catch a glimpse of the train that carried the state's most noble soul on his final journey. His duty faithfully performed, Stephen D. Lee was tenderly laid to rest alongside his beloved wife in Friendship Cemetery.

Vicksburg NMP

This statue of Stephen D. Lee stands on the grounds of Vicksburg National Military Park along the portion of the defense line his gallant troops occupied during the siege.

In recognition of Lee's life of service to his nation and the American people, his fellow commissioner William T. Rigby had sought to erect and dedicate within the general's lifetime a monument of bronze on the grounds of the battlefield at Vicksburg. Without Lee's knowledge, Rigby solicited contributions making himself the first donation. Even President Theodore Roosevelt made a financial contribution.[34]

Fortunately, Captain Rigby had taken advantage of Lee's visit to Vicksburg in May and asked the general to pose for a photograph on the spot from which he watched the charge against Railroad Redoubt. Lee went to the very place, stood erect with the posture of a soldier, and with his head turned slightly to the north, the fire of younger days returned to his eyes for the final time. Lee passed away four days after the photograph was taken.

The photo taken that day was the basis for the monument that now stands on the grounds of Vicksburg National Military Park and was dedicated on June 11, 1909. The monument of stone and bronze serves as a reminder of courage, duty, honor, and stands as a enduring symbol of the love and respect that former enemies had for men turned brothers. It is a fitting tribute to the man who had worked tirelessly by example in the post war era to take Yankees and Rebels and make them Americans and of his efforts to make an American shrine that would honor them all.[35]

Epilogue

Although the siege of Vicksburg ended on July 4, 1863, the lives of those who survived the ordeal continued to unfold. It may interest the reader to learn the individual destiny which awaited the actors—large and small—who participated in the Vicksburg drama and were the subjects of these essays. Here are but a few:

Brig. Gen. John E. Smith, whose Union brigade splashed across Little Bayou Pierre at Askamalla Ford on May 2, 1863, and led the advance across Big Bayou Pierre at Grindstone Ford the following day, was a native of Switzerland. (His father had served as an officer under Napoleon at Waterloo.) Although a jeweler and goldsmith by trade, Smith was active in Galena, Illinois, politics and it was he who recommended Grant to Governor Richard Yates stating he "ought to know how to organize a regiment." He exhibited a penchant for military life and developed into a solid combat officer. Elevated to division command, he served with great credit in this capacity during the Atlanta campaign and the March to the Sea. At war's end he was in command of the District of Western Tennessee. Brevetted major general of volunteers for his wartime service, Smith remained in the army and was appointed colonel of the Twenty-seventh Infantry. Brevetted brigadier and major general, Smith retired in 1881 and spent the remainder of his life in Chicago.

Col. Francis M. Cockrell. Considered by many to be the finest combat brigade in either army during the Vicksburg campaign, Cockrell's Missourians helped avert disaster along the banks of Kennison Creek on May 3, 1863, as John Bowen's Confederate force, that had evacuated Grand Gulf, withdrew north of Big Black River. Born in Warrensburg, Missouri, in 1834, Cockrell was a lawyer by training who entered the Missouri State Guard as a private in 1861. Once in Confederate service, he rose rapidly through the ranks and became colonel of the Second Missouri Infantry. Though he had no formal military training, Cockrell was a stern disciplinarian who developed into a combat officer without peer. During the Vicksburg campaign, his brigade fought at Grand Gulf, Port Gibson, Champion Hill, and Big Black River Bridge, and manned the city's defenses during the siege. Exchanged almost immediately after the city's surrender, Cockrell was promoted to brigadier general on July 18 and remained in brigade command for the duration of the war. His daring and bravery on the field of battle earned him the Thanks of Congress on May 23, 1864. During his service, he gained the dubious distinction of being wounded five times and was captured on three occasions. Cockrell resumed the practice of law in Missouri following the Civil War and in 1874 was elected to the United States Senate. A life-long Democrat, he served in the Senate for thirty years and played a prominent role in gaining Southern support for the establishment of Vicksburg National Military Park. Upon his retirement from the Senate, President Theodore Roosevelt appointed him to the Interstate Commerce Commission on which he served from 1905 until 1910. Cockrell died in 1915 and is buried in his hometown.

Sgt. Osborn Oldroyd. Only 19 when he mustered into service on October 15, 1861, Oldroyd was a sergeant in Company E, Twentieth Ohio Infantry during the Vicksburg campaign. Following the Civil War, he served as steward of the National Soldier's Home in Dayton, Ohio, and pursued with a passion collecting items associated with Abraham Lincoln. In 1884 he and his family moved to Springfield, Illinois, where Oldroyd rented Lincoln's home and operated it as a museum. In 1893, when the home was donated to the State of Illinois, Oldroyd moved his

family and Lincoln collection to Washington where he lived in the
Petersen House, the building in which the sixteenth president died. He
operated the Petersen House as a museum until 1925 when he sold his
3,000-item Oldroyd Lincoln Memorial Collection to the United States
government for $50,000. A prolific writer, Oldroyd wrote *The Lincoln
Memorial: Album-Immortelles* (1882), *The Words of Lincoln* (1895), *The
Assassination of Lincoln* (1901), and *The Poet's Lincoln* (1915). Perhaps
his most enduring work is *A Soldier's Story of the Siege of Vicksburg*
(1885).

   Col. Manning Force. The hard-fighting commander of the Twentieth
Ohio Infantry whose troops captured the bridge across Big Black River
on May 3, 1863, before it could be destroyed by retreating Confederate
soldiers, was born on December 17, 1824, in Washington, D.C. where his
father, Peter Force, worked on compiling his famous work *American
Archives*. From a young age, Manning Force desired a military life and
prepared for West Point. Instead, he ended up at Harvard and graduated
from its law school in 1848. Following graduation, he moved to
Cincinnati, was admitted to the Ohio bar, and practiced law until
mustered into service as major of the Twentieth Ohio at the outbreak of
hostilities in 1861. Force saw action at Fort Donelson, Shiloh, and
throughout the Vicksburg campaign and was awarded the XVII Corps
Gold Medal for his service. Elevated to brigadier general, he commanded
a brigade in the Atlanta campaign and was awarded the Medal of Honor.
The citation reads: "Charged upon the enemy's works, and after their
capture defended his position against assaults of the enemy until he was
severely wounded." (It was a facial wound that disfigured him for life.)
Brevetted major general of volunteers, Force declined numerous civil
and military posts and returned to his law practice. Elevated to the bench,
he served first in the common pleas court and later on the superior court.
From 1887 until his death in 1899, he was the commandant of the Ohio
Soldiers' and Sailors' Home in Sandusky, Ohio. Throughout the
post-war period Force wrote extensively about law, history, and
archaeology, including *From Fort Henry to Corinth* (1881) which is
included in the ever-valuable Scribner's Campaigns of the Civil War
series.

Alice Shirley. Although born in Vicksburg on May 2, 1844, Alice Eugenia Shirley was a staunch Unionist. (Her parents were both from New England.) While attending the Central Female Institute in Clinton, she witnessed Union Maj. Gen. James B. McPherson's XVII Corps enter town on May 13, 1863. Her father, Judge James Shirley, had just arrived by rail from Vicksburg to take her home for safety. But as the tracks were destroyed by Federal soldiers, Judge Shirley left her with relatives in Clinton and he walked back to Vicksburg. Following the surrender of Vicksburg, Alice returned to her home where she found her father ill.

Shirley was a student at the Central Female Institute in Clinton when troops of McPherson's XVII Corps marched into town on May 13, 1863, en route to Jackson. *Vicksburg NMP*

(Judge Shirley died on August 9 at the age of 69 from the effects of heat exhaustion suffered during the long walk from Clinton.) During the occupation of Vicksburg, Alice caught the eye of Union Chaplain John Eaton who was in the city serving as general superintendent of freedmen. The two "eloped up the river" and were married in Toledo, Ohio, on September 29, 1864. Eaton was brevetted brigadier general in 1865, but resigned from the army the following year. He became editor of the *Memphis Post*, and later served as superintendent of schools in Tennessee. In 1870 he was appointed by President Grant as U.S. Commissioner of Education, a post he held until 1886, and later was U.S. superintendent of schools in Puerto Rico. General Eaton died in 1906 (prior to publication of his memoirs) and Alice followed on June 5, 1927. They now rest in Arlington National Cemetery. Her childhood home withstood the ravages of siege and occupation, and is today the only surviving wartime structure in Vicksburg National Military Park.

Lt. Col. James H. Wilson. The man who gleefully delivered the note relieving John McClernand of command of the XIII Corps then in the trenches at Vicksburg, was born in 1837 in Shawneetown, Illinois. Referred to as the "most distinguished" of the "boy generals," Wilson graduated from West Point in 1860, standing sixth in a class of forty-one cadets. Although he took part in the reduction of Ft. Pulaski in Georgia and served on the staff of Maj. Gen. George B. McClellan at Antietam, Wilson's rise to fame and glory came through his association with U. S. Grant, whose staff he joined in October 1862. After the siege of Vicksburg, he was promoted to brigadier general and given a combat command. Energetic, bold, and talented, Wilson rose to command the cavalry in Sherman's Military Division of the Mississippi and led his horse soldiers during the Atlanta campaign and in response to Hood's invasion of Tennessee. In the spring of 1865, he defeated what was left of Nathan Bedford Forrest's proud command at Selma then swung east into Georgia as the war came to a close. Although mustered out of service in 1870 to pursue railroad construction, Wilson returned to duty as a major general of volunteers during the war with Spain. He also served during the Boxer Rebellion in China. A prolific writer, his most famous work, the two-volume *Under the Old Flag*, was published in 1912. He died in 1925 and was survived by only three other men who held full-rank commissions during the Civil War: Nelson Miles, John R. Brooke, and Adelbert Ames.

Charles A. Dana, the man sent to "spy" on Grant, was a newspaperman by profession. Born in Hindsdale, New Hampshire, on August 8, 1819, Dana served as managing editor of Horace Greeley's *New York Tribune* (a leading organ of anti-slavery sentiment) from 1848-1862. He resigned at Greeley's request due to a difference in their views on the proper conduct of the war. Appointed as assistant secretary of war, Dana was won over by Grant and the positive reports he sent Washington were a major factor in the decision to retain the general in command of the Army of the Tennessee. He returned to the newspaper business following the Civil War and organized the *New York Sun* of which he served as editor until his death 1897. (During the presidency of U. S. Grant, Dana was critical of civil maladministration. In July 1873, the administration attempted to charge him with libel and take him from New York to Washington to stand trial in police court without a jury, but the warrant was refused by Samuel Blatchford, U. S. District Court judge for the Southern District of New York.) Dana authored *The Life of Ulysses S. Grant* (1868) and *Recollections of the Civil War*, which was not published until after his death.

Rear Adm. David Dixon Porter is one of the most distinguished naval officers in American history. Born in 1813, the Pennsylvania native was son of Commodore David Porter, and began his naval career when only ten years of age. In 1827 he was commissioned a midshipman in the Mexican navy and two years later joined the United States Navy. Thus, by the outbreak of the Civil War, Porter had already served on the high seas for more than thirty-five years. Instrumental in securing control of the Mississippi River, the luster to Porter's reputation gained during the Vicksburg campaign was somewhat tarnished by association with Maj. Gen. Nathaniel Banks during the Red River campaign in 1864 that proved an embarrassment to U. S. forces. Given command of the North Atlantic Blockading Squadron, his forces assisted in the reduction of Fort Fisher in North Carolina. Following the Civil War, he was named superintendent of the United States Naval Academy, a position he held from 1865-1869. Promoted full admiral in 1870, he served as head of the Board of Inspection and Survey from 1877 until his death on February

13, 1891. A prolific writer, in addition to his *Memoirs* (1875), Porter wrote *Incidents and Anecdotes of the Civil War* (1885) and *The Naval History of the Civil War* (1886). He is buried in Arlington National Cemetery, a short distance from the Custis-Lee mansion. Nearby is the final resting place of his grandson and namesake, Maj. Gen. David Dixon Porter.

Cmdr. George Mifflin Bache, the commander of the ill-fated gunboat *Cincinnati*, was Benjamin Franklin's great-great-grandson. Born in Washington, D.C. on November 12, 1840, Bache was the son of Commander George Mifflin Bache who won renown with the United States Coast Survey and perished in a gale off Cape Hatteras on September 8, 1846. The younger Bache entered the U. S. Naval Academy in 1857 and graduated four years later at the commencement of active operations. During the Civil War, Bache served on *Jamestown*, *Powhatan*, and *New Ironsides* prior to taking command of *Cincinnati*. In 1864, he commanded a division of sailors during the assault on Fort Fisher in North Carolina, where he was wounded. Following the Civil War, Bache served on *Sacramento* and commanded *Juniata*. Retired from service in 1875, he died in the city of his birth on February 11, 1896. On November 14, 1942, DD 470 was commissioned USS *Bache*. The ship, sponsored by Bache's daughter, received eight battle stars for her service in World War II.

Rev. William W. Lord. Returning to the Confederacy after the fall of Vicksburg, Reverend Lord and his family went first to New Orleans, then on to Mobile, and eventually settled in Charleston, South Carolina. There he continued to preach the gospel to citizens and soldiers alike until February 1865, when the Federals occupied Charleston and the family fled inland to Winnsboro. After the war the Lords returned to Charleston where William served as rector of St. Paul's Episcopal Church until 1869. Beckoned to return to Vicksburg, Reverend Lord and his family returned to the Hill City where he became rector of the newly established Trinity Episcopal Church. (The magnificent edifice in which he led worship services still stands and its beauty is enhanced by six Tiffany windows.) In 1880, at the age of 62, William Lord finally returned to his native state, New York, and spent the remainder of his life at Cooperstown where he died on April 22, 1907.

Confederate Secretary of War James A. Seddon was born in Falmouth, Virginia, on July 13, 1815. Following graduation from the University of Virginia, Seddon practiced law in Richmond where he lived for a time in the building that later served as the White House of the Confederacy. Elected to Congress in 1845, poor health caused him to decline a bid for reelection. However, he returned to Congress in 1849, but continued poor health restricted him to just a single term. (One of his secretaries wrote of Seddon, that he resembled "an exhumed corpse after a month's interment.") Retiring to his estate, Sabot Hill, Seddon remained active politically and turned down the nomination to run as James Buchanan's running mate on the Democratic ticket in 1856. He was a member of the failed Washington Peace Conference in 1861 that was the last attempt at conciliation on the slavery question prior to the outbreak of hostilities between the states. Following the secession of Virginia, he was appointed to the Confederate Congress where he was a political ally of President Jefferson Davis. When George Randolph resigned as secretary of war in November 1862, Davis appointed Seddon to the post.

The Virginian quickly demonstrated that he was one of the administration's most capable members, though one critic claimed that his "principal effect was a vast capacity for indecision." Faced with an almost impossible situation, Seddon was never able to overcome the difficult challenges that faced his department. As the Congress and nation lost confidence in Davis, they too lost confidence in Seddon who resigned on February 6, 1865, and returned to his home in Goochland County. Although he took the oath of amnesty in May, he was arrested and imprisoned at Fort Pulaski, Georgia, along with Archibald Campbell, Robert M. T. Hunter (secretary of state), and George A. Trenholm (secretary of the treasury). In the aftermath of war, Seddon returned to the practice of law and the management of his plantations in Virginia and Louisiana. He died in 1880 and is interred in Richmond's Hollywood Cemetery within a few feet of two U.S. presidents: John Tyler and James Monroe.

Brig. Gen. William H. "Red" Jackson. The Confederate cavalry commander whose attempt failed to capture Sherman's artillery train during the siege of Jackson was a native of Tennessee. Born in Paris on October 1, 1835, Jackson stood 38 out of 49 cadets in the West Point

Class of 1856. After service on the frontier and in Indian fighting, he resigned in 1861 and offered his sword to the Confederacy. Wounded at Belmont, he was promoted colonel and given command of the First Tennessee Cavalry which he led during Van Dorn's Holly Springs Raid in December 1862. Elevated to brigadier general, he served in Mississippi throughout the Vicksburg/Jackson campaign and during the Meridian Expedition in 1864. Given command of the cavalry corps of the Army of Mississippi, which he led during the Atlanta campaign, Jackson was attached to Hood's command during the advance on Nashville. Following the war, he lived at "Belle Meade," near Nashville where he bred thoroughbred horses. Sporting scarlet and gold colors, his championship horses included "Iroquois," the first American-foaled winner of the English Derby (1881).

Maj. Gen. John Grubb Parke. The Coatesville, Pennsylvania, native was born on September 22, 1827. At the time of graduation from West Point in 1849, Parke stood second in a class of 43 cadets and entered the prestigious Topographical Engineers with which he served until the outbreak of the Civil War. Promoted to brigadier general, Parke was given command of a brigade that he led during Ambrose Burnside's North Carolina Expedition in 1862. Elevated to division command, Parke continued to demonstrate that he was an extremely competent troop commander. He served as Burnside's chief of staff during the Maryland campaign and at Fredericksburg, in which action Burnside commanded the army. Parke went on to command the IX Corps during the Vicksburg campaign and in the operations around Knoxville later in the year. In the spring of 1864 he again served as Burnside's chief of staff, but following the debacle at The Crater at Petersburg, Parke was given command of the IX Corps. In the winter of 1865, the Pennsylvanian commanded the Army of the Potomac while George G. Meade was on leave, during which time Parke successfully repulsed the last tactical assault of the Army of Northern Virginia at Fort Steadman on March 25. Brevetted major general for his service, Parke remained in the army rising to become assistant chief of engineers. His final two years in the army (1887-89) were spent at West Point, where his career began, serving as superintendent of the United States Military Academy. He died in Washington, D.C. on December 16, 1900, at the age of 73 and is buried in Philadelphia.

We now come to the two men who best reflect the "triumph & defeat" that was Vicksburg:

John C. Pemberton. The Pennsylvanian in gray who commanded the Army of Vicksburg and surrendered the city on July 4, 1863, was immediately paroled and exchanged. For all intent and purpose his military career was destroyed. Although he continued in Confederate service until the end of the war, Pemberton did so at a lower rank, that of lieutenant colonel. Following the war, he eventually returned to the city of his birth, Philadelphia, and attempted to forget the obloquy from which he could never escape. In 1874, Joseph E. Johnston published his *Narrative of Military Operations* in which he placed the blame for the loss of Vicksburg squarely at Pemberton's feet. Spurred into action by this savage critique of his generalship, Pemberton wrote a lengthy rebuttal for publication. As fate would have it, Pemberton's account of the Vicksburg campaign failed to get published in his lifetime and the pages of his manuscript lay forgotten and collected dust until it surfaced for sale at a flea market in Loveland, Ohio, in 1995. Found among the papers of former Confederate general Marcus J. Wright, who helped compile *War of the Rebellion: The Official Records of the Union and Confederate Armies*, Pemberton's manuscript was purchased by Civil War collector Alan Hoeweler. Edited by David M. Smith of the Cincinnati Civil War Round Table, *Compelled to Appear in Print* was finally published in 1999. People can now read and assess for themselves the actions of John Pemberton during the decisive campaign for Vicksburg, one which sealed the fate of the Southern Confederacy.

Ulysses S. Grant. The Ohio-born commander of the Union Army of the Tennessee, which triumphed at Vicksburg, needs no further acclamation here as his achievements are known to all who read these pages. Following the Civil War, Grant returned only once to "the scene of his greatest victory" when he visited Vicksburg in 1880. "An immense concourse of people gathered on Washington street in front of the Lamadrid house," reported the *Vicksburg Daily Herald* on April 12. "There was hardly standing room on any of the public thoroughfares in the vicinity of the building. The main hall of the hotel was crowded to its utmost capacity, and a larger or more enthusiastic gathering we have never seen assembled in this city." Speaking on behalf of the citizens of Vicksburg, William McCardle welcomed Grant:

> There was a time when your presence here was less welcome than it is to-day. You were then, with a large retinue of your friends, anxious to make a visit to this city, and those of us who were then present were equally anxious that you should forgo that pleasure. For forty-seven weary days and nights, beneath the pitiless hail of shot and shell, we sought to avoid having you with us, but your attentions were so pressing and persistent that we finally concluded to receive you.

The former president, always mindful of his soldiers' sacrifice, visited Vicksburg National Cemetery to pay his respects to the gallant men who perished during the campaign. When asked if he would like to see the battlefield, he replied, "No thanks, I've been there before."

Of all the other people whose names have become synonymous with Vicksburg, the most significant (yet least publically appreciated) is saved for last:

William T. Rigby. Born in Red Oak Grove (near present-day Stanwood), Iowa, on November 3, 1840, he was the first child born to Washington Augustus and Lydia Barr Rigby. The oldest of four children, Will, as he was called by family and friends, was anxious to enlist in the Union army following the firing on Ft. Sumter. His father, who was opposed to the war on religious grounds, forbade him to join. Although a company was raised locally, Will lamented, "Father gave them $20 instead of letting me go. I guess that is more than I am worth so the company does not lose any thing." Finally in July 1862, he gained his father's consent and entered service as a second lieutenant in Company B, Twenty-fourth Iowa Infantry. During the course of his service he saw action at Vicksburg, on the Red River campaign, and in the Shenandoah Valley, and rose to captain in command of the company. Following the Civil War, Rigby attended Cornell College in Mt. Vernon, Iowa, from which he received his diploma in 1869. For the next thirty years he worked on the family farm and in the banking business. Then in 1895, at the urging of his brother-in-law John F. Merry, Rigby helped organize the Vicksburg National Military Park Association of which he became secretary. Upon passage of the park bill four years later, Rigby was appointed to the three-man commission charged with oversight of operations. Along with his wife, Eva Cattron Rigby and their youngest child, a daughter named Grace, Will moved to Vicksburg where he established the park's office—which doubled as their residence. For the final thirty years of his life, he labored with boundless energy to make Vicksburg the finest of the national military parks. During his tenure as resident commissioner, then later as chairman, Rigby secured the necessary land that encompassed the Union and Confederate lines, contracted for the construction of roads and bridges, conducted exhaustive correspondence with siege veterans to ensure the accuracy of tablet inscriptions and their placement on the field, and worked with state legislatures North and South to provide impressive monuments honoring the men in blue and gray who had struggled at Vicksburg in 1863. On May 10,1929, he breathed his last and is interred in Vicksburg National Cemetery along with his comrades in arms whose sacrifice helped to shape the nation he so faithfully served as citizen and soldier.

*   *   *

Vicksburg National Military Park

The park in development of which Rigby and Lee devoted their very souls was the fifth Civil War battlefield to be set aside in perpetuity by Congress and thus established as only the seventh national park. (Today, our national park system consists of almost 400 units.) Known as the "art park of the world," Vicksburg boasts of 1,330 monuments, markers, tablets, and plaques that make it one of the more densely monumented battlefields in the world. Although many changes have occurred in the years that have passed since these veterans of the siege managed the park, their stamp on the landscape is indelible and will serve to inspire future stewards of this national shrine. In recent years, Congress has expanded the interpretive mandate of the park to include the history of Vicksburg under Union occupation during the Civil War through Reconstruction. Congress has also authorized expansion of the park to include the remaining vestige of the Williams-Grant Canal across the Mississippi River from Vicksburg in Madison Parish, Louisiana, and the addition of the building that served as the headquarters of Confederate Lt. Gen. John

C. Pemberton. It was in the hallowed rooms of this building that Pemberton, in the company of his subordinate officers, made the fateful decision to surrender Vicksburg to Grant. The National Park Service is currently working with a network of partners, public and private, to enhance preservation and interpretation of sites along the Vicksburg Campaign Trail. At places such as Port Gibson, Raymond, and Champion Hill land on which the lifeblood of a nation was spilled is currently being acquired through this partnership and will be preserved for future generations to enjoy and enable visitors to follow in the footsteps of the soldiers in blue and gray who struggled for control of the Mississippi River.

The triumph & defeat that was the Vicksburg campaign is an American story the pages of which continue to be written through the evolution of Vicksburg National Military Park. As the park, established to commemorate American valor, enters its second century of service to the nation, may those entrusted with stewardship of its unique resources remain ever faithful to the legacy of Stephen D. Lee and William T. Rigby. May they always honor the memory of those who struggled here, citizens and soldiers alike, whose sacrifice in the crucible of war forged a national identity that binds those of North and South and make us unique among the peoples who inhabit the earth.

Notes

Chapter One: Beyond the Rubicon: The Union Army Secures its Beachhead on Mississippi Soil

1. Michael Ballard, *Pemberton: A Biography* (Jackson, 1991), p. 140.

2. Diary of Israel Ritter, Regimental Files, 24th Iowa Infantry, Vicksburg National Military Park.

3. Thomas B. Marshall, *History of the Eighty-third Ohio Volunteer Infantry: The Greyhound Regiment* (Cincinnati, 1912), p. 76. Port Gibson is nestled along the left bank of Little Bayou Pierre. Big Bayou Pierre, which flows north of town, confluences with Little Bayou Pierre west of Port Gibson to form Bayou Pierre. All three streams are referenced in this essay.

4. Mark M. Boatner, *The Civil War Dictionary* (New York, 1959), pp. 417-418. Benjamin Grubb Humphreys commanded the Twenty-first Mississippi Infantry that served as part of Brig. Gen. William Barksdale's Brigade in the Army of Northern Virginia. On July 2, 1863, Humphreys assumed command of the brigade when Barksdale was mortally wounded and captured at Gettysburg. Promoted to brigadier general on August 14, 1863, he led the brigade until he too was wounded at Berryville, Virginia, in September 1864. Following the Civil War, Humphreys was elected governor of Mississippi and served from October 1865, until he was ejected from office by Federal military authorities in June 1868. He died in 1882 and is buried in Wintergreen Cemetery in Port Gibson.

5. Brig. Gen. Edward D. Tracy had been killed in the battle of Port Gibson on May 1 while in command of the Alabama brigade. Brig. Gen. Stephen D. Lee was given command of the brigade on May 2.

6. Diary of Henry S. Keene, Regimental Files, 6th Wisconsin Battery, Vicksburg National Military Park.

7. Ephraim McD. Anderson, *Memoirs: Historical and Personal; including the Campaigns of the First Missouri Confederate Brigade*, edited by Edwin C. Bearss (Dayton, 1972), p. 302.

8. *Ibid.*, pp. 302-303.

9. *Ibid.*, pp. 303-304.

10. U. S. War Department, *The War of the Rebellion: The Official Records of the Union and Confederate Armies*, 128 vols. (Washington, D.C., 1890-1901), series I, vol. 24, part 1, p. 645. Hereinafter cited as *OR*. All references are to series I unless otherwise noted; Edwin C. Bearss, *The Vicksburg Campaign*, 3 vols. (Dayton, 1985-1986), vol. 2, p. 427; Osborn H. Oldroyd, *A Soldier's Story of the Siege of Vicksburg* (Springfield, 1885), p. 6.

11. Ulysses S. Grant, *Personal Memoirs of Ulysses S. Grant*, 2 vols. (New York, 1885), vol. 1, p. 410.

12. John Y. Simon, ed., *The Papers of Ulysses S. Grant*, 30 vols. (Carbondale, 1967-2006), vol. 8, pp. 132, 155.

13. *Ibid.*, p. 148.

Chapter Two: Blitzkrieg: Grant Style

1. This rail line had been the target of a Union cavalry raid led by Col. Benjamin Grierson whose horse soldiers had ridden south out of La Grange, Tennessee, on April 17. On April 24, the daring cavalrymen managed to cut the line at Newton Station, between Jackson and Meridian. They then raced to the security of Union lines at Baton Rouge, Louisiana, where they arrived on May 2, having ridden more than 600 miles. Grant learned of the success of the raid through Southern newspapers when he arrived in Port Gibson on May 2. Unwilling to run the risk that the damage inflicted by the raiders was superficial, he determined to knock the railroad out of commission, isolate his opponent in Vicksburg, and approach the city from the east. For a detailed account of the raid, see Chapter 3, "Playing Smash With the Railroads: The Story of Grierson's Raid," *Triumph & Defeat*, vol. 1.

2. *OR* vol. 24, pt. 3, p. 268.

3. Benjamin F. Stevenson, *Letters From the Army* (Cincinnati, 1884), pp. 218-219; William H. Bentley, *History of the 77th Illinois Volunteer Infantry, Sept. 2, 1862,—July 10, 1865* (Peoria, 1883), p. 139.

4. Thomas H. Bringhurst and Frank Swigart, *History of the Forty-sixth Regiment Indiana Volunteer Infantry September, 1861—September, 1865* (Logansport, 1888), p. 59; Diary of Henry Clay Warmoth, Letters and Diaries Files, Vicksburg National Military Park.

5. *OR* vol. 24, pt. 3, p. 285.

6. Marshall, *History of Eighty-third Ohio*, p. 77.

7. John A. Bering and Thomas Montgomery, *History of the Forty-eighth Ohio Vet. Vol. Inf.* (Hillsboro, 1880), p. 81.

8. Diary of William B. Halsey, Regimental Files, 72d Ohio Infantry, Vicksburg National Military Park.

9. Ezra J. Warner, *Generals in Gray* (Baton Rouge, 1959), pp. 118-119.

10. The Ron Sheffield Collection, copy contained in Bearss, *The Vicksburg Campaign*, vol. 2, p. 482.

11. Oldroyd, *A Soldier's Story*, pp. 16-17.

12. *OR* vol. 24, pt. 1, p. 715.

13. Grant, *Memoirs*, vol. 1, p. 454n; Bearss, *The Vicksburg Campaign*, vol. 2, p. 514.

Chapter Three: The National Colors Are Restored O'er the Capitol

1. *OR* vol. 24, pt. 1, p. 147.

2. *Ibid.*

3. Diary of William H. Raynor, Regimental Files, 56th Ohio Infantry, Vicksburg National Military Park.

4. Ezra J. Warner, *Generals in Blue* (Baton Rouge, 1964), p. 455.

5. Diary of Henry S. Keene, Regimental Files, 6th Wisconsin Battery, Vicksburg National Military Park.

6. John Eaton, *Grant, Lincoln and the Freedmen* (New York, 1907), p. 78.

7. *Ibid.*, pp. 79-80.

8. Warren Grabau, *Ninety-eight Days: A Geographer's View of the Vicksburg Campaign* (Knoxville, 2000), p. 242.

9. *OR* vol. 24, pt. 1, p. 215.

10. S. C. Beck, "A True Sketch of His Army Life," Letters and Diaries File, Vicksburg National Military Park; Diary of Henry S. Keene; Diary of Richard C.

Hunt, Regimental Files, 20th Ohio Infantry, Vicksburg National Military Park; Oldroyd, *A Soldier's Story*, p. 20.

11. Aaron Dunbar and Harvey M. Trimble, *History of the Ninety-third Regiment Illinois Volunteer Infantry from Organization to Muster Out* (Chicago, 1898), p. 25.

12. *OR* vol. 24, pt. 1, p. 638.

13. Robert J. Burdette, *The Drums of the 47th* (Indianapolis, 1914), p. 37; Byron Bryner, *Bugle Echoes: The Story of Illinois 47th Infantry* (Springfield, 1905), p. 79.

14. Burdette, *Drums*, p. 49.

15. *Ibid.*

16. Bryner, *Bugle Echoes*, p. 79.

17. Burdette, *Drums*, p. 49.

18. *OR* vol. 24, pt. 1, p. 766.

19. Letter, Lt. Col. Jefferson Brumback to his wife, Kat, May 20, 1863, Regimental Files, 95th Ohio Infantry, Vicksburg National Military Park.

20. Burdette, *Drums*, pp. 57-58; Charles B. Clark and Roger B. Bowen, *University Recruits—Company C, 12th Iowa Infantry Regiment U.S.A. 1861-1866* (Elverson, 1991), p. 176.

21. Diary of Henry S. Keene.

22. *Ibid.*

23. *Ibid.*

24. *Ibid.*

25. Wilbur F. Crummer, *With Grant at Fort Donelson, Shiloh and Vicksburg* (Oak Park, 1915), pp. 100-101.

26. Oldroyd, *A Soldier's Story*, p. 21.

27. Sylvanus Cadwallader, ed. by Benjamin P. Thomas, *Three Years with Grant as Recalled by War Correspondent Sylvanus Cadwallader* (New York, 1955), pp. 73-74.

28. *OR* vol. 24, pt. 1, p. 772.

29. Oldroyd, *A Soldier's Story*, p. 21.

30. Diary of Henry S. Keene; Diary of George W. Huff, Regimental Files, 80th Ohio Infantry, Vicksburg National Military Park; Diary of Enoch Williams, Letters and Diaries Files, Vicksburg National Military Park.

31. Bryner, *Bugle Echoes*, pp. 80-81.

32. William T. Sherman, *Memoirs of General William T. Sherman*, 2 vols. (New York, 1875), vol. 1, p. 350.

33. Charles A. Willison, *A Boy's Service with the 76th Ohio* (Menasha, 1908), p. 53.

34. *Ibid.*, p. 53; *Official Roster of the Soldiers of the State of Ohio in the War of the Rebellion and in the War With Mexico*, 12 vols. (Akron, Cincinnati, Norwalk, 1886-1895), vol. 6, p. 291.

35. *OR* vol. 24, pt. 1; Willison, *A Boy's Service*, p. 53.

36. Bryner, *Bugle Echoes*, p. 82.

37. Grant, *Memoirs*, vol. 1, p. 446.

Chapter Four: John A. McClernand: Fighting Politician

1. Richard Kiper, *Major General John Alexander McClernand: Politician in Uniform* (Kent, Ohio, 1999), p. xii.

2. On June 23, 1863, McClernand notified President Abraham Lincoln that "I have been relieved for an omission of my adjutant. Hear me." *OR* vol. 24, pt. 1, p. 158.

3. John Fiske, *The Mississippi Valley in the Civil War* (New York, 1900), p. 225.

4. Historian Edwin C. Bearss write emphatically of Grant's decision: "The third alternative was full of dangers and risks. Failure in this venture would entail little less than total destruction [of his army]. If it succeeded, however, the gains would be complete and decisive." *The Vicksburg Campaign*, vol. 2, page 21.

5. Letter from McClernand Butler Crawford (great-great-great grandson of General McClernand) to author, May 26, 1998. Quoted by Mr. Crawford from *Past and Present of Sangamon County* (n.p., n.d.).

6. Warner, *Generals in Blue*, pp. 293-294; Boatner, *Civil War Dictionary*, p. 525.

7. *OR* vol. 3, p. 288.

8. *Ibid*, pp. 271, 277; Simon, *The Papers of Ulysses S. Grant*, vol. 3, pp. 138, 148.

9. Grant, *Memoirs*, vol. 1, p. 246; *OR* vol. 7, p. 178.

10. Kiper, *McClernand*, p. 84; *OR* vol. 7, pp. 159-160.

11. *OR* vol. 7, pp. 160, 170-182; Charles A Dana and James H. Wilson, *The Life of Ulysses S. Grant* (Springfield, IL, 1868), p. 65.

12. Grant, *Memoirs*, vol. 1, p. 282; *OR* vol. 10, pt. 1, p. 110.

13. The reader may recall the famous photographs of Lincoln and McClellan taken at the Grove farm during the president's visit to the battlefield near Sharpsburg. A lesser known photograph of the same group shows McClernand standing next to the president, while another photograph taken on the same occasion shows McClernand with President Lincoln and Alan Pinkerton. McClernand was no doubt telling Lincoln, "Give me command Mr. President and I'll whip those Rebs."

Personal conjecture, but McClernand could have done as well as Ambrose Burnside, who Lincoln selected to replace McClellan.

14. The Battle of Chickasaw Bayou occurred on December 27-29, 1862. The principal attack was launched on December 29 during which Sherman's troops were repulsed with ease suffering the loss of 1,776 men compared to only 187 casualties for the Confederates. *OR* vol. 17, pt. 1, p. 671.

15. *OR* vol. 17, pt. 2, p. 553.

16. *OR* vol. 24, pt. 1, pp. 11, 13.

17. Grant, *Memoirs*, vol. 1, pp. 358-359.

18. *OR* vol. 24, pt. 1, pp. 141, 159.

19. Bearss, *The Vicksburg Campaign*, vol. 2, pp. 402-404; *OR* vol. 24, pt. 1, p. 160.

20. Bearss, *The Vicksburg Campaign*, vol. 2, pp. 646-651.

21. *Ibid.*, pp. 680, 686-689; *OR* vol. 24, pt. 1, p. 617. In his memoirs, Grant glosses over McClernand's success at Big Black River, writing simply of the engagement: "The assault was successful. But little resistance was made. The enemy fled from the west bank of the river, burning the bridge behind him and leaving the men and guns on the east side to fall into our hands." (Grant, *Memoirs*, vol. 1, p. 440.)

22. Bearss, *The Vicksburg Campaign*, vol. 3, pp. 773-778.

23. *OR* vol. 24, pt. 1, p. 172.

24. Bearss, *The Vicksburg Campaign*, vol. 3, pp. 862-864.

25. James H. Wilson, *Under the Old Flag* (New York, 1912), pp. 182-183.

26. *OR* vol. 24, pt. 1, pp. 159-161.

27. *Ibid.*, pp. 162-163. Sherman's, and McPherson's notes that follow, is quoted here at length to illustrate the vitriolic nature of the relationship between McClernand and his fellow corps commanders and the lack of harmony, which was detrimental to the army, that existed among Grant's subordinates.

28. *Ibid.*, p. 164.

29. *Ibid.*, pp. 159, 162.

30. Ed Longacre, *From Union Stars to Top Hat* (Harrisburg, PA, 1972), p. 83.

31. *OR* vol. 24, pt. 1, p. 16.

32. *Ibid.*, p. 167.

33. *Ibid.*, pp. 167-168.

34. *Ibid.*, p. 157.

35. *Ibid.*, p. 169.

36. Bearss, *The Vicksburg Campaign*, vol. 1, p. 27.

37. Simon, *The Papers of Ulysses S. Grant*, vol. 7.

38. *OR* vol. 24, pt. 1, p. 172.

39. Kiper, *McClernand*, p. 308.

40. Warner, *Generals in Blue*, p. 293.

Chapter Five: Companion to the Fishes: The Saga of the Gunboat *Cincinnati*

1. Lloyd Lewis, *Sherman: Fighting Prophet* (New York, 1932), p. 252; *OR* vol. 30, pt. 3, p. 694.

2. "Letters of General Thomas Williams, 1862," *American Historical Review*, Vol. XIV (1908-1909), p. 311.

3. *OR* vol. 31, pt. 3, p. 459.

4. *OR* vol. 24, pt. 1, p. 22.

5. David Dixon Porter, *Incidents and Anecdotes of the Civil War* (New York, 1885), pp. 95-96.

6. *New York Times*, January 14, 1863. Quote is taken from Davis' speech to the Mississippi legislature on December 26, 1862.

7. Mary Boykin Chesnut, ed. Ben Ames Williams, *A Diary From Dixie* (Boston, 1949), p. 215.

8. *OR* vol. 1, pp. 500-501.

9. *OR* vol. 53, pp. 491-492.

10. *Official Records of the Union and Confederate Navies in the War of the Rebellion*, 30 volumes (Washington, D.C., 1894-1922), series 1, volume 22, p. 481. Hereinafter cites as *ORN*. All references are to series 1 unless otherwise noted.

11. Kenneth Williams, *Lincoln Finds a General: A Military Study of the Civil War*, 5 volumes (New York, 1949-1959), vol. 3, p. 200.

12. Letter Foote to wife, February 6, 1862, Area File 5, Box 1, RG 45, National Archives and Records Administration.

13. Benjamin F. Cooling, *Forts Henry and Donelson: The Key to the Confederate Heartland* (Knoxville, 1987), p. 106.

14. Letter, Foote to wife, February 6, 1862.

15. *ORN*, vol. 22, p. 544.

16. *Ibid.*, p. 651.

17. *ORN*, vol. 23, p. 17.

18. *Ibid.*, pp. 14, 16, 56.

19. *Ibid.*, pp. 23, 94.

20. *Ibid.*, p. 23.

21. *Ibid.*, pp. 112, 115.

22. *Ibid.*, pp. 104, 166-167, 180-182. On June 17, 1862, during the course of the expedition, *Mound City*, *St. Louis*, *Lexington*, and *Conestoga* came under attack near St. Charles. At the height of the action, a well directed round penetrated the port casemate of *Mound City* and exploded her steam drum which filled the boat with searing steam killing or scalding almost everyone on board. Out of a crew of 175 officers and men, 140 were killed or wounded. It was the single deadliest shot fired during the Civil War.

23. *Ibid.*, p. 259.

24. *Ibid.*, pp. 372, 476.

25. *Ibid.*, p. 470.

26. A. A. Hoehling, *Vicksburg: 47 Days of Siege* (Englewood Cliffs, 1969), p. 64.

27. Diary of A. Hugh Moss, Copy in the Library of Congress dated 1948.

28. *Medal of Honor, The Navy, 1861-1949* (Washington, D.C., 1949), pp. 16, 20, 23, 28, 32, 38.

29. *ORN*, vol. 25, p. 41.

30. William H. Tunnard, *A Southern Record: The History of the Third Regiment Louisiana Infantry* (Baton Rouge, 1866), p. 241; Diary of Emma Balfour, Letters and Diaries Files, Vicksburg National Military Park.

31. Diary of A. Hugh Moss; Tunnard, *A Southern Record*, p. 242.

32. *The Daily Citizen.*

33. *OR* vol. 24, pt. 2, p. 422.

Chapter Six: The Lords of Vicksburg

1. William W. Lord, Jr., "A Child at the Siege of Vicksburg," *Harpers Monthly Magazine*, December 1908.

2. George Downing, unpublished history of Christ Church provided to the author courtesy of Mr. Downing; Boatner, *Civil War Dictionary*, pp. 657-658.

3. *In and About Vicksburg* (Vicksburg, 1890), p. 137.

4. Census Records, 1860, City of Vicksburg, courtesy of Gordon Cotton, Director, Old Court House Museum, Vicksburg.

5. Lida Lord Reed, "A Woman's Experiences During the Siege of Vicksburg," *Century Magazine*, Vol. LXI, April 1901, pp. 923-924.

6. *OR* vol. 18, p. 492.

7. *Vicksburg Daily Whig*, July 1, 1862.

8. Lord, Jr., "A Child at the Siege of Vicksburg." Historically called "Oakland," the Flowers' plantation is known today as "Ceres" and the home in which the Lords stayed is still standing.

9. *Ibid.*

10. *Ibid.* There in conflict among the Lord's children as to how long they stayed at Flowers' plantation and when they returned to Vicksburg. Willy Lord noted that, "I was not long to enjoy the delights of this plantation paradise," indicating an early return to the city. Yet, his older sister Lida recorded "Scared from our home by the gunboat shelling, we had passed the entire winter, an unusually severe one for Mississippi, on a lonely plantation in Warren County." Presented here is the author's own interpretation of their activities.

11. Margaret Lord, *A Journal Kept by Mrs. W. W. Lord* (not published), transcribed copy provided courtesy of Old Court House Museum, Vicksburg, Mississippi. The location of the original journal is no longer known. Flemens Granger, whom Margaret also calls Mr. Fleming in her journal, cannot be positively identified based on the Warren County census for 1860. However, it is believed that he was a relative of Uriah Flowers and that his home was situated on the Flowers' "Oakland" plantation.

12. Reed, "A Woman's Experiences," p. 922.

13. Lord, *A Journal Kept by Mrs. W. W. Lord.*

14. *Ibid.*; Reed, "A Woman's Experiences," p. 922.

15. Reed, "A Woman's Experiences," p. 923; Lord, *A Journal Kept by Mrs. W. W. Lord.*

16. Lord, *A Journal Kept by Mrs. W. W. Lord*; Reed, "A Woman's Experiences," p. 923.

17. Lord, *A Journal Kept by Mrs. W. W. Lord.*

18. *Ibid.*; Diary of Emma Balfour.

19. Reed, "A Woman's Experiences," p. 923.

20. *Ibid.*, p. 923; Lord, Jr., "A Child at the Siege of Vicksburg."

21. Reed, "A Woman's Experiences," p. 924; *General Directory, City of Vicksburg* (Vicksburg, 1860), p. 34; *Herald Directory, City of Vicksburg* (Vicksburg, 1866), pp. 68, 72. Gerard Stites, whose first name is also given as Girard, lived only a few blocks north of the Lords on Locust Street. His residence was situated between Fayette and Jefferson Streets. Mr. Stites worked for Hamilton Wright and Co., cotton factors and commission merchants. He later purchased the business which became known as Stites, Green & Co.

22. Lord, Jr., "A Child at the Siege of Vicksburg;" Reed, "A Woman's Experiences," p. 923.

23. Lord, Jr., "A Child at the Siege of Vicksburg." Mrs. Lord provides the names of the following individuals who also occupied the cave: "Mrs. Stiles, Mrs. Hopkins, Mrs. Houghton, Mrs. Yakes, Mrs. Gunn, Mrs. McRoss, and Mrs. Shaw." Mrs. Hopkins and Mrs. Houghton lived on Locust Street, a few blocks

north of Christ Church. The others cannot be identified. It is important to remember that this information is based on a transcribed copy of Mrs. Lord's original journal. It is very likely that the transcription is incorrect. For example, Mrs. Stiles is probably Mrs. Stites and Mrs. McRoss is probably Mrs. McRae. Mrs. McRae and her daughter Lucy lived on Main Street, three blocks west of the rectory.

24. Lucy McRae Bell, "A Girl's Experience in the Siege of Vicksburg," *Harper's Weekly*, Vol. LVI, June 8, 1912, pp. 12-13.

25. *Ibid.*

26. Diary of Emma Balfour. All of the original windows, save one, were shattered or so badly damaged during the siege that they had to be replaced.

27. Lord, Jr., "A Child at the Siege of Vicksburg."

28. Bell, "A Girl's Experience in the Siege of Vicksburg," pp. 12-13.

29. *Ibid.*

30. Lord, Jr., "A Child at the Siege of Vicksburg;" Reed, "A Woman's Experiences," p. 924.

31. Bell, "A Girl's Experience in the Siege of Vicksburg," pp. 12-13. William Siege Green, the son of Duff and Mary Lake Green, was not destined for a long life as he died on October 24, 1874.

32. Lord, Jr., "A Child at the Siege of Vicksburg."

33. *Ibid.*; Lord, *A Journal Kept by Mrs. W. W. Lord*; Reed, "A Woman's Experiences," p. 924.

34. Lord, Jr., "A Child at the Siege of Vicksburg."

35. Reed, "A Woman's Experiences," p. 924; Lord, Jr., "A Child at the Siege of Vicksburg."

36. Reed, "A Woman's Experiences," p. 925; Lord, Jr., "A Child at the Siege of Vicksburg."

37. *Ibid*, both sources.

38. Diary of Emma Balfour.

39. Reed, "A Woman's Experiences," p. 925.

40. *Ibid.*; Lord, *A Journal Kept by Mrs. W. W. Lord.*

41. Lord, Jr., "A Child at the Siege of Vicksburg;" Reed, "A Woman's Experiences," p. 926.

42. Lord, *A Journal Kept by Mrs. W. W. Lord.*

43. *Ibid.*; Reed, "A Woman's Experiences," p. 927.

44. Lord, Jr., "A Child at the Siege of Vicksburg;" Lord, *A Journal Kept by Mrs. W. W. Lord.*

45. Lord, *A Journal Kept by Mrs. W. W. Lord.*

46. *Ibid.*

47. *Ibid.*

48. *Ibid.*

49. Lord, Jr., "A Child at the Siege of Vicksburg."

Chapter Seven: "I Am Too Late": Joseph E. Johnston and the Army of Relief

1. *OR* vol. 24, pt. 1, p. 215.

2. Boatner, *The Civil War Dictionary*, p. 441.

3. Shelby Foote, *The Civl War: A Narrative*, 3 vols. (New York, 1958-1974), vol. 2, p. 16.

4. *Ibid.*

5. William C. Davis, *Jefferson Davis: The Man and His Hour* (New York, 1991), p. 502.

6. Joseph E. Johnston, *A Narrative of Military Operations During the Late War Between the States* (New York, 1874), p. 152.

7. *OR* vol. 24, pt. 3, p. 807.

8. *OR* vol. 24, pt. 1, p. 215.

9. *OR* vol. 24, pt. 3, p. 870.

10. Bearss, *The Vicksburg Campaign*, vol. 3, p. 530; Edwin C. Bearss and Warren Grabau, *The Battle of Jackson/The Siege of Jackson* (Baltimore, 1981), p. 12.

11. *OR* vol. 24, pt. 3, p. 888.

12. *Ibid.*, p. 892; *OR* vol. 24, pt. 1, pp. 217, 219.

13. *OR* vol. 24, pt. 1, pp. 193-194, 222.

14. *Ibid.*, pp. 194-195.

15. *Ibid.*, p. 224.

16. Diary of William A. Drennan, Letters and Diaries Files, Vicksburg National Military Park; *OR.*, vol. 24, pt. 3, p. 953.

17. *OR* vol. 24, pt. 3, pp. 953, 963.

18. *Ibid.*, pp. 917, 953, 971.

19. Diary of William A. Drennan.

20. *OR.*, vol. 24, pt. 1, p. 227; *OR.*, vol. 24, pt. 3, p. 965.

21. *OR.*, vol. 24, pt. 3, pp. 974, 980.

22. *Ibid.*, p. 897.

23. Ballard, *Pemberton: A Biography*, p. 181.

24. Frank Vandiver, ed., *The Civil War Diary of General Josiah Gorgas* (University, Alabama, 1947), p. 50.

Chapter Eight: "No Longer a Point of Danger": The Siege of Jackson

1. *OR.*, vol. 24, pt. 3, pp. 460-61; William T. Sherman, *Memoirs of William T. Sherman*, 2 vols. (New York, 1875), vol. 1, p. 358.

2. *OR.*, vol. 24, pt. 3, pp. 974, 980.

3. Johnston, *Narrative of Military Operations*, p. 205.

4. *OR.*, vol. 24, pt. 3, pp. 994-95.

5. *OR.*, vol. 24, pt. 2, pp. 522, 525.

6. *OR.*, vol. 24, pt. 3, pp. 502-503.

7. *Ibid.*, vol. 24, pt. 3, p. 503.

8. *OR.*, vol. 24, pt. 2, p. 604.

9. *Ibid.*, p. 524; Johnston, *Narrative of Military Operations*, p. 207.

10. *OR.*, vol. 24, pt. 2, p. 528.

11. *Ibid.*; Eugene Beauge, "The Forty-fifth in Kentucky and Mississippi," Allen D. Albert, ed., *History of the Forty-fifth Regiment of Pennsylvania Veteran Volunteer Infantry 1861-1865* (Williamsport, 1912), p. 75.

12. *OR.*, vol. 24, pt. 2, p. 529.

13. *Ibid.*, p. 537.

Chapter Nine: Crucial to the Outcome: Vicksburg and the Trans-Mississippi Supply Line

1. Albert Castel, "Vicksburg: Myths and Realities," *North & South*, Vol. 6, Number 7, November 2003, p. 69.

2. Porter, *Incidents and Anecdotes of the Civil War*, pp. 95-96.

3. *OR* vol. 31, pt. 3, p. 459; *OR* vol. 24, pt. 1, p. 22.

4. John C. Pemberton, *Pemberton: Defender of Vicksburg*, Chapel Hill, 1942, p. 261.

5. Jerry Korn, *War on the Mississippi*, Alexandria, 1985, p. 16.

6. Henry Steele Commager (editor), *The Blue & Gray: The Story of the Civil War as Told by Participants*, 2 vols., Indianapolis, 1950, vol. 2, p. 677; OR., vol. 24, pt, 3, pp. 460-461; Vandiver (ed.), *The Civil War Diary of General Josiah Gorgas*, p. 55.

7. *OR* vol. 24, pt. 2, p. 178; *OR* vol. 24, pt. 1, p. 62; Alexander S. Abrams, *A Full and Detailed History of the Siege of Vicksburg*, Atlanta, 1863, p. 67.

8. Larry J. Daniel and Riley W. Gunter, *Confederate Cannon Foundries*, Union City, 1977, p. vii.

9. *Ibid.*, pp. 52-54.

10. Lewis, *Sherman: Fighting Prophet*, p. 252; *OR* vol. 30, pt. 3, p. 694.

11. *OR* vol. 17, pt. 2, p. 334.

12. Ulysses S. Grant, "The Vicksburg Campaign," in Robert U. Johnson and Clarence C. Buell, eds. *Battles and Leaders of the Civil War*, 4 vols., New York, 1884-1889, vol. 3, p. 538.

13. Davis, *Jefferson Davis the Man and His Hour*, p. 375.

14. *Ibid.*, p. 485; Letter, Jefferson Davis to Theophilus Holmes, December 21, 1862, quoted in William Cooper, *Jefferson Davis: The Essential Writings*, New York, 2003, p. 274.

15. Davis, *Jefferson Davis*, p. 487.

16. Larry Estaville, *Confederate Neckties: Louisiana Railroads in the Civil War*, Ruston, 1989, pp. 64-65. After mid-July 1862, the VS&T only operated between Delhi and Monroe. It did not operate east of Delhi.

17. Preliminary Report Eighth Census, 1860.

18. Peter Walker, *Vicksburg: A People at War, 1861-1865*, Chapel Hill, 1960, p. 12.

19. *Ibid.*, p. 11.

20. Orville V. Burton and Patricia D. Bonnin, "Cotton," in Richard N. Current, ed., *Encyclopedia of the Confederacy*, 4 vols., New York, 1993, vol. 1, pp. 416-420.

21. Memorandum, Benjamin F. Butler to Edwin M. Stanton, January 1862, Edwin M. Stanton Papers, Division of Manuscripts, Library of Congress; *DeBow's Review*, Vol. II (Revised Series, 1866), p. 419.

22. Preliminary Report Eighth Census, 1860.

23. *OR* Series IV, vol. 2, p. 250; *OR* vol. 24, pt. 1, p. 288.

24. Castel, "Vicksburg," p. 65; Michael Wright, "Vicksburg and the Trans-Mississippi Supply Line (1861-1863)," *The Journal of Mississippi History*, XLIII, No. 3, August 1981, p. 212.

25. *OR* vol. 24, pt. 1, p. 288.

26. *OR* vol. 23, pt. 2, pp. 786, 817, 840.

27. Ella Lonn, *Salt as a Factor in the Confederacy*, University, Alabama, 1965, p. 146; *OR* Series IV, vol. 2, p. 486.

28. Wright, "Vicksburg and the Trans-Mississippi Supply Line," pp. 216, 222.

29. Castel, "Vicksburg," p. 68.

30. Francis V. Greene, *The Mississippi*, New York, 1882, pp. 170-171.

31. FM 100-5, Washington, D. C., 1986, pp. 91, 94.

Chapter Ten: Stephen D. Lee
and the Making of an American Shrine

1. Lee was born on September 22, 1833, in Charleston, South Carolina, and graduated from the United States Military Academy in 1854, standing seventeenth in a class of forty-six cadets. *Encyclopedia of the Confederacy*, 4 vols. (New York, 1993), vol. 2, pp. 920-21.

2. Lee married Regina Harrison, daughter of James Thomas Harrison and Regina Blewett Harrison, on February 9, 1865. Lilly's grandfather presented them with the 770-acre plantation, *Devereaux*, in Noxubee County. The couple had only one child, a son, Blewett Harrison Lee, born on March 1, 1867. Oral interview with Carolyn Neault, curator Lee Home and Museum, 15 April 1999.

3. Elected to the State Senate in 1878, to fill the unexpired term of W. H. Simms who became lieutenant governor. While in the Senate, Lee supported a bill to create Mississippi Agricultural and Mechanical College (now Mississippi State University) of which he was appointed first president in 1880. He served in that capacity until 1899 and his appointment to the Vicksburg National Military Park Commission. Herman Hattaway, *General Stephen D. Lee* (Jackson, 1976), 168-69.

4. The Louisiana Monument, which stands in the city rose garden on Monumental Square, was dedicated on Saturday, June 11, 1887. During the ceremony, letters of regrets from Stephen D. Lee, Jefferson Davis, P. G. T. Beauregard, and Francis Shoup were read to the audience. Included in Lee's command at the Battle of Chickasaw Bayou were the 17th, 22d, 26th, 29th, and 31st Louisiana Infantry regiments. *Vicksburg Evening Post*, June 13, 1887; Bearss, *The Vicksburg Campaign*, vol. 1, p.225.

5. "Administrative History Vicksburg National Military Park." Draft manuscript by Edwin C. Bearss. Edwin C. Bearss Series, Box 2, Vicksburg National Military Park (VNMP), Vicksburg, Mississippi.

6. Lee was elected to the honorary position of vice president of the Shiloh Battlefield Association on April 10, 1893. Administrative Records, Shiloh National Military Park, Shiloh, Tennessee.

7. Letter, Stephen D. Lee to S. A. Cunningham, January 16, 1908, quoted in Hattaway, *Stephen D. Lee*, p. 224.

8. Hattaway, *Stephen D. Lee*, 224; *Vicksburg Evening Post*, April 25, 1893.

9. The Governor's Greys from Dubuque, Iowa, arrived in Vicksburg on Thursday, February 8, 1894, after having participated in the Mardi Gras festivities in New Orleans. The group stayed at the New Pacific House Hotel on Washington Street. *Vicksburg Evening Post*, February 9, 1894.

10. *Vicksburg Evening Post*, October 22, 1895; Minutes, Vicksburg National Military Park Association, Administrative Series, Box 7, Folder 158, VNMP.

11. Minutes, Vicksburg National Military Park Association, Administrative Series, Box 7, Folder 158, VNMP; *Vicksburg Evening Post*, Nov. 22, 1895.

12. Minutes, Vicksburg National Military Park Association, Administrative Series, Box 7, Folder 158, VNMP.

13. *Ibid.*

14. *Ibid.*

15. *Ibid.*

16. Letter, James K. P. Thompson to William T. Rigby, January 14, 1896, Rigby Papers, Box 1, Folder 28, VNMP; *Ibid.*

17. Catchings introduced the bill on January 20, 1896.

18. Letter, Lee to Rigby, September 1, 1896, William T. Rigby Series, Box 1, Folder 28, VNMP.

19. Letter David Henderson to John F. Merry, November 6, 1896; Letter, Frederick D. Grant to Rigby, November 9, 1896; Letter, Henderson to Rigby, 14 December 1896. William T. Rigby Series, Box 1, Folder 28, VNMP.

20. Minutes, Vicksburg National Military Park Association, Administrative Series, Box 7, Folder 158, VNMP.

21. Letter, Lee to Rigby, February 7, 1897. William T. Rigby Series, Box 1, Folder 29, VNMP.

22. Letter, Lee to Rigby, October 29, 1897. William T. Rigby Series, Box 1, Folder 29, VNMP.

23. Letter, Lee to Rigby, January 5, 1898. William T. Rigby Series, Box 1, Folder 29, VNMP.

24. The Association met in Vicksburg on December 28, 1898. Rigby arrived in Washington on February 4, 1899, and checked into the Hotel Normandie on McPherson Square. Minutes, Vicksburg National Military Park Association, Administrative Series, Box 7, Folder 128, VNMP.

25. *Vicksburg Evening Post*, February 7, 1898.

26. Minute Book, Vicksburg National Military Park Commission, VNMP; Hattaway, *Stephen D. Lee*, p. 226.

27. Letter, Lee to Secretary of War Elihu Root, December 20, 1899.

28. Letter, Lee to Rigby, November 21, 1901.

29. *Vicksburg Evening Post*, May 28, 1908.

30. *Ibid.* The Rigby home, which also served as the park office, was situated at 100 N. Cherry Street. The building is no longer standing.

31. *Ibid.*

32. *Ibid.*

33. *Ibid.*

34. Letter, William Loeb, Jr., Secretary to the President, to Rigby, September 25, 1908, check enclosed for $50.00 Monumentation Series, Box 4, Folder 123, VNMP. The bronze figure of Lee standing was sculpted by the renowned artist Henry Hudson Kitson. Donors in 27 states and the District of Columbia contributed $6,337 for the monument. The balance was provided by the general's son Blewett for a total of $8,000.

35. Monumentation Records, VNMP.

Epilogue

1. Warner, *Generals in Blue*, p. 459; Boatner, *Civil War Dictionary*, p. 772.

2. Warner, *Generals in Gray*, pp. 57-58; Boatner, *Civil War Dictionary*, p. 161; Current, *Encyclopedia of the Confederacy*, vol. 1, p. 366.

3. Oldroyd, *The Siege of Vicksburg*, preface.

4. Warner, *Generals in Blue*, pp. 155-156; Boatner, *Civil War Dictionary*, pp. 287-288.

5. Terrence J. Winschel, *Alice Shirley and the Story of Wexford Lodge* (Conshohocken, 1993).

6. Warner, *Generals in Blue*, pp. 566-568; Boatner, *Civil War Dictionary*, pp. 930-931.

7. Boatner, *Civil War Dictionary*, p. 221.

8. *Ibid.*, p. 661.

9. Website: United States Naval Academy.

10. Records, Christ Episcopal Church, Vicksburg, Mississippi; Records Holy Trinity Episcopal Church, Vicksburg, Mississippi.

11. Current, *Encyclopedia of the Confederacy*, vol. 3, pp. 1383-1384.

12. Warner, *Generals in Gray*, pp. 152-153; Boatner, *The Civil War Dictionary*, p. 433.

13. Warner, *Generals in Blue*, pp. 359-360; Boatner, *The Civil War Dictionary*, pp. 618-619.

14. David Smith, ed., *Compelled to Appear in Print* (Cincinnati, 1999), pp. xi-xiii.

15. *Vicksburg Daily Herald*, April 12, 1880

16. Letter, William T. Rigby to Rhoda Rigby, April 1861, Rigby Papers, MsC 82, Special Collections Department, University of Iowa Libraries, Iowa City, Iowa.

Bibliography

Manuscripts

Memorandum, Benjamin F. Butler to Edwin M. Stanton, January 1862, Edwin M. Stanton Papers, Division of Manuscripts, Library of Congress.

"Administrative History Vicksburg National Military Park." Draft manuscript by Edwin C. Bearss, Edwin C. Bearss Series, Box 2, Vicksburg National Military Park (VNMP), Vicksburg, Mississippi.

Administrative Records, Shiloh National Military Park, Shiloh, Tennessee.

Minutes, Vicksburg National Military Park Association, Administrative Series, Box 7, Folder 158, VNMP.

Records, Christ Episcopal Church, Vicksburg, Mississippi; Records Holy Trinity Episcopal Church, Vicksburg, Mississippi.

Newspapers

Vicksburg Daily Whig, July 1, 1862
New York Times, January 14, 1863
The Daily Citizen
Vicksburg Daily Herald, April 12, 1880
Vicksburg Evening Post, June 13, 1887
Vicksburg Evening Post, April 25, 1893
Vicksburg Evening Post, February 9, 1894
Vicksburg Evening Post, October 22, 1895
Vicksburg Evening Post, November 22, 1895
Vicksburg Evening Post, February 7, 1898
Vicksburg Evening Post, May 28, 1908

Official Publications

The War of the Rebellion: The Official Records of the Union and Confederate Armies, 128 vols., Washington, D.C., 1890-1901.

Official Records of the Union and Confederate Navies in the War of the Rebellion, 30 volumes, Washington, D.C., 1894-1922.

Official Roster of the Soldiers of the State of Ohio in the War of the Rebellion and in the War With Mexico, 12 vols., Akron, Cincinnati, Norwalk, Ohio, 1886-1895.

FM 100-5, Washington, D. C., 1986.

Medal of Honor, The Navy, 1861-1949, Washington, D.C., 1949.

Preliminary Report Eighth Census, Washington, D.C., 1860.

Letters

Letter Andrew H. Foote to wife, February 6, 1862, Area File 5, Box 1, RG 45, National Archives and Records Administration.

Letter, Lt. Col. Jefferson Brumback to his wife, Kat, May 20, 1863, Regimental Files, 95th Ohio Infantry, Vicksburg National Military Park (VNMP).

Letter, James K. P. Thompson to William T. Rigby, 14 January 1896, Rigby Papers, Box 1, Folder 28, VNMP.

Letter, Stephen D. Lee to William T. Rigby, September 1, 1896, William T. Rigby Series, Box 1, Folder 28, VNMP.

Letter David Henderson to John F. Merry, November 6, 1896, William T. Rigby Series, Box 1, Folder 28, VNMP.

Letter, Frederick D. Grant to William T. Rigby, November 9, 1896, William T. Rigby Series, Box 1, Folder 28, VNMP.

Letter, David Henderson to William T. Rigby, December 14, 1896, William T. Rigby Series, Box 1, Folder 28, VNMP.

Letter, Stephen D. Lee to William T. Rigby, February 7, 1897, William T. Rigby Series, Box 1, Folder 29, VNMP.

Letter, Stephen D. Lee to William T. Rigby, October 29, 1897, William T. Rigby Series, Box 1, Folder 29, VNMP.

Letter, Stephen D. Lee to William T. Rigby, January 5, 1898, William T. Rigby Series, Box 1, Folder 29, VNMP.

Letter, Stephen D. Lee to Secretary of War Elihu Root, December 20, 1899, William T. Rigby Series, Box 1, Folder 32, VNMP.

Letter, Stephen D. Lee to William T. Rigby, November 21, 1901, William T. Rigby Series, Box 1, Folder 33, VNMP.

Letter, William Loeb, Jr., Secretary to the President, to William T. Rigby, September 25, 1908, Monumentation Series, Box 4, Folder 123, VNMP.

Letter, William T. Rigby to Rhoda Rigby, April, 1863, Rigby Papers, MsC 82, Special Collections Department, University of Iowa Libraries, Iowa City, Iowa.

Diaries

Diary of Emma Balfour, Letters and Diaries Files, Vicksburg National Military Park.

Diary of William A. Drennan, Letters and Diaries Files, Vicksburg National Military Park.

Diary of William B. Halsey, Regimental Files, 72d Ohio Infantry, Vicksburg National Military Park.

Diary of George W. Huff, Regimental Files, 80th Ohio Infantry, Vicksburg National Military Park.

Diary of Richard C. Hunt, Regimental Files, 20th Ohio Infantry, Vicksburg National Military Park.

Diary of Henry S. Keene, Regimental Files, 6th Wisconsin Battery, Vicksburg National Military Park.

Diary of A. Hugh Moss, Copy in the Library of Congress dated 1948.

Diary of William H. Raynor, Regimental Files, 56th Ohio Infantry, Vicksburg National Military Park.

Diary of Israel Ritter, Regimental Files, 24th Iowa Infantry, Vicksburg National Military Park.

Diary of Henry Clay Warmoth, Letters and Diaries Files, Vicksburg National Military Park.

Diary of Enoch Williams, Letters and Diaries Files, Vicksburg National Military Park.

Books and Articles

Abrams, Alexander S., *A Full and Detailed History of the Siege of Vicksburg*, Atlanta, Georgia, 1863.

Anderson, Ephraim McD., *Memoirs: Historical and Personal; including the Campaigns of the First Missouri Confederate Brigade*, edited by Edwin C. Bearss, Dayton, Ohio, 1972.

Ballard, Michael, *Pemberton: A Biography*, Jackson, Mississippi, 1991.

Bearss, Edwin C. and Warren Grabau, *The Battle of Jackson/The Siege of Jackson*, Baltimore, Maryland, 1981.

Beauge, Eugene, "The Forty-fifth in Kentucky and Mississippi," Allen D. Albert, ed., *History of the Forty-fifth Regiment of Pennsylvania Veteran Volunteer Infantry 1861-1865*, Williamsport, Pennsylvania, 1912.

Beck, S. C., "A True Sketch of His Army Life," Letters and Diaries File, Vicksburg National Military Park.

Bell, Lucy McRae, "A Girl's Experience in the Siege of Vicksburg," *Harper's Weekly*, Vol. LVI, June 8, 1912.

Bentley, William H., *History of the 77th Illinois Volunteer Infantry, Sept. 2, 1862,—July 10, 1865*, Peoria, Illinois, 1883.

Bering, John A. and Thomas Montgomery, *History of the Forty-eighth Ohio Vet. Vol. Inf.*, Hillsboro, Ohio, 1880.

Boatner, Mark M., *The Civil War Dictionary*, New York, New York, 1959.

Bringhurst, Thomas H. and Frank Swigart, *History of the Forty-sixth Regiment Indiana Volunteer Infantry September, 1861—September, 1865*, Logansport, Indiana, 1888.

Bryner, Byron, *Bugle Echoes: The Story of Illinois 47th Infantry*, Springfield, Illinois, 1905.

Burdette, Robert J., *The Drums of the 47th*, Indianapolis, Indiana, 1914.

Cadwallader, Sylvanus, ed. by Benjamin P. Thomas, *Three Years with Grant as Recalled by War Correspondent Sylvanus Cadwallader*, New York, New York, 1955.

Castel, Albert, "Vicksburg: Myths and Realities," *North & South*, Vol. 6, Number 7, November 2003.

Chesnut, Mary Boykin, ed. Ben Ames Williams, *A Diary From Dixie*, Boston, Massachusetts, 1949.

Clark, Charles B. and Roger B. Bowen, *University Recruits—Company C, 12th Iowa Infantry Regiment U.S.A. 1861-1866*, Elverson, Iowa, 1991.

Commager, Henry Steele, ed., *The Blue & Gray: The Story of the Civil War as Told by Participants*, 2 vols., Indianapolis, Indiana, 1950.

Cooling, Benjamin F., *Forts Henry and Donelson: The Key to the Confederate Heartland*, Knoxville, Tennessee, 1987.

Cooper, William, *Jefferson Davis: The Essential Writings*, New York, New York, 2003.

Crummer, Wilbur F., *With Grant at Fort Donelson, Shiloh and Vicksburg*, Oak Park, Illinois, 1915.

Current, Richard N., ed., *Encyclopedia of the Confederacy*, 4 vols., New York, New York, 1993.

Dana, Charles A. and James H. Wilson, *The Life of Ulysses S. Grant*, Springfield, Illinois, 1868.

Daniel, Larry J. and Riley W. Gunter, *Confederate Cannon Foundries*, Union City, Tennessee, 1977.

Davis, William C., *Jefferson Davis: The Man and His Hour*, New York, New York, 1991.

DeBow's Review, Vol. II (Revised Series, 1866).

Dunbar, Aaron and Harvey M. Trimble, *History of the Ninety-third Regiment Illinois Volunteer Infantry from Organization to Muster Out*, Chicago, Illinois, 1898.

Eaton, John, *Grant, Lincoln and the Freedmen*, New York, New York, 1907.

Estaville, Larry, *Confederate Neckties: Louisiana Railroads in the Civil War*, Ruston, Louisiana, 1989.

Fiske, John, *The Mississippi Valley in the Civil War*, New York, New York, 1900.

Foote, Shelby, *The Civil War: A Narrative*, 3 vols., New York, New York, 1958-1974.

General Directory, City of Vicksburg, Vicksburg, Mississippi, 1860.

Grabau, Warren, *Ninety-eight Days: A Geographer's View of the Vicksburg Campaign*, Knoxville, Tennessee, 2000.

Grant, Ulysses S., *Personal Memoirs of Ulysses S. Grant*, 2 vols., New York, New York, 1885.

Grant, Ulysses S., "The Vicksburg Campaign," in Robert U. Johnson and Clarence C. Buell, eds. *Battles and Leaders of the Civil War*, 4 vols., New York, New York, 1884-1889.

Greene, Francis V., *The Mississippi*, New York, New York, 1882.

Hattaway, Herman, *General Stephen D. Lee*, Jackson, Mississippi, 1976.

Herald Directory, City of Vicksburg, Vicksburg, Mississippi, 1866.

Hoehling, A. A., *Vicksburg: 47 Days of Siege*, Englewood Cliffs, New Jersey, 1969.

In and About Vicksburg, Vicksburg, Mississippi, 1890.

Johnston, Joseph E., *A Narrative of Military Operations During the Late War Between the States*, New York, New York, 1874.

Kiper, Richard, *Major General John Alexander McClernand: Politician in Uniform*, Kent, Ohio, 1999.

Korn, Jerry, *War on the Mississippi*, Alexandria, Virginia, 1985.

"Letters of General Thomas Williams, 1862," *American Historical Review*, Vol. XIV, 1908-1909.

Lewis, Lloyd, *Sherman: Fighting Prophet*, New York, New York, 1932.

Longacre, Ed, *From Union Stars to Top Hat*, Harrisburg, Pennsylvania, 1972.

Lonn, Ella, *Salt as a Factor in the Confederacy*, University, Alabama, 1965.

Lord, Margaret, *A Journal Kept by Mrs. W. W. Lord* (not published), transcribed copy provided courtesy of Old Court House Museum, Vicksburg, Mississippi.

Lord, William W., Jr., "A Child at the Siege of Vicksburg," *Harpers Monthly Magazine*, December 1908.

Marshall, Thomas B., *History of the Eighty-third Ohio Volunteer Infantry: The Greyhound Regiment*, Cincinnati, Ohio, 1912.

Oldroyd, Osborn H., *A Soldier's Story of the Siege of Vicksburg*, Springfield, Illinois, 1885.

Pemberton, John C., *Pemberton: Defender of Vicksburg*, Chapel Hill, North Carolina, 1942.

Porter, David Dixon, *Incidents and Anecdotes of the Civil War*, New York, New York, 1885.

Reed, Lida Lord, "A Woman's Experiences During the Siege of Vicksburg," *Century Magazine*, Vol. LXI, April 1901.

Sherman, William T., *Memoirs of General William T. Sherman*, 2 vols., New York, New York, 1875.

Simon, John Y., ed., *The Papers of Ulysses S. Grant*, 30 vols., Carbondale, Illinois, 1967-2006.

Smith, David, ed., *Compelled to Appear in Print*, Cincinnati, Ohio, 1999.

Stevenson, Benjamin F., *Letters From the Army*, Cincinnati, Ohio, 1884.

Tunnard, William H., *A Southern Record: The History of the Third Regiment Louisiana Infantry*, Baton Rouge, Louisiana, 1866.

Vandiver, Frank, ed., *The Civil War Diary of General Josiah Gorgas*, University, Alabama, 1947.

Walker, Peter, *Vicksburg: A People at War, 1861-1865*, Chapel Hill, North Carolina, 1960.

Warner, Ezra J., *Generals in Blue*, Baton Rouge, Louisiana, 1964.

Warner, Ezra J., *Generals in Gray*, Baton Rouge, Louisiana, 1959.

Williams, Kenneth, *Lincoln Finds a General: A Military Study of the Civil War*, 5 vols., New York, New York, 1949-1959.

Willison, Charles A., *A Boy's Service with the 76th Ohio*, Menasha, Ohio, 1908.

Wilson, James H., *Under the Old Flag*, New York, New York, 1912.

Winschel, Terrence J., *Alice Shirley and the Story of Wexford Lodge*, Conshohocken, Pennsylvania, 1993.

Wright, Michael, "Vicksburg and the Trans-Mississippi Supply Line (1861-1863)," *The Journal of Mississippi History*, XLIII, No. 3, August 1981.

INDEX